Under the Molehill

Michel de Castelnau, Seigneur de Mauvissière. British Library.

UNDER THE MOLEHILL

An Elizabethan Spy Story

John Bossy

NB

Yale Nota Bene
Yale University Press
New Haven & London

First published as a Yale Nota Bene book in 2002.

For information about this and other Yale University Press publications please contact:
  U.S. office: sales.press@yale.edu
  Europe office: sales@yaleup.co.uk

Designed by Adam Freudenheim

Printed in Great Britain

The Library of Congress catalogued the previous edition as follows:
  Bossy, John.
  Under the molehill: an Elizabethan spy story/John Bossy.
  p. cm.
  Includes bibliographical references and index.
  ISBN 0–300–08400–5 (hbk.)
  ISBN 0–300–09450–7 (pbk.)
  Great Britain–History–Elizabeth, 1558–1603
  00–043802

A catalogue record for this book is available from the British Library.

10 9 8 7 6 5 4 3 2 1

For Pete and Miggy,
with love

Contents

Illustrations

Acknowledgements

My first debt is to Simon Adams, for his generosity in passing on to me his knowledge of Elizabethan policy and the fruits of his compendious investigation of relevant archives; then to Stuart Carroll and Gayle Brunelle for information turned up in their labours in French notarial archives; to Margaret Aston (Buxton), Peter Biller, Nick Furbank, Mary Heimann and the reader(s) of Yale University Press for careful readings and criticism of the typescript in its various stages; to Louise Harrison for word-processing it (three times); to Amanda Lillie for directing me to the jacket picture; and to Adam Freudenheim for his watchfulness and professionalism as an editor. I am very grateful to them all.

I also thank the Marquess of Salisbury for permission to publish Document (a) and to quote other pieces from the Cecil Papers, and Robin Harcourt Williams for kind assistance; the Trustees of the British Library for Documents (b), (c) and (d), Plates IV, V, VI and VIII and the portrait of Castelnau; the Keeper of the Public Records for Document (e) and Plates I, II, III, VII, IX and X; the Director of the National Portrait Gallery for the portrait of Walsingham; and the Museo Thyssen-Bornemisza, Madrid, for the painting used on the jacket. Likewise, for the use of material in their care, the authorities of: in England, the Bodleian Library, Oxford, the British Library, the Chapter Library, Canterbury (and Cressida Annesley), Durham University Library (and Beth Rainey and Jan Rhodes), the Guildhall Library, London, and the Public Record Office (and Amanda Bevan); in France, the Archives du Ministère des Affaires Etrangères, the Archives Nationales and the Bibliothèque Nationale, Paris, and the Archives Départementales de la Seine-Maritime, Rouen; and, in Rome, the Archivio Segreto Vaticano and the Archives of the Ven. English College.

John Bossy
York, January 2001

Abbreviations used in the Footnotes

BL   British Library, Department of Manuscripts,
              followed by title of collection.

BN   Bibliothèque Nationale, Paris, Département des
              Manuscrits:
                  fr – Manuscrits français;
                  V^{c}C – Cinq Cents de Colbert.

Chéruel   A. Chéruel, *Marie Stuart et Catherine de Médicis*
              (Paris, 1856).

CRS   Catholic Record Society publications, followed by
              volume number.

CSP   *Calendars of State Papers of the Reign of Queen
              Elizabeth*, followed by title of series (as, 'Foreign')
              and dates covered by volume.

Diary   Office Diary of Sir Francis Walsingham, April 1583
              to December 1584: BL Harleian Ms. 6035.

DNB   *Dictionary of National Biography* (Compact Edition in
              2 volumes, London, 1975).

GB   John Bossy, *Giordano Bruno and the Embassy
              Affair* (London, 1991); referred to in the text as
              Bruno.

HMC   Historical Manuscripts Commission, followed by
              title of collection (as, 'Hatfield').

Labanoff   Alexandre Labanoff (ed.), *Lettres, instructions et
              mémoires de Marie Stuart* (7 vols, London,
              1844–5).

Murdin   William Murdin (ed.), *A Collection of State Papers
              [of] Lord Burghley* (London, 1759).

OED   *Oxford English Dictionary* (Compact Edition in 2
              vols, London, 1971).

PRO	Public Record Office, London: SP – State Papers, followed by call number of series and volume number.
Read, *Walsingham*	Conyers Read, *Mr. Secretary Walsingham and the Policy of Queen Elizabeth* (3 vols, Oxford, 1925–7; reprinted 1967).
SP	See PRO.
Numbers	A number may be used in three ways in the footnotes: (1) with a small 'n' ('no.'), in reference to a primary source, to indicate the number of the document in the volume; (2) with a capital 'N' ('No.') to indicate the number of the letter in 'Appendix: Letters Passed from Salisbury Court, July 1583–November 1584'; where the plain number may be mysterious, I add 'Appendix' before it; (3) with 'Text' before it, and a small 'n', to indicate the number of the document in the series of *Texts* printed in *GB* (see above). See also the 'Note' at the beginning of 'A Note on the Date of Fagot's Letter'.
Documents	At pp. 171–9. I have included the text of five letters and extracts referred to in the footnotes, where they will be described as Document (a), (b), (c) (d) or (e).
Dates	See 'Note' in *GB*, p. xi. Here I use old-style dates throughout in the text, in the footnotes old and new styles together. For usage in 'A Note on the Date . . .' and 'Appendix II', see the notes prefixed to each. I begin the year on the first of January.

Characters

ELIZABETH, Queen of England

Michel de CASTELNAU, seigneur de Mauvissière, ambassador from King Henry III of France to Elizabeth 1575–85, moderate Catholic, had tried unsuccessfully to arrange a marriage between Elizabeth and Henri III's brother François, Duke of Anjou

Jean ARNAULT, secretary of Castelnau

Giordano BRUNO, house-guest of Castelnau, Neapolitan ex-friar, philosopher, polemicist, poet

Claude de COURCELLES, secretary of Castelnau

Henri FAGOT, presumably pseudonymous chaplain of Castelnau, perhaps identical with Bruno

Laurent FERON, clerk of Castelnau

GIRAULT de la Chassaigne, butler of Castelanu

Sir Francis WALSINGHAM, councillor and Secretary of State of Elizabeth, promoter of Protestant politics, practitioner of secret intelligence

Walter WILLIAMS, servant of Walsingham, intelligencer

William FOWLER, Scottish ex-minister and poet, familiar of Castelnau, intelligencer for Walsingham

Archibald DOUGLAS, Scottish nobleman, political exile, familiar of Castelnau and Walsingham, later Scottish ambassador to Elizabeth

William Cecil, Lord BURGHLEY, principal councillor of Elizzabeth

Sir Edward STAFFORD, courtier, friend of Castelnau, Burghley and Howard (*see below*), English ambassador in France 1583–9

William HERLE, servant of Burghley, intelligencer, diplomatic agent, later ambassador

Robert Dudley, Earl of LEICESTER, favourite and councillor of Elizabeth

Sir Philip SIDNEY, courtier, poet, Protestant, nephew of Leicester, son-in-law of Walsingham 1583

MARY, Queen of Scots, refugee from Scotland in custody at Sheffield, Catholic, potential successor or alternative to Elizabeth, sister-in-law of Henri III of France, executed 1587

Thomas MORGAN, servant of Mary living in Paris, political secretary, conspirator against Elizabeth

Charles PAGET, Catholic nobleman living in Paris, friend and collaborator of Morgan

Thomas BALDWIN, servant of Mary's guardian the Earl of Shrewsbury

Lord Henry HOWARD, Catholic nobleman, courtier, friend of Castelnau, author, devotional writer, later Earl of Northampton

Francis THROCKMORTON, Catholic, friend of Castelnau, conspirator, executed 1584

William PARRY, intelligencer, Catholic convert, M.P. 1584, alleged conspirator, executed 1585

Bernardino de MENDOZA, Spanish ambassador to Elizabeth 1578–84

Guillaume de l'Aubépine, baron de CHÂTEAUNEUF, French ambassador to Elizabeth 1585–9

INTRODUCTION

SOME YEARS AGO I published *Giordano Bruno and the Embassy Affair*, a book which claimed to disentangle part of a spying operation in Elizabethan London; to identify a principal figure in the story, known under the alias, possibly comic, of 'Henri Fagot', as the philosopher named in the title; and to attempt the writing of the life of the hero which was required if the identification were correct. This book will be an account of the substance of that spy story.[1] It therefore occurred at the same time: between the spring of 1583 and the summer of 1585, years when the temperature of relations between the crowns of England and Spain, and between Queen Elizabeth and some of her subjects, rose steadily to the boil. It occurred in the same place: in and around the house of the French ambassador, a comfortable but dilapidated mansion known as Salisbury Court, sitting above its garden at the top of the slope running down from Fleet Street to the Thames, with the City on its left and Westminster to its right, the pleasure-houses of Southwark on the far bank, and a panorama of boats and boatmen plying up and down or back and forth between them. The two books share a topic: the defence of the realm by the acquisition of intelligence about subversion and potential invasion; and they share most of their characters, though here you will have the pleasure, I hope, of meeting a couple of new ones.

Under the Molehill differs from *Giordano Bruno and the Embassy Affair* in at least two respects. The first is that the hero of it, so to call him, is not an individual of world-historical significance. I hope the reader will find himself warming to him as a person, but the concern will be rather with

---

1 New Haven/London, 1991; various translated editions, notably in Italian, *Giordano Bruno e il mistero dell'ambasciata* (Milan, 1992), with a 'postfazione' indicating second thoughts and revisions and responding to some critics who have found the identification unconvincing. My rejoinder to one critical point will be found in 'A Note on the Date of Fagot's Letter', below, pp. 157ff, and relevant new details at various points in the book. They do not settle the issue whether Bruno and Fagot were the same person, and I have proceeded here on the assumption that this is not certain. I can say that this second trawl of the evidence about Castelnau's household has turned up nothing to contradict the identification and (thanks to Simon Adams) one thing which is rather in favour of it (see pp. 136–8).

what he does than with what he is, and with the consequences of his
doing it rather than with his intentions in doing it. It will also be, as was
not the case in *Bruno*, with the *sort* of thing he does, that is to say with
the passing of information or intelligence; this sort of thing, though
nothing to do with what has been called a 'culture of surveillance',[2] or
indeed with any sort of culture at all, is of interest for the history of Elizabethan England, of the Europe of the wars of religion, and perhaps of
other times and places as well.

The second difference is, as my title indicates, that this will be a story
about a mole, as which I could not describe the former. I take a mole to
be someone with a permanent and confidential position in an establishment dealing with matters of state who uses his special access to documents and other sources of knowledge to convey them or their contents
to a foreign and hypothetically hostile power; he does this systematically
and over a period of some time. By contrast I take a spy to be a relative
outsider and a more occasional contributor. If we follow that distinction,
Fagot was a spy, and the hero of the present book a mole. It is true that
a full-grown mole, nowadays, may have got into his position by way of a
long-term and complicated manoeuvre on the part of his principals. This
is not the case here, nor could it be. Such manoeuvres require long-term
institutions to conceive and run them, and these did not, in our period,
exist. But I think the general silhouette of a mole is recognisable enough,
and that my man fits it.

In the preface to *Bruno* I made some claims about facts which have
turned out to be unwarranted. It was not the case, as I said, that the identification which formed the basis of the book was an addition to knowledge whose correctness could not be doubted. I thought so at the time,
but have turned out to be mistaken. Less fundamental things in the book
have proved to be mistaken too: I misidentified the person whom Fagot
recruited as a mole; I got at least one important date wrong. The story
there told was more hypothetical and more approximate than I thought,
though to my mind it remains highly probable in principle and substantially exact in detail.

Here I should like to day something, not about facts, but about events.
Since the late Fernand Braudel published his *Mediterranean* in 1949, events
have had a fairly bad press: Braudel dismissed them as a sort of froth
buzzing about meaninglessly above the deep water of real history;[3] for
others, they are there to illustrate generalities like 'structure', 'culture',

2   John Michael Archer, *Sovereignty and Intelligence* (Stanford, Cal., 1993), pp. 2, 3 etc.
3   *La Méditerranée et le monde méditerranéen à l'époque de Philippe II* (2nd edn, 2 vols, Paris, 1966), i, 16;
    English translation (2 vols, London, 1972–3), i, 21.

'society'. This will not do. Events are things that happen. They count as events by forming part of stories. I particularly like the description of an event given by John Holloway from the point of view of a reader of fiction: an event is something that happens in a story to alter or reverse the reader's supposition about how the story will turn out in the end. On that very strict definition, the story to be told here contains three or four events. We need not be as strict as that, so long as we recognise that events occur in stories; that stories occur in life; and that, to quote W. B. Gallie, 'history is a species of the genus story'. It is not at all necessary to concede that, if history consists of stories, it must restrict itself to a narrow band of trivial doings. This would be to misunderstand what it is that goes to make up a story. I quote Holloway: 'stories comprise (1) events which happen in (2) states of affairs'. A state of affairs is a *terminus a quo*, a context, a scene. It is also moving and cumulative: it consumes events as they happen, and is likely to be changed by them. It may ramify as broadly, and penetrate as deeply, as the story requires.[4]

Here then is the state of affairs in the spring of 1583, when we begin. It was some sixty years since the outbreak of Luther's Reformation. In that time the Reformation had complicated itself, adding an unquiet Calvinism to the now contented followers of Luther. It had provoked in the Roman Church, not the give and take which some of its luminaries had shown in the early days, and which continued to attract the more humane of its followers, but the zeal of unquestioning anti-Protestantism which was now personified by the Society of Jesus. In 1555 the German lands had achieved a peace between Lutherans and Catholics: to the west such accommodation was proving impossible to secure, and wars of religion between or within states becoming the norm. The Rome of Pope Gregory XIII, fortified by the glamour of missionary ventures from China to Peru, was promoting various kinds of war in the West with the lack of inhibitions of an institution which had seen off many a dissident faith and troublesome ruler in the past. The relative prudence of the alternative centre of loyalty, Calvin's Geneva, was compensated by the zeal and solidarity, the courage, even the messianism which marked so many of those it had inspired.

Pressure for war between states was rarely welcome to their rulers. Neither King Philip II of Catholic Spain, who wielded the greatest power in the West, nor Queen Elizabeth of more shakily Protestant England, had

---

4   John Holloway, *Narrative and Structure* (Cambridge, 1979), pp. 1–19, at pp. 5, 15f; W.B. Gallie, *Philosophy and the Historical Understanding* (London, 1964), p. 66, and chaps 1–5 in general. Also Paul Veyne, *Comment on écrit l'histoire* (Paris, 1979 edn), pp. 35ff, on facts and 'intrigues'. On Gallie, Paul Ricoeur, *Time and Narrative* (3 vols, Chicago, 1984–8), i, 149–54, 157–61; cf. Peter Burke's piece cited below, n. 10.

been at all anxious for the grand confrontation in arms which would finally occur when Philip sent his Armada up the Channel in 1588. The Catholic King Henri III of France and the young Protestant king of Scotland, James VI, both managed to keep out of it. All of them, even Philip, would have much preferred that their relations should be kept within the bounds of the personal and familial, the law of real property, the political saws and commercial connections which governed their own instincts and those of many of their advisers. But the current of sanctified enthusiasm proved stronger than the prudence of both Philip and Elizabeth, and would shortly sweep away Henri III, assassinated by a Catholic enthusiast in 1589.

Long before they had determined war between princes, the breaking waves of contrary religious passion had cracked the interior structure of two western states. King Philip, who was alone in having no diversity of such passions within his Iberian kingdoms, had had to confront them in his inheritance of the Netherlands: here a vigorous Protestant rebellion had found a sanctuary in the seaward provinces of Holland and Zealand and a leader in William of Orange, and was now defending its freedom against a Spanish or Catholic army led by Alessandro Farnese, Prince of Parma. This war in the wetlands was the largest fact in view in the spring of 1583, and for the time being Parma's army was having the better of it to a degree which alarmed all faithful Protestants.

Like the artillery from Flanders' fields heard from the shores of Kent during the war of 1914, this muddy struggle formed the background to the events I shall be recording; it will not be directly part of them. Their location is between England and France, neither of whom was as yet officially involved in the Netherlands, though they were both intimately concerned by what happened there. France bordered them, and had a historic claim to part of them; England faced them across the narrow seas, and intercourse between the two had always been a dominant feature of English geography and policy. In the past these interests had generally been in conflict; it remained to be seen whether the two countries could transcend their history, and their religions, in a joint intervention to thwart a Spanish reconquest.

The French were unlikely to do much, since in France the passions of confessional zeal had been almost as destructive as they had been in the Netherlands. Potentially the greatest power in the West, the strength of the kingdom had been drained and its motions hobbled by conflicts of religion which had now been endemic for some twenty years; when, as at the moment, actual warfare was not going on, the state of antagonism in the country was such as virtually to paralyse all active policy. A policy of intervention in the Netherlands on the side of the rebels had been stymied by the massacres of Calvinists on and after St Bartholomew's day in 1572. The party of massacre was now quietly assembling its forces in what was to become the Catholic League or Holy Union. The government of King Henri III, against which this confederation of the zealous was finally to come out in arms, was still just about in control of the country, and would remain so for another year; after this, an extra strain on the machinery of state would disable it pretty completely during some ten years of internecine conflict.

In England religious passions were not obviously less intense, but they had been, so far, contained. Elizabeth, whose preferences were on the pacific side of the Reformation, had done her best to construct a comprehensive church, and in doing so had had to confront powerful and growing forces of Protestant zeal. She had now also to cope with the zeal of a revivified and aggressive Catholicism. During the last few years, an influx of missionary priests had been undermining the natural constituency of her regime, and presenting a more direct political threat in that their coming could not be kept apart from the pope's attempts to find indigenous collaborators for a military enterprise against her. Unwillingly, but pressed by willing counsellors, she had been obliged to resort to persecution to contain them.

Scotland, still an independent actor in the affairs of Christendom, did not have this problem. It was the only sizeable state in the West to possess a Calvinist establishment, vigorous though as yet insecure. It had got rid of its Catholic queen Mary Stewart, and turned out to have little to fear from missionary Catholicism: there were plenty of Scottish Jesuits, but they preferred to stay in France. Political Catholicism could exert some leverage from its entanglement with political Catholicism in France, from the historic if rusty link between French intervention and the country's independence, and from the chronic Scottish resentment towards England. Scottish Calvinism was also beginning to be disturbed by the moderating intentions of the young King James, who wanted a church of more traditional shape. For a year or two around 1580 political Catholicism, in the person of the Franco-Scottish Esmé Stuart d'Aubigny, Duke of Lennox, had seemed to have the ear of the king. Lennox had been sent back to France late in 1582, and the prospects of political Catholicism had probably gone with him; but pending the outcome of future battles in France and the Channel this could not be assumed.

Two topics had governed the relation between the French and English crowns during the past few years, and Scotland, for which Henri III had no time, was not one of them. The first was the attempt to consolidate the common interest of the two kingdoms by a marriage between Elizabeth and the king's younger brother François, Duke of Alençon and Anjou.

This attempt to bridge the religious divide had recently broken down, mainly because of intense opposition to it from English Protestants. Anjou, funded by Elizabeth, had gone off to fight the Spaniards with William of Orange in the Low Countries. But by attempting a *coup d'état* at the beginning of this year in Antwerp, the chief city of the Netherlands, he had turned the Netherlanders whose side he was supposed to be on violently against him, and nobody knew what he might do next.

Meanwhile, the forces of Catholic intransigence which were mobilising at home against Henri III had received an access of strength from England. This second problem arose from the removal to France of a number of English Catholics, and of a powerful engine of Catholic zeal, the English College at Reims, where a hundred or so young men were being trained to return to England on their clandestine and often heroic mission as Catholic priests. The persecution of these priests and their lay audience offered fine opportunities of propaganda to the diehard Catholic movement in France; and the presence in England of the fifth wheel in the carriage of contemporary western sovereigns, Mary Stewart, Queen or ex-Queen of Scots, provided a strong political reason for taking advantage of them.

Mary, to speak whose name is to arouse passion, had now been in more or less lax captivity in England since she had escaped from a Scottish rebellion fifteen years before. She was living in Sheffield Castle. Her son James was now generally recognised as king of Scotland, and her actual power was virtually nil. But her influence was very considerable; not because of her personality or political talents, but because of what she represented. She was, to any reasonable observer, the legitimate successor to Elizabeth's crown. Though no *dévote*, she represented Catholicism, and could be portrayed as another object of persecution. She represented the House of Lorraine, which for twenty-five years had dominated the forces of intransigent Catholicism in France and was now led by her first cousin, Henri, Duke of Guise. She represented, regrettably as Henri III considered, the crown of France which had been worn by her first husband, his short-lived eldest brother. She represented, not very graciously, the French interest in Scotland. She was a magnet for many who were discontented with the state of affairs in Elizabeth's England; and her establishment in power was the object of those schemes of military intervention now being canvassed by the pope. Mary had done what she could to sabotage the marriage of Elizabeth and Anjou, which would have left her out in the cold; now that that danger was over, her enmity with Elizabeth re-emerged unqualified. For many years, enthusiastic Protestants in England had been demanding her death; Elizabeth had resisted them, on the grounds that those who wanted rid of Mary would soon want rid of her. She was now, in some desperation, trying to fix up an accommodation between the two of them. Mary, feeling that the world was going her way, responded with public civility and secret contempt. She was aware that, while the present regime in France was not going to do her much good, it might before long succumb to the hostility of her friends; and she was delighted to discover that King Philip, long unwilling to support her ambitions, was coming round to her side. A *Te Deum* in Westminster Abbey was beginning to loom on her horizon.[5]

The chance of such a *peripeteia*, which we shall see being read in the stars by no less a person than the philosopher Jean Bodin, made swift and reliable intelligence an urgent necessity for Elizabeth and her ministers; it added an undertone of melodrama to the conventional exchanges of diplomacy which occupied most of the time of the two principal characters in our story. As Elizabeth's Secretary of State, Sir Francis Walsingham is known for workaholic habits and a penchant, perhaps exaggerated, for secret information; both of them in the service of a dour commitment to the Protestant cause. In this cause he kept a sharp eye on Mary. He had deplored as much as she had the prospect of a marriage between Elizabeth and Anjou, and viewed with stony hostility the revival of Romanism in England and elsewhere. He had been English ambassador in Paris during the massacre of 1572. We might suppose him to have looked with a baneful eye on any non-Protestant Frenchman. If so, we should be discounting some attractive traits: a fascination with Italy, where he had been a student, and with Italians; and a fondness for trees.[6] And we should miss his genuine friendship, ripening over twenty years, with the victim of the intelligence operation to be recounted. The victim was Michel de Castelnau, seigneur de Mauvissière, who was to be ambassador from Henri III to Elizabeth for ten whole years. He had staked a great deal on the Anjou marriage; the missionary priests, whose coming had exacerbated the nerves of English

5 A short list of essential reading on the state of affairs in north-west Europe at this time would include J. H. Elliott, *Europe Divided, 1559–1598* (London, 1968); Geoffrey Parker, *The Dutch Revolt* (London, 1977); J. H. M. Salmon, *Society in Crisis: France in the Sixteenth Century* (London, 1975); A. O. Meyer, *England and the Catholic Church under Queen Elizabeth* (London, 1916; repr. 1967); Wallace MacCaffrey, *Queen Elizabeth and the Making of Policy, 1572–1588* (Princeton, NJ, 1981). Biographies: J. E. Neale, *Queen Elizabeth* (London, 1935); Antonia Fraser, *Mary Queen of Scots* (London, 1969) and, for her reign in Scotland, the critical Jenny Wormald, *Mary Queen of Scots: a Study in Failure* (London, 1988); Mack Holt, *The Duke of Anjou and the Politique Struggle during the Wars of Religion* (Cambridge, 1986); for Walsingham, see 'Abbreviations used . . .', under 'Read'. On the Anjou marriage scheme, Susan Doran, *Monarchy and Matrimony: the Courtships of Elizabeth I* (London, 1996), chaps. 6 and 7.

6 Read, *Walsingham*, iii, 432, n. 2 (trees). For Italy, *Ibid.*, i, 22; iii, 433 (Italians at i, 56, 68, 147, 263f; iii, 438); *CSP Foreign 1575–77*, no. 694 (Valentine Dale to Walsingham, Paris, 25-iii-1576, sending over one Pietro Capponi, who had asked for a recommendation to him, 'nothing needful considering [Walsingham's] goodwill to that nation'.)

Protestants and hence had been most inconvenient for that project, he had nevertheless come to view with a nervous respect. He had a brief to represent the interests of Mary, which he had fulfilled coolly enough in the past; now, as the vision of a French marriage faded away and her own prospects seemed to brighten, he was trying to repair some of the damage. He was a Catholic, who thought of French Protestants, en masse, as enemies of his country, and of the Church of England as a self-interested muddle. In these respects he could be obstinate, but he was ecumenical in his interests: all told, Elizabeth was more his kind of person than Mary. He had assembled a markedly pluralistic establishment at Salisbury Court, which was fun for its less committed members and probably fruitful for inward intelligence; but not half so fruitful as it was of outward leakages. 'Good, easy man', he has been called,[7] and hence a sitting target for Walsingham's gambits; he was also a Renaissance figure of omnivorous and cultivated curiosity who set great store by friendship and whose range of friends included many of the intellectual luminaries of the age: Bruno and Bodin, the poet Ronsard, Philip Sidney and Walter Raleigh. He was not, so far as I know, an acquaintance of Michel de Montaigne, though surely a reader of him;[8] like Montaigne, he concealed under a sociable exterior the frustrations and contrary passions attendant on being a patriotic Frenchman in an age of national calamity.

Formally speaking, both Walsingham and Castelnau were agents, not principals: Walsingham of Elizabeth, Castelnau, in practice and on this occasion, of Mary. We shall be following an episode in the celebrated duel of the queens, which ended with Mary's execution eighteen months after our story ends. They did not simply duel by proxy: we shall see Elizabeth, her passions aroused, intervening most vigorously in the course of events. If Mary seems the more passive participant it is partly because she was hampered by her lack of freedom; partly because she was successful in destroying the part of the evidence nearest the bone; and partly because she was a more predictable person than her cousin. But even Elizabeth gives the impression of making periodic attempts to run a show which Walsingham, not she, was really master of, and I shall be suggesting that his most imaginative move was rather made against her than on her behalf. On the other side, it was Castelnau who decided exactly what line to tread in the exceptionally difficult task of reconciling his obligations to Mary, to Henri III and to Elizabeth, as well as his own disparate feelings.

7   J. H. Pollen, *The English Catholics in the Reign of Queen Elizabeth* (London, 1920), p. 315n.
8   John Florio, who lived in Salisbury Court 1583–1585, tutored Castelnau's daughter and looked after his affairs when he went home, wrote his famous translation of the *Essais* in 1599–1603; the first two books of the *Essais* had been published in 1580.

For the narrator, the sharpest competition to Walsingham and Castelnau comes, not from those they served, but from those who served them: what happens in the story happens not directly between them, but somewhere along the chains of human connection which led from one to the other, through their respective bodies of servants and agents and their mutual friends. One of the rewards of exploring the history of Elizabethan intelligence is that it takes us into that otherwise dim world as nothing else does. We shall come out of it, not with a big fish like Bruno, though he will be around, but with people worth knowing, and sometimes more knowable than their betters. We shall also become acquainted with a class of person whose doings were such that intelligence of them was always welcome and sometimes urgent: victims, in this case on the Catholic side, of the state of public affairs, enthusiasts and malcontents, vindictive exiles, conspirators, potential assassins. Such people appear a great deal in the story, and one of them has a sizeable role in it. But they will be the material of the story rather than the subject of it: we shall be seeing them either from the enemy side (Walsingham's) or from that of an embarrassed and uncertain ally (Castelnau). The subject is an intelligence operation conducted in the space between the two of them: who was involved in it, what they did, when and how they did it, and with what consequences. In due course I shall offer some thoughts about the practice of Elizabethan secret intelligence in general. For the moment I have two things to say.

First, I shall be dealing with something rather simple: individuals, pieces of handwritten paper, meetings and conversations face to face. The human feelings and relationships which pertain to the craft of spying are surely universal: the machinery, physical and administrative, will change. There will not be much technology here: it will be human intelligence in a pretty strict sense. Second, I shall be dealing with a story that has been concealed: concealed indeed most efficiently. Unravelling such stories requires a pair of spectacles adapted for the kind of close work conventionally thought to be more proper to policemen than to historians. It will generally require a certain amount of conjecture. I think that the general shape of the story, its major events and my interpretation of them, will survive the critical tests to which any work of history is subject. In details, I have allowed conjecture a little room: so, when a person mentioned in a document is referred to only as somebody's servant, I have taken the liberty of identifying him as the particular servant I think he is most likely to have been. I may not always have acknowledged this instantly in the text or in a footnote.

I have taken no liberties, I believe, in the identification with which, to the contrary of detective fiction, I must begin the story; for it is by this

identification, to borrow again from John Holloway, that we find our ini-
tiating event.[9] Or rather: we do not exactly find it, but detect it by trian-
gulation, which is natural considering the sort of event it is. There remains
the task of giving it a set of exact and visible features, which takes time;
unlike Holloway's model, Boccaccio, we cannot briskly invent the meeting
of a priest and the mother of his godchild. Peter Burke has suggested that
we might liven up the practice of historical narration by experimenting
with alternative endings:[10] this sounds perverse. Alternative beginnings are
another matter. They seem to be embedded in the sequence of historical
investigation, at least where one is trying to find out something which has
been concealed. In short, I spend three chapters figuring out exactly what
was the event with which the story starts. I do not think this is two chapters too many. I might say that they amount to a description of the milieu
or a history of the question; and that the reader will get a clearer view of
the event by seeing precisely what it was not. There would be something
to be said for all of these proposals. But what I really mean is that they
tell a good but accessory story which needs to be got out of the way
before we can proceed with the real one. The first story is partly a story
about the historian himself, and so far may be thought to conform to E.
H. Carr's injunction to 'study the historian before you begin to study the
facts'.[11] The average reader will judge this a dreary suggestion, and rightly:
Carr's facts were more interesting than Carr, and mine are more interesting than me. We have come, writer and reader, to find out what actually
happened; we can now get on with it.

---

9   *Narrative and Structure*, p. 5.
10 Peter Burke, 'History of Events and the Revival of Narrative', in P. Burke (ed.), *New Perspectives
    in Historical Writing* (Oxford, 1991), p. 240. I should say that Burke's alternative endings only differ
    by stopping the narrative at different times, which is perfectly reasonable.
11 E. H. Carr, *What is History?* (2nd edn by R. Davies, London, 1987), p. 23.

PART I

Secrets and Secretaries

I

A POT OF MARMALADE

WHEN WALSINGHAM DIED in London in April 1590 he took many of his secrets with him. One he did not take was reported not long afterwards by his brother-in-law Robert Beale: as clerk of the Privy Council, and as Walsingham's stand-in as Secretary of State for some of the relevant time, he is a good authority. For the later use of a candidate who was applying for Walsingham's position, Beale described how he, Walsingham, had gone about the job, and came to the doings in intelligence for which he was renowned. For instance: 'In the time of the Ambassages of Monsieur la Mott [La Mothe-Fénelon, French ambassador 1568–75] and Monsieur Mauvesier [1575–85], he had some of his [i.e. their] secretaries that bewrayed the secretts both of the French and Scottish dealinges.' Beale did not know, and said the queen had doubted, whether the secrets had been worth the money spent on them.[1]

This is surprising, because the French and Scottish dealings in question were dealings with or about Mary, Queen of Scots, for whom the ambassadors held a brief; if there were secrets to be revealed about them, they were probably secrets affecting the security of the realm. True, Beale was not talking about the most famous case of Walsingham's extraction of secret intelligence from the French embassy, which occurred in 1586 and led to the execution of Mary and that of a number of her English admirers who had been conspiring in what is known as the Babington Plot:[2] neither of the ambassadors mentioned had been in London at the time. He must have meant some earlier chapter in the same sorry tale. I do not know why he included among Walsingham's victims M. de la Mothe-Fénelon, whose stint as ambassador overlapped with Walsingham's secretaryship by only a year or so and was not, at that time, raising any political problems; perhaps he was referring to a period Fénelon spent in London early in 1583, on the way back from an official trip to Scotland. This was indeed

1 Read, *Walsingham*, i, 435–6; from BL Yelverton Mss, 162.
2 Described below, pp. 139–42.

a time when relations were sensitive; the person in charge of them was Fénelon's host, Michel de Castelnau (Mauvesier).

Beale's applicant did not get the job, and his briefing stayed in the family archives until it was printed in 1925. It took a long time for historians, working from the other end of the evidence, to catch up with him. They were French, not English. During the 1760s the medieval scholar Louis de Bréquigny went through English manuscript collections copying material of French interest, which he deposited in the Royal Library in Paris. In the British Museum he came upon Harleian Manuscript 1582, which turned out to contain the principal documents in the case. It was a volume of Elizabethan papers relating to France, and contained a number of copies of letters of Mary, Queen of Scots. It had come from Walsingham's files, and a good deal of it, including the letters from Mary, consisted of documents originating in Castelnau's office. How they had got to Walsingham was made plain by a note attached to the copy of one of Mary's letters written by whoever had sent it. Bréquigny observed that the handwriting of this note was identical with that in which Mary's letters had been copied; and hence that the leakage was the work of a single person. It was a piquant fact that the letter to which the culprit's note was attached was one from Mary to Castelnau, dated 25 February 1584, in which she told him that someone in his house was leaking their correspondence.[3] Bréquigny's discovery was made public by Louise de Kéralio, historian and novelist, who on the eve of the Revolution attempted in vain to persuade her countrymen of the political virtues of Queen Elizabeth,[4] and exploited by Prince Alexander Labanoff in the classic edition of Mary's letters and papers which he published in 1844–5. Labanoff's trawl of the sources has scarcely been surpassed, and by fitting the evidence in the Harleian manuscript with what was to be found elsewhere he claimed to identify the mole and to give some account of him. His name was Chérelles, and he was the secretary of the embassy. He had begun, as far as Labanoff could see, in the autumn of 1583, and had continued until at least October or November of the following year, from which time Labanoff found, elsewhere in the British Museum, another confidential and anonymous note from him to, presumably, Walsingham. This was not the end of Chérelles'

3 J. Balteau *et al.* (ed.), *Dictionnaire de biographie française*, vii (Paris, 1956), *Bréquigny*; the volume was no. 97 of the 100 containing his copies.

4 Louise Guinement de Kéralio [*afterwards* Robert], *Histoire d'Élisabeth, reine d'Angleterre* (5 vols, Paris, 1786–8); extracts from Harleian Ms.1582 (via Bréquigny) printed in vol. v, 345–95, the one mentioned at p. 361. Her interesting career is discussed by Carla Hesse in Barbara Diefendorf and Carla Hesse (ed.), *Culture and Identity in Early Modern Europe: Essays in Honour of Natalie Zemon Davis* (Ann Arbor, 1993), pp. 237–59.

treachery. In the spring of 1585, when he was back in Paris, he had got
hold of the collection of ciphers used for correspondence between Mary
and her friends in England and abroad; he had managed to do this when
his superiors, ignorant of his betrayal, had employed him to go through
the papers of one Thomas Morgan, a servant of Mary living in Paris.[5]

Morgan, who will be a constant though invisible presence in our story,
was a Catholic gentleman of energy and ambition who came from south
Wales. He had become secretary to George, Earl of Shrewsbury, shortly
after Queen Elizabeth had appointed Shrewsbury guardian of Mary, her
guest or prisoner. Mary had secured Morgan for herself and her cause;
after a short imprisonment on this account he had left for France. There
he entered the establishment which Mary maintained in Paris as dowager
queen, and soon acquired the position of a virtual secretary of state, communicating with her through the French embassy in London and otherwise, and setting on foot a multitude of schemes and conspiracies on her
behalf.[6] In March 1585, at Elizabeth's request, Henri III had arrested him,
put him in prison, and seized a pile of his papers which Chérelles was told
to investigate. According to Labanoff Chérelles extracted the collection of
ciphers which Morgan had used for his correspondence, and in the
summer, when he returned to London as secretary to the next ambassador, he passed over the collection to Walsingham. This windfall enabled
Walsingham and his staff to decipher the large quantity of new correspondence to and from Mary which came into their hands in the first half
of 1586, and from it to assemble the evidence of conspiracy with Anthony
Babington and others on which she was executed. Labanoff had no
evidence that Chérelles had contributed to the success of the intricate
arrangements by which this correspondence had been acquired, but since
these involved the French embassy his collaboration could probably be
assumed. He was not there to witness his work come to fruition, as it did
in July 1586: four months before that his treachery had been discovered
in Paris, and he had been summoned home. Nothing was known of his
career thereafter.

The evidence Labanoff had was direct and indirect. Chérelles had
personally been charged with the offence, and had defended himself in
letters written to Mary at the time of his recall home.[7] Otherwise there
were the two anonymous notes which had been found by Bréquigny and

5 Labanoff, v, 361n, 430n; vi, 14ff, 150n, 260n; vii, 175.
6 *DNB*; Leo Hicks, *An Elizabethan Problem: Some Aspects of the Careers of Two Exile-Adventurers* (London, 1964); Mark Greengrass, 'Mary, Dowager Queen of France', *The Innes Review*, xxxviii (1987), 171–88.
7 Labanoff, vii, 175; *CSP Scotland 1585–6*, pp. 255f, 290, 297; and below, p. 23–5.

himself,[8] and the copies of Mary's letters in the same hand. Having read Chérelles' acknowledged letters in the State Paper Office, Labanoff was prepared to state that these were in the same handwriting. Hence the charge against Chérelles was correct. He had been for some three years a traitor to both the ambassadors who employed him, to his king, and to the Queen of Scots. He had been the instrument of the queen's undoing.

Labanoff's discovery thickened the atmosphere of pathos and melodrama attending the downfall of his heroine. It might have furnished Verdi with a strong role if he, rather than Donizetti, had written an opera about her. But nineteenth-century historians, who were rather above such things as espionage, did not make much of it. In a brief round-up of Walsingham's work in the field, James Anthony Froude observed that 'Chérelles, the secretary of the French ambassador, was bought to watch his master', and left it at that.[9] The excellent historian of the underside of Elizabethan policy, the Jesuit John Hungerford Pollen, does not seem to have thought that Chérelles was a traitor at all. He poured cold water on Labanoff's story about the ciphers which, he claimed, would not have done Walsingham any good if he had had them; so far as I know he never commented publicly on the leakages of 1583–4. I have the feeling that he had checked up on Labanoff's identification of the handwriting of the copied letters, and found it unpersuasive.[10] His reticence is the more remarkable since a document had been published in 1910, which appeared to bring sensational confirmation to Labanoff's conclusion. It was a letter written to Walsingham by another informant in Castelnau's household, who called himself Henri Fagot, apparently in April 1583. It said that the writer had talked to the ambassador's secretary, and that the secretary had said that he was willing, for a consideration, to communicate to Walsingham the contents of his master's correspondence with Mary and the cipher in which it was written. April 1583 was close to the date of the earliest of Labanoff's leaked copies; it seemed quite clear that Fagot had recorded the origins of the leakage, and it was now certain that the source of it was Castelnau's secretary. Chérelles was Castelnau's secretary. He was consequently the man to whom Fagot had talked, and the man responsible for the copies and the notes to Walsingham.[11]

8   Labanoff, v, 429; vi, 26f; from BL Harleian 1582, f. 312ᵛ, and BL Cottonian Nero B vi, ff. 371ᵛ–2ʳ.

9   James Anthony Froude, *History of England from the Fall of Wolsey to the Defeat of the Spanish Armada* (12 vols, London, 1870, repr. 1893), vii, 102.

10   J. H. Pollen (ed.), *Mary, Queen of Scots and the Babington Plot* (Scottish History Society, 3rd series, iii, Edinburgh, 1922), introduction, pp. xxx f, lv, lx.

11   *GB*, pp. 18–20, and Text no. 4; *CSP Scotland 1581–83*, pp. 430–1.

Hence, when the American Conyers Read published his full political biography of Walsingham in 1925–7, Chérelles emerged into the light. He was indeed the party to whom Fagot had talked; thenceforth he had given Walsingham a copy of practically all the letters which passed between Mary and Castelnau, and in particular of the one dated 25 February 1584 to which his note was attached. Chérelles was re-established as the mole-secretary of 1583–4. Read's account of him was not quite so confident as Labanoff's. He followed Pollen in silently acquitting him of Labanoff's second phase of treachery, in 1585 and 1586. He also revealed that there was a difficulty in the evidence by noticing that in November 1583, when the leakage from the embassy was running strongly, Walsingham had had a conversation with Castelnau's secretary, who appeared to be somebody else than Chérelles. So, when he talked about Chérelles' treachery, he described him as 'one of [Castelnau's] secretaries'.[12] A pedantic reader might have observed that, if Castelnau had had more than one secretary, Fagot's information, which certainly confirmed that there was a mole in the establishment, did not confirm that the mole was Chérelles. On that point there was still no more evidence than Labanoff's, that the leaked letters were in Chérelles' handwriting.

Some of Read's conclusions about Elizabethan espionage, as that the then English ambassador in Paris, Sir Edward Stafford, was working for the Spaniards, did not satisfy everybody;[13] in the case of Chérelles his authority has not been contested. He was followed by Leo Hicks, who succeeded to Pollen's position as historian of the English Jesuits; in 1964, in a book about Thomas Morgan and his friends, he made even more of Chérelles than Read had done. He seems to have conceded that there were no grounds for attributing treachery to him in connection with the Babington Plot; but he saw Chérelles as coming from farther back than that. In Hicks's view this shadowy secretary had been a force in Eliza-bethan history, not because of his betrayal of Mary's letters, which did not seem to have had anything to do with the queen's downfall, but because of his relationship with Morgan. Hicks believed of Morgan what Read believed of Stafford, that he was in the pay of the other side: doing Walsingham's work by concocting spurious conspiracies to discredit Mary and sowing internecine conflict among those labouring in the English Catholic cause. In the scheme by which Mary was finally destroyed, Morgan's intermediary had been the renegade seminary student Gilbert Gifford, who had organised the delivery to her enemies of a quantity of

---

12 Read, *Walsingham*, ii, 380f, 389, 395 (cf. *CSP Scotland 1581–83*, p. 654); iii, 5. I suppose he was fol-lowing Robert Beale (above, n. 1).
13 'The Fame of Sir Edward Stafford', *American Historical Review*, xx (1915), 292–313.

Mary's correspondence; before Gifford, the job had been Chérelles'. By his own account, Chérelles had in 1585 been in touch with Morgan secretly for several years, including the years when he was passing letters to Walsingham. This, thought Hicks, was sufficient to damn them both. When he came to Morgan's papers he constructed a new version of Labanoff's story, which Pollen seemed to have disbelieved: under instructions from England, Chérelles was removing the evidence of Morgan's communications with Walsingham, preserving his cover, and enabling him to conclude his operations by planting on Mary Gifford and the other agents by whom she was entrapped.[14] This was a hazardous conjecture; but it had in its favour the very reasonable inference that, if Chérelles was working for Walsingham (as everyone agreed), and if Chérelles had attended to Morgan's papers (as he certainly had), he must have been attending to them in Walsingham's interest.

In the end the moral of Hicks's story about Morgan and Chérelles was that knowledge may triumph over intention. His intention was to show that dirty tricks were the Elizabethan government's way of resisting the momentum of the Catholic movement in England, and that Chérelles' operations were essential to the pulling off of one of the most effective of them. It was probably misguided, and certainly unsubtle; but in stubbornly pursuing it Hicks advanced the subject not a little. He added two more points of fact. He discovered that Chérelles was identical with a man called Arnault who had appeared in Read's footnotes, confusingly, as yet another informant in the French ambassador's household; and that when he was dealing with Morgan's papers he was not the embassy secretary, though he had been before and was to be again.[15] Both these points were to prove important, especially the first: among other things, it revealed that a number of letters written to Walsingham from Paris around the same time, and signed 'Arnault', were letters from Chérelles.[16] There was now a chance of putting together some kind of a biography of him; and Hicks took the sensible view that his doings would only be got into perspective when fitted into a coherent account of the conduct towards Elizabethan Catholicism of his employers, the government of France. He was disposed

14 Hicks, *An Elizabethan Problem*, esp. pp. 172–84, 77–90; the key passage is from *CSP Scotland 1585–86*, p. 290 (Chérelles to Mary, 20/30-iii-1586). I have made Fr. Hicks's views rather more definite than they appear in his book, but this is what they amounted to.

15 Hicks, *An Elizabethan Problem*, pp. 173, 178, 181; cf. Read, *Walsingham*, ii, 380.

16 Arnault to Walsingham, 17/27-x-1584, 25-i/4-ii-1585, 16/26-ii-1585, 4/14-iii-1585 (PRO SP 78/12, no. 93 and Plate I; 78/13, nos. 17, 31, 49[bis]; *CSP Foreign 1584–85*, pp. 109, 260, 285, 323).

to believe that the French crown, out of hostility to all the forces which had invested in the English Catholic cause – popes, Spaniards, his own Society of Jesus – was likely to have been sympathetic to Elizabethan dirty tricks against it, perhaps to have collaborated in pulling them off. In that case, Chérelles, or Arnault, or whatever he ought to be called, would not have been simply a venal secretary, but the instrument of a clandestine Anglo-French entente. In 1956 he found a student looking for a research topic, who proved willing to investigate the larger subject on roughly these lines.

The first thing to do about Chérelles was to clear up the problem of his name: it might be thought to count against him that he had had two. But Frenchmen of the time might be known by their family name or by the name of their *seigneurie* or lordship, if they possessed one, and this turned out to be the case here. A letter from Chérelles of November 1585 could be found in the Bibliothèque nationale in Paris, signed 'Arnault de Chérelles':[17] he must have acquired his title the previous summer, just before his return to London as secretary to Castelnau's successor. That settled, one could now discover that he came from towards the top of the French administrative and political élite, a much-intermarried body of people who carried the burdens and rewards of immediate royal service. His father had been only a provincial official, but his mother came from two eminent families: the Myrons, who included both Henri III's physician and his chief financial officer; and the Morvilliers, whose head, Jean de Morvillier, bishop of Orléans, had been a principal royal councillor for twenty years before his death in 1577. Morvillier had sponsored Castelnau for the embassy in London; he had found him a wife, and had surely found him a secretary as well. Arnault was related to both the ambassadors he served, and to almost everybody who was anybody around the king; his brother or brother-in-law ran the finances of Queen Mary's establishment in France, and sat on its council with Thomas Morgan and others.[18] One of the hardest things to find out

---

17 Arnault to [ ] Pasquier, London, 13/23-xi-1585 (BN V^{c}C 472, p. 179). The full signature is stuck in the binding, but the endorsement says the letter is from '[?Monsieur] de Chérelles'. He is referred to by his brother[-in-law?] Antoine de Chaulnes as 'Chérelles' in a letter of 18/28-vii-1585 (*Ibid*. p. 149), and had therefore acquired the *seigneurie* since 27-iv/7-v-1585, the (probable) date of a letter of his to Castelnau signed 'Arnault' (*Ibid*. p. 189).

18 J. le Laboureur (ed.), *Mémoires de Michel de Castelnau* (3 vols, Brussels, 1731), iii, 166f: François Myron, Henri II's doctor, married Geneviève de Morvillier (the bishop's niece), and among their children were Robert, seigneur de Chenailles, 'contrôleur-general et intendant des finances' to Henri III; Marc, the king's doctor; and Marie, who married Jean Arnaud, 'lieutenant-général d'Angoulême'. Our Arnault is identified as the son of the last two by his references to Chenailles as his uncle (*CSP Scotland 1585–86*, p. 297; BN V^{c}C 472, p. 189). On Morvillier, G. Baguenault de Puchesse, *Jean de Morvillier*, (Paris, 1870), and N.

about him was his Christian name, which eventually emerged from a list of Henri III's household in 1586: this gave 'Maistre Jehan Arnault', certainly our man, as the first of five men holding the office of Secretary of the king's Chamber, who were under-secretaries to the four Secretaries of State.[19]

In London or in Paris Arnault, as I shall now call him, was in an extraordinarily good position to act as an English mole; he was equally well placed to serve as confidential instrument of the clandestine accord between Henri III and Elizabeth for which Hicks had been looking. So it was with some anticipation that one turned to the four letters written by Arnault to Walsingham from Paris between 17 October 1584 and 4 March 1585, which was three days after Morgan's arrest, in a large, loopy and blessedly legible italic hand. It was disappointing to discover that they appeared to be mainly about pots of jam: for Walsingham 'quelques boîtes de Cotignac d'Orléans', which is quince marmalade or jelly, a box of 'confitures' for Mary. With a French sense of the priorities proper in a period of cold war, Arnault was concerned that they should not be hacked about ('margouillés') by customs officers or the guardians of Mary's household. Still, he might have been writing in code; he said he was keen to do services for Walsingham both in Paris and, when he had returned, in London; the last of the letters was sent by one of Walsingham's servants, perhaps the famous organizer of dirty tricks Thomas Phellippes. One other thing emerged from what seemed, on the face of it, a charming correspondence. By the end of it, as Hicks had said, Arnault was no longer Castelnau's secretary even *in absentia*, since he sent his third letter, in February 1585, by a man whom he so described; and he seemed to have been back in Paris for longer than one had supposed, not just from October 1584 but for some time before that, since in his first letter he referred to a previous despatch of marmalade which Walsingham had acknowledged with enthusiasm.[20] *Cotignac d'Orléans* was not to be had in London.

Sutherland, *The Massacre of St Bartholomew and the European Conflict* (London, 1973), pp. 252–55. For Arnault's and Castelnau's connections with him, Labanoff, v, 11; PRO Transcripts 31/3/27, [ ]-viii-1575, 8-xi-1577 – Castelnau's wife, Marie Bochetel, was another of Morvillier's nieces. For the 'brother', Antoine de Chaulnes, Labanoff, v, 118; vi, 174 and elsewhere. For the milieu in general, N. Sutherland, *The French Secretaries of State in the Age of Catherine de Medici* (London, 1962).

19 Archives nationales (Paris), KK 139 (Comptes de la Maison du Roy, 1586), f. 37f.

20 Above, n. 16; Phelippes returned to London from Paris with a packet from Stafford on 10/20 April (*CSP Foreign 1584–85*, p. 410).

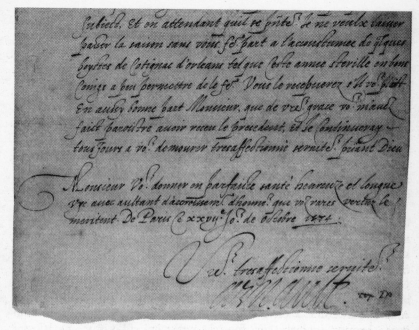

Plate I   Jean Arnault to Sir Francis Walsingham, Paris, 17/27 October 1584. Holograph. Public Record Office SP, 78/12, no. 93. 'The marmalade letter'.

Two difficulties arose from this surprising correspondence about Arnault's career as a mole. One was the handwriting: if Arnault was Chérelles, they ought to have had the same handwriting, but there was no resemblance at all between the elegant italic hand of the marmalade letters and the plain secretary hand of the mole's notes and copies. Well: people in the sixteenth century might have several hands, and it would be natural for a mole, while moling, to use a hand different from his normal one. The other difficulty was about dates. Labanoff's evidence of Arnault's treachery extended to dealings between some time in 1583 and his return to England in the summer of 1585. The two occasions for which there was explicit documentary evidence from the culprit himself, in his two notes to Walsingham, had occurred during 1584, and the second of them could not be dated much earlier than the middle of October, since the note accompanied a letter written by Mary on the 1st of the month.[21] How could Arnault have written it in London if he had sent the marmalade letter to Walsingham from Paris on the 17th, and appeared to have been in Paris for some time before that? True, he could have been in London between one despatch of marmalade and the next, and if he had not been there recently it was hard to see why he was corresponding with Walsingham at all. Secretaries of the London embassy made their way back and forth across the Channel pretty frequently, carrying confidential letters and messages. Journey times in the sixteenth century were unpredictable. The author of a detective story which had Arnault as a suspect could probably, wind and weather permitting, just about find time for him to send his copy of Mary's letter, nip across the Channel, pick up his marmalade and put it in the post by 17 October. But it sounded improbable, and only to be contemplated if we could be sure that Arnault had still been Castelnau's secretary in those October days.

According to the English ambassador Sir Edward Stafford, who was writing in May 1585, Arnault was then Castelnau's *ex*-secretary, now Secretary of the king's Chamber;[22] this must, by Arnault's own account, have already been so in February. How long before that? This proved difficult to determine exactly, but a little investigation produced a decisive result. One of Castelnau's letters in the Harleian volume, which had been sent by the mole along with the first of his notes, had been written in or about April 1584: we shall need to return to it fairly frequently. All we need from it now is that Castelnau, describing the personnel of his office, mentioned Arnault as someone who did not belong to it any more: 'Arnault, when he was here'.[23] Since Arnault and Chérelles were the same person, Chérelles had already ceased to be Castelnau's secretary at precisely the time when the principal leakage of documents was occurring; and some six or seven months before the last one had occurred. He could not be the secretary who had written a note to accompany a leaked letter which said that he was not the secretary. When one pursued the question further, it emerged that Arnault had not been Castelnau's secretary for rather a long time.

As far back as May 1582, when he was in Paris, we could find him being described by the two people who were employing him as already both Castelnau's former secretary and a Secretary of the king's Chamber. Hence he had changed jobs before that, and in fact we cannot find him in Castelnau's service after 1581.[24] He had in short disappeared beyond the horizon, and must have left London around the beginning of 1582, well over a year

---

22 *CSP Foreign 1584–85*, p. 457.

23 Castelnau to Mary, [22-iii/1-iv-1584] (Document (d)).

24 *CSP Foreign 1582*, p. 42 (Horatio Pallavicino); PRO Transcripts 31/9/79, 1-vi-1582 (Catherine de Medici); R. Toupin (ed.), *Correspondance du nonce en France G. B. Castelli, 1581–83* (Rome/Paris, 1967), pp. 328, 353. Other references to Arnault in Paris, July and November 1581, in BL Cottonian Galba E vi, f. 67 (Cobham); *HMC Hatfield*, ii, 441.

before the leakage of Castelnau's correspondence had begun. In so far as the charge against Arnault had been the leaking of Castelnau's letters, Labanoff and Read and Hicks had got the wrong man.

This leaves us with the second charge against him, tinkering dishonestly with Morgan's papers.[25] Since this will take us beyond the frame of this book in time and place, I insert a chronology of Arnault's career. From (probably) 1575 to about the end of 1581 he was in London as secretary to Castelnau. From early 1582 he was back in Paris. From the summer of 1582 to about May 1584 he was mainly in Rome, for reasons we shall see. From then until August 1585 he was in Paris, where he acquired his *seigneurie*. He also corresponded with Walsingham, in preparation for his second period as secretary to the embassy in London, under Castelnau's successor Guillaume de l'Aubépine, baron de Châteauneuf. He was back in England in August 1585, bringing to Mary objects of art and devotion collected in Italy. He served Châteauneuf from September 1585 to March or April 1586, when he was recalled to Paris, seemingly under a cloud. In the summer of 1586 he left for Rome again, on the way to Malta.

In the middle of this busy career we find the occasion when, as Labanoff and Hicks claimed, Arnault had served English interests while dealing with Thomas Morgan's papers. He might have subtracted Morgan's collection of ciphers and passed it over to England; or he might have got rid of sensational evidence that Morgan had been corrupted by Walsingham. He was, after all, corresponding with Walsingham at the time: was it not reasonable to suppose that there was something underneath, even inside, the marmalade? There is no shortage of evidence about the incident of the papers, and although the central contribution is Arnault's own, made in a letter to Mary a year later when he was defending himself against the charge of having betrayed her, it is generally supported from both the French and the English side.[26]

Morgan was arrested at his lodgings in the south-west of the city on 1 March 1585, and taken to the Bastille. His papers were impounded, and deposited with Pinart, the secretary of state who dealt with England. They were presumed to contain compromising matter concerning conspiracies against Elizabeth, whence Stafford was demanding that they should be sent to England; he had also claimed that Morgan had been conspiring against the crown of France. The French would need to inspect them on either ground, and rather more on the first than on the second: Henri III's crown

25 Above p. 15.
26 Arnault (Chérelles) to Mary, London, 20/30-iii and 23-iii/2-iv-1586 (*CSP Scotland 1585–86*, pp. 290ff, 297); Hicks, *An Elizabethan Problem*, pp. 179f. Evidence from the French side in Le Laboureur, *Mémoires de Castelnau*, i, 619 and G. Baguenault de Puchesse (ed.), *Lettres de Catherine de Médicis*, viii (Paris, 1901), p. 454; from the English side (Stafford), *CSP Foreign 1584–85*, pp. 309ff, 457ff; from Morgan and Charles Paget in Murdin, pp. 440–41; *CSP Scotland 1584–85*, p. 630; *1585–86*, p. 255 (misdated).

was in danger from an impending mass revolt of French Catholics, who regarded Mary Stewart as a martyr for the faith, and if the king was found to have exposed her loyal followers to Elizabeth's vengeance, that might very possibly be the end of him. Whoever was to look at the papers will almost certainly have been told that if he found any compromising items he was to make them disappear: Arnault was chosen for the job. As an under-secretary, he will have been working for one of the principal secretaries, probably for Villeroy. Having worked for Castelnau, he was *au fait* with the subject; he was, as the marmalade letters show, reasonably well regarded in England; and he was almost certainly the only member of Henri III's secretariat who could read English. Arnault himself implies political motives for the choice: one of the reasons he had been picked, he told Mary, was that he had been on friendly terms with Morgan for a long time, though this was not generally known. Hicks had thought this sinister: I think Arnault meant that he had been dealing, in London and probably in Paris, with the conveyance of Mary's correspondence to and from Paris through the French diplomatic bag.[27] In that case, he will have been appointed to do Morgan and Mary a good turn on the quiet; which I think he was, and did.

Morgan had had some time to deal with his papers before the arrest, so there was probably not too much inflammatory matter left in them; but there were a lot of letters, a collection of thirty-two ciphers for correspondence, an account book and a memo-book. Much could have been extracted from these. Arnault says that he simply removed all letters and papers of political interest and handed them back to Morgan's friend and stand-in Charles Paget; he probably burned the account book and the memo-book. After a hiatus caused by political crisis in France, he was instructed to bring the papers to the Council, and brought a modest collection of odds and ends, which included some ciphers. The councillors told him to take these to Stafford, which he did. The only worthwhile thing among them was the ciphers, which Stafford was keen to have because he had himself got hold of a packet of Morgan's letters which he intended to decipher with their aid. There were nine ciphers in the packet returned: Arnault had made them up himself, and put them in instead of Morgan's original thirty-two, which he had removed. Stafford sat up all night, and gave himself a bad headache trying to use them to decipher the letters he had; Arnault went back to the Council and told them what he had done, and not being very sympathetic to Stafford they laughed a great deal. I have no idea what happened to the authentic thirty-two, but there

27 Above, p. 18; *GB*, pp. 54–6. Cf. Paget in *CSP Scotland 1585–86*, p. 26: Arnault depends on Villeroy.

is no evidence that Arnault sent or brought them to England, and I suppose he either gave them to Paget or burned them.

In short, the story of Arnault's dealings with Morgan's papers is of his doing Morgan and his friends a favour, under instructions, I suspect, directly from Villeroy and indirectly from Henri III. Anyone may disbelieve it if they will; but there is a lot of good evidence for it, and no evidence for any other story at all. The only reason for supposing that Arnault was doing something different from what he appeared to be doing had been that he was thought to have been working for Walsingham for two years already; but we have no reason to believe this. He emerges, not as a scoundrel, but as a civilised and conscientious person with a sense of humour.[28] This does him the more credit in view of a fact of some importance in Arnault's life: his father, and namesake, had been something of a Catholic martyr in the wars of religion. Jean Arnault *père* had been *lieutenant-général*, or principal royal justice, in the city of Angoulême. In 1568, Gaspard de Coligny's Huguenot army had been consolidating its ethnic territory in south-west France and had seized and sacked the town. Arnault *père* was perhaps the chief royal officer in Angoulême; the Huguenots had arrested him, beaten him up and finally, so the Catholics said, strangled him in his house. His fate was widely publicised by the Anglo-Dutch polemicist Richard Verstegan as a superior instance of Protestant barbarity.[29] I do not know whether Arnault *fils*, who must have been in his teens at the time, was in his father's house when he was murdered: in any case it will now be hard to imagine him growing up into a fellow-traveller of the Protestant cause or the instrument of an anti-Catholic Anglo-French entente. The father was a Catholic royalist, and so was the son.

That being so, why has the charge been made against him? It was originally brought in the spring of 1586, when Arnault was eight months into his second period in London, as secretary to Castelnau's successor Châteauneuf. We do not know exactly what he was accused of doing in England, and so far as I can see the accusation was extremely vague: Arnault was not actually the man who dealt with Mary's business under the Châteauneuf regime. The only precise charge against him related to what he had been doing, not in England, but in Rome. He had indeed been in Rome for most of the time between 1582, when he seems to have left London, and 1584, when we have found him back in Paris. The charge

---

28 It would spoil Arnault's story if Charles Paget had been an English 'spy' or 'agent', as suggested by Hicks, *An Elizabethan Problem*, pp. 7–11, 21–9, followed less cautiously by Fraser, *Mary Queen of Scots*, pp. 552f; but there is no good reason to believe this.

29 Richard Verstegan, *Theatrum crudelitatum haereticorum nostri temporis* (Antwerp, 1592), p. 36. I owe this to Dr Anne Dillon: it appears in the volume of appendices to her thesis, 'The Construction of Martyrdom in the English Catholic Community, to 1603' (Cambridge Univ. Ph.D., 1998), ii, 192.

was that he had been spreading the word there that Mary was hostile to the idea of military intervention against Elizabeth on her behalf, and had been discouraging the papacy and the Catholic powers from proceeding with it. It was presumably being alleged that he had been doing this as an English agent.[30]

The grounds for the making and believing of this accusation, if it was an accusation, are not hard to discover. Arnault had been in Rome for two periods: certainly during the summer of 1582, and probably for the best part of a year ending in May 1584. On the first occasion he had been acting, with the concurrence of Henri III and Catherine de Medici, as the representative of a Genoese financier now resident in England, Horatio Pallavicino. The purpose of his mission was to rescue from the prisons of the Inquisition Pallavicino's brother Fabrizio, who had been in custody for four years on a charge which had little theology in it, but was connected with infighting between financial syndicates about control of the export of alum from the papal territories: a profitable business on which the clothiers of northern Europe depended. For a hostile observer this seemingly innocent mission of mercy was dubious in itself, and would appear increasingly so in retrospect, as Horatio Pallavicino emerged as a pillar of the Elizabethan regime: Elizabeth's financier, ambassador and hirer of Protestant armies, convert to the Church of England, supervisor of spying on English Catholics abroad.[31] I should not in fact be surprised if there had not been more to Arnault's trip to Rome than a service to Pallavicino's brother: the ambassador with whom he stayed in 1582, and to whose household he returned for eight months in 1583–4, was Paul de Foix, a cultured aristocrat and *politique*, who had barely escaped burning as a Protestant in the 1550s and had views virtually indistinguishable from Elizabeth's own. In Rome his systematic policy was to prevent a Catholic attack against her. We can well believe that while Arnault was there he had done his best to bring specific detail to the support of the ambassador's line: in the Curia they had cultivated Cardinal Montalto, who as Sixtus V

30 Arnault bought by Walsingham: Labanoff, vii, 176 (*CSP Scotland 1585–86*, p. 255); *CSP Foreign 1586–88*, p. 34. Returned to France by 16/26-iv-1586: BN fr 3305, f. 24. Mary's reaction: Labanoff, vi, 418 (*CSP Scotland 1585–86*, p. 554). A useful addition is Albert Fontenay to Mary, Paris, 28-iii/7-iv-1586, deciphered by Shiela Richards, *Secret Writings in the Public Records* (London, 1974), p. 35, written while awaiting Arnault's return; he put the credence given to the charge down to the bad odour of Arnault's trip to Rome; cf. *CSP Scotland 1585–86*, p. 146. The secretary who dealt with Mary's business under Châteauneuf was called Cordaillot: A. Teulet (ed.) *Relations diplomatiques de la France . . . avec l'Écosse au XVIe siècle* (5 vols, Paris, 1862), iv, 96; he is called 'Cordaillot-Arnault' in *CSP Domestic Addenda 1580–1625*, p. 233, and may therefore have been a brother or other relation of our Arnault, and the writer of the otherwise perplexing letter of 'Arnault' to Courcelles, London, 27-viii/6-ix-1586 (*CSP Scotland 1585–86*, p. 629).
31 Laurence Stone, *An Elizabethan: Sir Horatio Palavicino* (Oxford, 1956), *passim*, and pp. 4ff, 10ff, 41–64, 102f, for the incident. For Arnault's part, *CSP Foreign 1582*, pp. 42, 77, 104, 224 (Pallavicino), and above, n. 24; and *Lettres de Messire Paul de Foix . . . au Roy Henri III* (Paris, 1628), pp. 519f (Arnault in Rome).

was to emerge a year later as a pope sceptical of enterprises against England. While there is no evidence that Arnault had any connection with England at this time, it is not impossible that in 1582 he had been sent to explore, ultimately on Elizabeth's behalf, whether there was any prospect of averting a final breach between England and Rome.[32] To that extent Hicks's bold hypothesis had something to be said for it.

We cannot be surprised that Catholic zealots regarded Arnault's doings in Rome as extremely suspect. And there were plenty of such zealots in Rome in the spring of 1586, even if the new pope had turned out not to be one of them. In the immediate context there were French envoys of the Duke of Guise and the Catholic League complaining bitterly that Henri III and his representatives in Rome were betraying the Catholic cause; and there was the English émigré establishment, whose base was a second English College, recently established, which worked in close relation with the Leaguers.[33] It was presumably from them that the accusation against Arnault came; and, even without the general state of Catholic paranoia which prevailed in Paris at the time, it was no great step from exposing Arnault as an agent of English influence in Rome, to assuming that he was using his position as secretary of the embassy in London to betray the secrets of Queen Mary. The conclusion was reported to Mary in a letter from a servant of hers in Paris called Albert Fontenay, who was not entirely convinced of it himself: its grounds, he said, were a general feeling that Arnault was 'peu catholique' (i.e., not a Leaguer) and an unscrupulous careerist, whose conduct in Rome had given him a very bad reputation all round. There was probably another influence at work. It appears that the information against Arnault was presented to the Queen Mother by a prominent English émigré gentleman called Charles Arundell who, according to a good source, had been put up to it by the ambassador Stafford, a crony of his.[34] That is not at all unlikely; and Stafford's motives, if he was involved, can readily be imagined. Our source thought that he was trying to make problems for Walsingham, whom he detested and claimed to be spying on him. But this implies that Stafford believed the accusation against Arnault, which I doubt: in his dealings about Morgan's papers, Arnault had given Stafford very good reason to know that he was a loyal servant of Henri III. I should suppose that, if Stafford

---

32 Arnault to Castelnau, Paris, [27-iv/7-v-1585] (BN V^{c}C 472, p. 189): election of Montalto 'que j'ai eu cest honneur de connaître et avoir souventesfois visité avec M. de Foix pendant que j'estois à Rome'; and to Nau, 12/22-iii-1586 (*CSP Scotland 1585–86*, p. 278) – eight months in Italy.

33 L. von Pastor, *History of the Popes*, xxi (London, 1952 repr.), 262ff; indications of connection between the English College and the Leaguers in BN fr 16045, f. 14r (Nicolas Pellevé, Cardinal of Sens), and Archives of the Ven. English College, Rome, Libri 262, c. 14/24-x-1586, etc.

34 Fontenay, above, n. 30; *CSP Foreign 1586–88*, p. 34.

was involved, he was simply getting his own back on Arnault for making a fool of him the year before.

Mary, who originally thought the charge absurd, and knew very well that Arnault could not have been the betrayer of her correspondence, was finally persuaded that he was guilty on the evidence of his conduct in Rome.[35] It does not appear that anyone else with a worthwhile opinion believed it: not Henri III or his council, not Arnault's master Châteauneuf, and not Thomas Morgan, who would have been a principal victim of Arnault's treachery if it had occurred. There was no investigation in Paris, and three months after his apparent disgrace, where do we find Arnault but back in Rome having an audience with Sixtus V, from whom Henri III was looking for help in reviving French influence in the international Order of the Knights of St John?[36] No sign of disgrace here; nor indeed, much as the pope might have appreciated it, of Arnault bringing another message to Rome from Queen Elizabeth.

Arnault was an officer of the French crown at a time of peculiar difficulty. He served his king faithfully, and both Mary and Elizabeth with dignity. I imagine that his private opinions were, roughly speaking, *politique*; but as an executant of the instructions of his superiors he did, very competently, what he was asked to do. Where he had a free hand, he applied the marmalade of civility; but it was not possible for him to be *persona grata* with everybody. That was the extent of his treachery. When we see him for the last time, as his boat disappears over the Tyrrhenian horizon, bound for Malta, there is no stain on his reputation. On all the evidence we have, Jean Arnault, seigneur de Chérelles, was a charming, witty and honourable man, who had risen above the murderous hostilities which had brought about his father's death; it is a pleasure to have been able to vindicate him. We must find our mole elsewhere.

35 *CSP Scotland 1585–86*, pp. 520, 554; Labanoff, vi, 367, 418.
36 Henri III to Châteauneuf, 16/26-iv-1586 (above, n. 30); Giglioli (agent in Paris) to Cardinal d'Este, 2/12-v-1586 (Archivio Segreto Vaticano, Francia 385, ff. 285 and ff), reporting an interview with Arnault, who had just had an informative letter from Châteauneuf; Thomas Morgan to Mary, 24-vi/4-vii-1586 (Murdin, *State Papers*, p. 524): Arnault off to Malta via Rome, Morgan has asked his friends in Rome to help him, so has Beaton, Archbishop of Glasgow, who had originally brought the charge against him. Arnault in Rome, August 1586: BN fr 16042, f. 366 (d'Este), 16045, f. 225 (Saint-Goard, the ambassador). H. J. A. Sire, *The Knights of Malta* (New Haven/London, 1994), pp. 74, 77, describes the revival of French influence.

A CASTLE IN SPAIN

SINCE ARNAULT WAS NOT OUR MOLE because he was not Castelnau's secretary at the relevant time, it followed that all one had to do to find the mole was to find who was then Castelnau's secretary. No problem here: it could be discovered by following up Conyers Read's references, since the secretary who had had an interview with Walsingham on 3 November 1583 was called (in the text which Read cited) Courcelles.[1] A mistranscription, perhaps – not an unusual thing in the *Calendar of State Papers, Scotland*? But no, for not long after, when Castelnau was telling Mary who the possible leakers in his establishment were, the first person he mentioned after Arnault was called Courcelles.[2] This Courcelles, who first appears in the records of the embassy in 1579, had succeeded Arnault on his departure to France – somewhere, that is, about the end of 1581 – and remained Castelnau's secretary for three years or so. He was a 'secretary' in the strong contemporary sense, i.e., a keeper of secrets. He had an autonomous role in the conduct of the ambassador's confidential affairs, and probably more scope than Arnault had had in his time: he was certainly the only one of Castelnau's servants in this position.[3] Castelnau had to send him home in March 1585, when he was accused of abetting conspiracy against the queen; at the end of the year he was on a mission to Scotland which ran until 1588.

Who, then, was he? I initially identified him as Nicolas Leclerc, seigneur de Courcelles, and referred for my authority to Jean Le Laboureur, the seventeenth-century editor of Castelnau's remains. This man, like the father of Jean Arnault, had a reasonably important royal office on the legal side, that of *lieutenant-général* at Tours, and was likewise under the patronage of Jean de Morvillier, into whose family he had married: Morvillier had died

---

1 Above, p. 17.
2 Castelnau to Mary, [22-iii/1-iv-1584] (Document (d)).
3 PRO Transcripts 31/3/27, 4-x-1579; 31/3/28, 11-i-1581; *CSP Foreign 1581–82*, p. 31. As well as from Castelnau's letter above, n.2, Courcelles' special position can be gathered from Labanoff, v, 479; vi, 21 & 48; *CSP Scotland 1584–85*, pp. 478, 489f; Murdin, pp. 457, 522.

in his house at Tours in 1577. Considering how close Castelnau stood to Morvillier, it was natural to suppose that Leclerc had migrated to London shortly after Morvillier's death.[4] My identification turned out to be hasty: in a number of documents written in Scotland a few years later, Courcelles gave his name as 'Claude de Courcelles'; and when it emerged from the genealogy given by Le Laboureur that Nicolas Leclerc's eldest son was called Claude, it was possible to identify this son as our Courcelles. We can thus accept Castelnau's statement that Courcelles had been working for him since about 1570, ever since Castelnau had been a figure at the court of Charles IX and Catherine de Medici. He had probably brought Courcelles to London with him in 1575, and Courcelles had certainly served him in a lesser capacity before being appointed secretary in 1581 or so.[5]

Although his background was similar to Arnault's, as would probably have been that of anybody holding the position, they were different kinds of people in a variety of ways. Arnault's connections gave him the entry into the highest circles of Henri III's court; Courcelles' circle, which we know about from a motley assortment of his papers which came into English hands after he left Scotland, included a number of friends and relations in the middling ranks of French officialdom, legal and financial.[6] Arnault was a civilised, cultivated, rather sceptical man, in amiable relations with everyone from Walsingham to the pope; Courcelles, by all accounts, was a Catholic zealot. His mother had a saint in the family, the Calabrian St Francis of Paola who walked across the Straits of Messina; his sister was a waiting-woman to Queen Mary at Sheffield, and was shortly to return to France with Mary's lifelong friend, Mary Seton. He is described in the genealogy as a *conseiller-clerc* in the Parlement of Paris, and as not having married, which suggests that at some point he took minor orders. He possibly, at the time of his return from England in 1585, became one of the earliest members of the inner ring of the Catholic League in Paris.[7] I doubt if it is accidental that his succession to Arnault

---

4   *GB*, pp. 20f; Le Laboureur, *Mémoires de Castelnau*, i, 505; iii, 163. Cf. above, p. 19.
5   *CSP Scotland 1586–88*, p. 442, etc. (PRO SP 52/42, nos. 50–2); Le Laboureur, *Mémoires*, iii, 163; Castelnau to Henri III, 16/26-iii-1585 (BN fr 4736, f. 189).
6   *CSP Scotland 1585–86*, pp. 186, 226ff, 338; *1586–88*, *passim*; Murdin, p. 444.
7   The saint: D. Attwater, *Penguin Dictionary of Saints* (London, 1965), p. 137; Le Laboureur, *Mémoires*, i, 502, 505; iii, 163; perhaps satirised by Bruno, *Spaccio della bestia trionfante* (Giordano Bruno, *Dialoghi italiani*, ed. G. Gentile; rev. G. Aquilecchia, Florence, 1958), pp. 803–5 – saints walking on the water. Courcelles' sister, called either Marie or Michelle: *HMC Bath*, v, p. 46; BL Harleian 6035 (see below, chap. 5), f. 12ʳ; BL Addnl. Mss. 48049 (= Yelverton Mss. 54), f. 311. A Courcelles and the League: P. Robiquet, *Paris et la Ligue* (Paris, 1886), pp. 202f; E. Barnavi, *Le parti de Dieu* (Brussels/Louvain, c. 1980), p. 45, identifies him with a *procureur*, Robert de Courcelles, R. Descimon, *Qui étaient les Seize?* (Paris, 1983), with Jacques de Courcelles, wine merchant. Descimon seems persuasive.

as Castelnau's secretary coincided with a distinct shift in the ambassador's position in England: a shift from the cultivation of Elizabeth in the hope that she would marry the Duke of Anjou, to the cultivation of Mary and her friends. It coincided with the beginnings of their secret correspondence, which became Courcelles' particular responsibility,[8] and probably with the systematic use of the embassy as a channel for Mary's confidential communications in general, and for the passage of letters between English Catholics in England and France.

It also coincided with an ominous event, symbolic of a sharp rise in tension between Elizabeth's government and her Catholic subjects, and of the general exacerbation of such tensions in north-west Europe. Among the missionary priests now coming into the country clandestinely to promote a hard-line Catholicism distinguished by recusancy, or refusal to participate in the services of the Elizabethan church, the most charismatic was the Jesuit humanist Edmund Campion. Campion had arrived in England with his colleague Robert Parsons in the summer of 1580, and had been arrested a year later. He was convicted of treasonable conspiracy and executed in December 1581.[9] Neither his mission nor his execution had had anything to do with Castelnau, and they had nothing directly to do with Courcelles; but Courcelles' enterprises brought them both into contact with Englishmen whose lives had been changed by himself or his fellow-priests.

According to Castelnau, Courcelles was the man who carried the packets of letters to their recipients, and spoke to people who were of Mary's party. Although these visits were necessarily clandestine – it was also said that he 'haunted the Court in the night season' – we know that he worked closely with Thomas Morgan in Paris, and that his contacts in London included three men who were to be executed for treasonable conspiracies in which Morgan was involved.[10] The one we shall be most interested in will be Francis Throckmorton, who was the longest and closest of them. For the moment we need to know that he was a rich and agreeable gentleman from an establishment of strong Catholic traditions, who had fairly recently undergone a conversion to recusancy, and was now undergoing another from loyalty to Elizabeth to loyalty to Mary. His relation with Courcelles began 'a little before Christmas [1581]', when

---

8 Below, n. 11; *CSP Foreign 1581–82*, no. 347, shows Castelnau in touch with Throckmorton on 1-x-1581 (?via Castelnau's wife).

9 To Evelyn Waugh's respectable *Edmund Campion* (London, 1935), add now T. McCoog (ed.), *The Reckoned Expense: Edmund Campion and the Early English Jesuits* (Woodbridge, Suff., 1996).

10 Above, n. 2; [R. Bell (ed.)], *Extract from the Dispatches of M. Courcelles, French Ambassador at the Court of Scotland (1586–87)* (Bannatyne Club, Edinburgh, 1828), p. 13; *GB*, p. 212, Text no. 10.

Throckmorton agreed to become a postman for clandestine correspondence with Mary; a year or so later, we find Throckmorton very thick
with Castelnau, and Courcelles busy funnelling and receiving correspondence through him.[11] Courcelles also tried to recruit the even younger and
even richer Anthony Babington for the same purpose; according to
Babington he rather bullied him into doing something he was not at all
keen on, and withdrew from in favour of distributing samizdat literature
from the embassy. Babington was, according to a good observer, on very
familiar terms with Courcelles, though his venture into conspiracy
occurred some time after Courcelles' return to France.[12] Both Throckmorton and Babington appear to have been part of a network of Catholic
gentlemen connected with Campion's mission,[13] and so will have steered
clear of Castelnau, to whose matrimonial project for Elizabeth the influx
of priests was a nuisance, possibly a fatal blow. When his project collapsed,
Castelnau's silence about the execution of Campion became an embarrassment; it seems that Courcelles' job was to repair the damage by cultivating the likes of Throckmorton and Babington and drawing them, fatally,
into the orbit of Mary.

The third conspirator, and a different case, was William Parry, the supposed devout assassin whose history we shall need to pursue later. Courcelles had known him in the earlier days of the embassy, when he acted
as a go-between for Castelnau and Lord Burghley. He would be dealing
with him again two years hence, when Parry returned from a stay on the
continent, now a Catholic convert but in the queen's favour; his conspiracy was leaked at the beginning of 1585, and Courcelles expelled from
the country as a participant in it. His expulsion, and numerous disparag-
ing observations made about him by Elizabeth and others, complete our
notion of him as a political Catholic of a fairly intense kind.[14]

In the spring of 1583, then, Courcelles had been running a secret correspondence between Castelnau and Mary for something over a year. It
was secret in the sense that it did not pass through the official post
controlled and inspected by Walsingham, by which he communicated

11 *A Discoverie of the Treasons* (below, 65 n. 1), p. 197; and n. 8 above. I discuss Throckmorton at
    pp. 84f below.
12 Below, pp. 139f; Babington's confession, 18–20/28–30-viii-1586, in Pollen, *Mary, Queen of Scots,
    and the Babington Plot*, pp. 49f; *GB*, pp. 23f, 209; Geoffroy le Brumen (Castelnau's doctor in
    London) to Castelnau, 29-x/8-xi-1586 (BN VcC 472, p. 205): '. . . ung jeune homme nommé
    Babynthon que j'ay sy souvent veu en votre logis et si familier avec Monsieur de Courcelles'.
    No credit can be given to Courcelles' own statement (Bell, *loc. cit.* above, n. 10) that he did not
    know Babington.
13 Robert Parsons, 'Of the Life and Martyrdom of Father Edmund Campian', *Letters and
    Notices of the English Province S.J.*, xii (privately printed, Roehampton, 1878), p. 29 (chap.
    21).
14 *CSP Foreign 1584–85*, p. 261; *CSP Scotland 1585–86*, p. 601; *1586–88*, p. 81 and below, pp. 96ff.

financial matters concerning the running of Mary's establishment in France, and whatever political matters he was happy for Walsingham to see. It was also secret in the sense that it was kept so secure that none of it has survived, and we therefore do not know what was in it. From an intercepted letter from Castelnau to France it had been known to have been going on since the previous autumn,[15] but there had been no other leaks. This was a big feather in Courcelles' cap, and probably not because Mary's correspondence with Castelnau was in itself of critical importance: Mary did not trust him sufficiently for that. Its importance to Mary, and its danger to Elizabeth, lay much more in what was being carried to and fro under the cover of Castelnau's packets. This included packets from Thomas Morgan and others in Mary's establishment in France, which appear to have been arriving at Salisbury Court in the diplomatic bag about once a month;[16] Mary's letters in reply; and her letters to other correspondents in England, which might be carried directly to their addressees by the messengers, as those to the Spanish ambassador probably were, or left at Salisbury Court to be forwarded from there. Francis Throckmorton ran the whole operation from his house at Paul's Wharf in London, whence communication with Salisbury Court, by river or otherwise, was simple: he appears to have received from Courcelles all the packets going to Mary, and to have sent them on to Sheffield by one George More.[17]

This was not quite the limit of the network of clandestine communications which Courcelles controlled. The packets which came from Morgan and others in Castelnau's diplomatic bag, and which probably nobody in Salisbury Court except Courcelles had access to, contained numerous letters to friends past, present and potential. Many of them might be innocent exchanges between friends and relations separated by the Channel, as between Charles Paget in Paris and his friend and former music-teacher William Byrd; they might equally well be, and taken as a whole surely were, links in the creation of a well-knit party which at the proper time would emerge to champion Mary's and the Catholic cause in England. As Castelnau said, Courcelles was the man who 'carr[ied] the packets to various people': there can be no doubt that, in his view, the passage of such packets through Salisbury Court was the effective spring of a political enterprise.[18] We can probably take it that Castelnau made it

---

15 Read, *Walsingham*, ii, 376; *CSP Scotland 1581–83*, p. 180.

16 To be gathered from William Parry to Thomas Morgan, London, 12/22-ii-1584 (PRO SP 15/28, f. 150; *CSP Domestic Addenda 1580–1625*, p. 113, and below, pp. 97–8): 'The letters of December and February were brought to us this week all together'.

17 Below, pp. 107–9.

18 For the important discovery of Byrd's relation to Charles Paget and the rest of the family we are all deeply indebted to David Crankshaw's unpublished paper, 'New Evidence of William Byrd's Aristocratic Catholic Friends'; which I hope will see the light shortly; also below, p. 97, n. 38. On Courcelles, above, n.2.

his business to interfere with it, and perhaps to know about it, as little as possible.

I shall be giving an account of the fortunes of this underground network, and in the first place of the entrance effected into it in the spring, or thereabouts, of 1583. It is quite surprising, and a tribute to Courcelles' competence, that the breach of security had been delayed for as long as it had. Forearmed with a knowledge of the history of Jean Arnault's affairs in Rome, we may easily suppose that Courcelles' sentiments and activities will not have been congenial to everyone in Castelnau's household. In Rome the French Crown and the Catholic League were soon to have their own separate embassies, which pursued a public feud against each other. In London the parties lived together in Salisbury Court. Mary had remarked back in 1576 that opinions in the house were so divided that if half of it was working on her side the other half would on principle be working against her.[19] Much the same was true in the years from 1583 to 1585. It consisted of a rabidly Catholic downstairs supporting an upstairs of professionals and intellectuals whose preferences ran from the simply Protestant through cultured middle-of-the-roaders like Arnault and eccentrics like Fagot and/or Bruno to zealous Catholics like Courcelles and Castelnau's wife. Castelnau presided amiably over them all, with the inscrutability proper to an ambassador, and fed them, surely to the kitchen's irritation, on a variegated diet of visitors, friends and useful connections.[20] His own thoughts, so far as we can grasp them, had probably been moving in a ruminative way towards a more positively Catholic position than he is generally credited with, and in due course were to start moving back again.

For the best part of six months Walsingham had been doing his best to insinuate an informant into the house in the person of a Scottish ex-minister and poet called William Fowler, recently returned from France with a reputation as an uncertain Protestant. Fowler continued to haunt Salisbury Court until July 1583, became quite intimate, at least in appearance, with Castelnau, and helped to persuade him to take into his confidence the intelligent but disreputable Scottish nobleman Archibald Douglas. But I rather doubt whether Castelnau was deceived by Fowler, and he had little access to the rest of the household. He seems to have had no knowledge of the secret correspondence, and only mentions Courcelles, incidentally, once; he mentions none of Courcelles' English contacts and only one of Castelnau's, an unnamed priest whose

19 Labanoff, iv, 329.
20 *GB*, pp. 181, 54f, 196, 225f, and *passim*; Frances Yates, *John Florio* (Cambridge, 1934), pp. 61–86 and *Giordano Bruno and the Hermetic Tradition* (London, 1964; repr. 1978), pp. 205–90.

conversation with the ambassador he was unable, or not encouraged, to stay for.[21]

So Walsingham's attempt to breach the security of Salisbury Court through Fowler appears to have had very little success indeed; the obstacle to their getting anywhere was probably that they were hunting for something in Castelnau's contacts with Scotland, which was not where the thimble was hidden at all. For the same reason I think Walsingham got less than he expected out of the planting of Archibald Douglas on Castelnau at the end of May. But in the meantime he had had a piece of luck which changed the fortunes of the game. In the course of April he began to receive messages from a new informant who was actually living in Salisbury Court, and so was able to penetrate its secrets as neither Fowler nor Douglas was able to do.[22] This was the priest who signed himself 'Fagot' and wrote in very bad French. I have argued elsewhere that he was the exiled Neapolitan philosopher, poet, searcher of the heavens and teacher of the art of memory Giordano Bruno, who did indeed come to live at Salisbury Court around the middle of April 1583 and remained there for the next two and a half years. I have also argued that a communication of his sent to Walsingham on 19 April was the first of his communications. Another view is that this was not the first of his communications, and that he was therefore not Giordano Bruno. We do not need to attempt to decide the argument. We do need to record what Fagot wrote in another missive to Walsingham whose date, according to one's opinion, will be early April, late May, or June. Most of it was about how the downstairs sector of the house was making a fortune importing Catholic literature into the country and selling it in London. He went on:

> Monseigneur, I also advise you that, if your excellency wishes, I have made the ambassador's secretary so much my friend that, if he is given a certain amount of money, he will let me know everything he does, including everything to do with the Queen of Scots and the cipher that is used with her. You must know that, after your excellency has inspected a packet addressed to her, he has a method of putting something else into the packet without anybody knowing. He has told me this himself.

> (Monseigneur je vous advertis aussy que si votre exelence veult que je tiens le segraitaire de monseigneur lambassadeur pour tant mon amy

---

21 *DNB*, Fowler, William; *CSP Scotland 1581–83*, pp. 196, 490, 244–569 *passim*; *GB*, Texts nos. 2, 3 & 4. Later he became secretary to Anne of Denmark, queen of James VI and I (*HMC Shrewsbury and Talbot Papers*, i, 166; ii, see index.). On Douglas, below, p. 58.

22 *GB*, pp. 14ff, 187f and *passim*.

que sil est considere de quelque peu de monnoye quil ne cest faict rien
quil ne me le donne a conoistre et que tout ce qui ce fera touchant la
Royne decosse et le segret et lecriture qui ce escript par lettre quar-
talle et fault que sachiez quapres que votre exelence a visite auchun
pacquet pour adresser vers icelle qui ne laisse a y en remectre dautre
dans ledit pacquet et que cela nest congneu nullement Je le say de par
luy.)

The secretary had also told Fagot to tell Walsingham not to trust Fowler,
who was betraying him.[23]

Since we already knew that the leakage of Castelnau's correspondence
with Mary had begun not so long afterwards, we could not dismiss Fagot's
report, as we might easily have otherwise done, as a product of invention,
fantasy or error. Fagot had talked to Castelnau's secretary, who was willing,
for a consideration, to betray his master's correspondence with Mary;
Courcelles was Castelnau's secretary, and there was only one of him; Courcelles had therefore been, through Fagot, the breaker of Walsingham's dead-
lock, and the betrayer of the correspondence he had spent the last eighteen
months organising. This was a surprise indeed. Courcelles the zealot, the
hub of the cross-Channel Catholic network, the tireless facilitator of
Mary's and Morgan's schemes, the expelled conspirator: Courcelles a
traitor to the Catholic cause? Well: stranger things have happened, and the
evidence appeared to speak for itself. How could we test it?

The first thing to do was to investigate one of Labanoff's pieces of
evidence: the handwriting in which the leaked letters were to be copied
and the notes to Walsingham written. Labanoff had claimed that this handwriting was Arnault's, which could not be so; it looked as if it would now
turn out to be Courcelles'. One could guess, in the first place, how
Labanoff's mistake had arisen. Following Bréquigny, he had found that all
the copies of Mary's letters in Harleian Ms. 1582 were in the same hand,
and so were the two accompanying notes. He had identified the hand as
Chérelles' by observing that there were 'several' of Chérelles' letters in the
State Paper Office, and that they were in the same hand. No such letters
exist. Of the eight items by Chérelles which do survive in the Public
Record Office, four are from the marmalade correspondence with
Walsingham of 1584–5: they are signed 'Arnault', which Labanoff had no
reason to recognise as Chérelles' signature, and written in a hand about as

23   *GB*, pp. 196, 198. I have altered the translation from 'You must know' onwards to indicate, what
     I did not see when I originally translated the letter, that what is being explained is that the
     secretary puts secret letters into the official packet, not that he can put them in if Walsingham
     wants him to. This reverses the sense. On the date, see the 'Note' below, pp. 157–69.

different from that of the leakages as it was possible to get in the sixteenth century. The others date from 1586, and are in decipher copies made by Thomas Phellippes,[24] so irrelevant. What do exist are some letters and some other pieces written by Courcelles, one in London in 1585 and the rest in Scotland in 1586–7: I suppose that Labanoff simply misread the signature 'Courcelles' as 'Chérelles'. In that case his identification was credible since, unlike Arnault, Courcelles wrote a conventional French secretary hand, as did the mole. True, the mole wrote it less carefully; but he was in a hurry. When one compared the two notes to Walsingham, and the copied letters to which they were attached, with the nearest legitimate letter from Courcelles that we had, also written to Walsingham, and not much later, nothing appeared to contradict the idea that they had been written by the same hand: one found the same letter-forms and word-connections, and signing-formulae which were practically identical.[25] To advance from this to a positive identification would have been risky; it was not necessary, since Fagot had identified the mole as Courcelles.

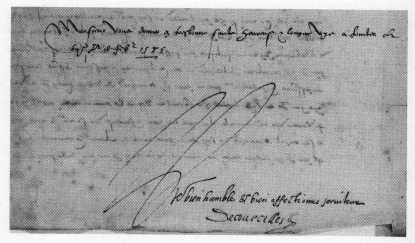

Plate II   Claude de Courcelles to Sir Francis Walsingham, London, 25 Feburary/7 March 1585 (wrongly dated 28 January/7 February). Holograph. Public Record Office SP 78/13, f. 41v.

24   Above, chap 1, n. 16; *CSP Scotland 1585–86*, pp. 278, 282, 290, 297.

25   For the handwriting, compare BL Harleian 1582, ff. 311–13 (the copy of Mary-Castelnau, 25-ii/6-iii-1584, with the first of the mole's notes attached) with PRO SP 78/13, f. 41 (Courcelles to Walsingham, 28-i/7-ii-1585: actually 25-ii/7-iii). See Plates II and IV. Courcelles certainly wrote, as well as signing, the second of these, because the handwriting is identical to that of the IOU 'written and signed' by Courcelles in Edinburgh, 20/30-vi-1587 (PRO SP 52/42, f. 51). Note the 'd's with a long, straight upward stroke at a very low

There was another point to be made. The corpus of leaked correspondence did not consist only of letters between Mary and Castelnau: there
was also a largish and apparently random collection of Castelnau's papers,
which seemed to represent a cross section of the productions of his office
over some time. The items in this collection had been written in three
easily distinguishable hands: Castelnau's own, scrawly, semi-italic and
unmistakable (Hand I); a very formal hand which was evidently that of
the final fair copies, and must have been written by the clerk, whom one
could see practising his craft in blank spaces (Hand III); and the hand of
the copies and notes to Walsingham (Hand II). The owner of this last had
occupied a place in the office procedure between Castelnau himself, who
mainly wrote drafts, and the fair-copyist.[26] Who would this be but the secretary, Courcelles? Labanoff had had the right idea, but had got the wrong
man.

That being so, we were to swallow our amazement that this notorious
promoter of Catholic politics had been persuaded to work for the other
side; had been, we were to conclude, the instrument of the destruction of
Francis Throckmorton and of who knew what other agents of the clandestine Catholic operations to which Courcelles had held the key. After
he was sent back to France he fell into a dispute with Thomas Morgan
about some money he had brought over from English Catholics, and
Morgan had told Mary that he could not press Courcelles for it without
risking that he would betray the entire network of her friends and relations in England: it appeared that this was exactly what he had done.[27]
Why had he then been expelled? That remained to be seen; but in the
meantime it could be said that Courcelles was to be expelled for his relationship with William Parry, and that if Parry, who had certainly been
working on behalf of Elizabeth and her ministers, had nevertheless been
executed for conspiracy against her, we ought not perhaps to be astonished at a comparable U-turn in the case of Courcelles.[28]

There were also, when we looked at Courcelles more closely, indications that he was the kind of oddball who might have been open to the

---

angle, practically horizontal; and the 'v/u's with a long, curling entrance stroke which, when
convenient, is joined to the previous word – thus 'ma vye' in the last line of Courcelles' letter,
and in the copy on f. 312ᵛ. For the *envoi*, Courcelles to Walsingham: '. . . et d'aussy bon coeur
que je prie Dieu Monsieur vous donner en tresbonne santé heureuse et longue vye'; the
mole's second note (BL Cottonian Nero B vi, f. 372ᵛ): '. . . d'aussy bon coeur que je prie Dieu
Monsieur qu'il vous donne en parfaite santé heureuse et longue vye avec accomplissement
de tous voz desirs'.

26 See Plates III–IV.
27 Murdin, pp. 451, 478, ?515, 522.
28 For Parry, see below, pp. 132–4; and L. Hicks, 'The Strange Case of Dr. William Parry', *Studies*
    (Dublin), xxxvii (1948), 343–62.

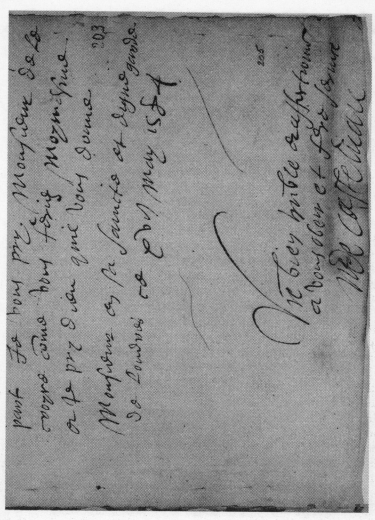

Plate III   Hand I (Castelnau): to Sir Francis Walsingham, London, 5/15 May 1584. Holograph. Public Record Office
SP 78/11, f. 205 (pencil numbering). Transcribed below, Document (e).

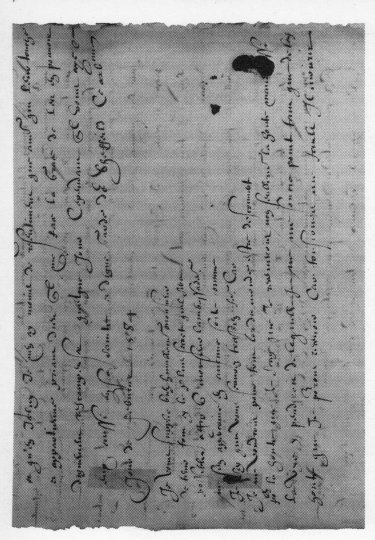

Plate IV Hand II (Hand of the copies): end of copy of Mary to Castelnau, Sheffield, 25 February/6 March 1584 with note added at the bottom. British Library, Harleian Ms. 1582, f. 312v (Appendix, no. 31); the note transcribed and translated below, p. 106.

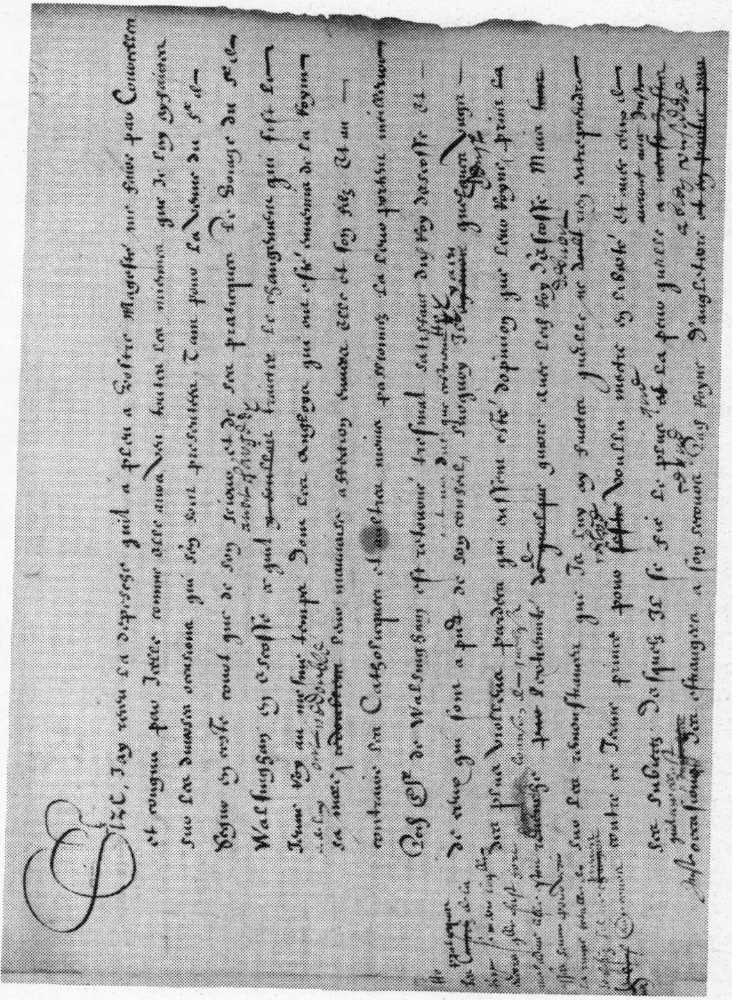

Plate V Hand III (Clerk's formal hand): Castelnau to Henri III, London, 12/22 November 1583. Abortive fair copy with interlinear corrections mostly in Hand I (Castelnau) and marginal additions in Hand II. British Library, Harleian Ms. 1582, f. 361r. Appendix, no. 9.

temptation Fagot had put in his way. From the end of 1585 he spent a couple of years in Scotland, originally as secretary of a young and inexperienced ambassador, M. d' Esneval, then on his own. When he went home he left behind some private correspondence with his friends in Paris which came into English hands. From this we get an impression of him as a figure from Shakespearean romance: melancholic, solitary, hypochondriac, with an obsessive imagination and a penchant for rambles in the woods; he took a lot of pills, and avoided the company of women. One friend wrote:

> Do not spend so much time day-dreaming and building castles in Spain. That is what builds up in you such melancholic humours as make you tiresome. Socialising is good for you, to talk and pass the time, and sometimes those of the feminine gender to purge the system ... I should like you to be here immediately after Easter, to go back and hear the nightingales singing where the woods come down to the meadows. I am told that they are already beginning to warble in the bushes.

> (Ne vous amusez plus tant a songer en vous mesmes et a bastir des chateaulx en Espaigne, c'est ce qui vous amasse tant d'humeurs melancholicques qui vous rendent ennuyeulx. Les compaignies vous sont bonnes tant a deviser qu'a passer le temps, et quelquefoys le foeminini generis pour purger rennes ... Je voudroys que fussiez icy pour incontynant apres pasques aller encore ouyr chanter les rossignolz dedans les boys conjoignant les prairies, sur les buissons l'on m'a dict qu'ilz commancent a gazouiller.)[29]

The nightingales may possibly have concealed a coded reference to the politics of the Catholic League, but evoking the pleasures of the valley of Chevreuse on a spring night would not be out of place for a friend in the grip of a Scottish winter, and altogether the portrait is fresh and convincing. The point about women is compatible with his not marrying, and perhaps becoming a cleric in later life, and I can well believe that he was a man given to fantasy and consumed with frustrated ambition. By comparison with Arnault's, his connections at home look unimpressive, and his conduct in Scotland suggests a chip on the shoulder. He changed his name, on the grounds that he needed to pass incognito since the English hated him so much. When he was left on his own he got a severe reprimand from his superiors for 'playing the great man' and assuming the status of

---

29 Maheut to Courcelles, 22-ii/4-iii-1586 (PRO SP 52/39, no. 18; *CSP Scotland 1585–86*, p. 226); cf. *Ibid.* p. 228f; *1586–88*, p. 171 (drugs).

ambassador to which he had no title. He certainly invested in spectacular clothes, and borrowed and spent a lot of money for which his government refused to reimburse him. He also carried on a campaign against Castelnau for letting him down in England, and there are signs that they had not been on the best of terms before Courcelles' departure from London. We may then want to see him, in the spring of 1583, already chafing at his position as Castelnau's secretary, and taking Walsingham's offer as an exciting opportunity to play the great man, as well as to earn a good deal of money.[30]

All the same, while Courcelles' doings in Scotland offered support to an explanation of his treachery by his character, they offered none at all to an explanation by his politics, which were solidly Marian and Catholic. Elizabeth pursued him with venom, and if she had cause to be grateful to him she gave no sign of it; he in turn was abusive about her.[31] Had he perhaps played a confidence trick on her and Walsingham, floated a spurious leakage to distract attention from a real conspiracy which was afoot? Short of that or a similar twist, we are left with the plain story that in the spring of 1583 or thereabouts this knotted-up, melancholy, possibly megalomaniac but certainly Catholic Frenchman was won over by Fagot to launch the betrayal of Catholic enterprises which ensued.

30 *CSP Scotland 1585–86*, p. 203 (alias); *1586–88*, pp. 45, 336ff (clothes), 484, 487 (playing the great man), 81 (Castelnau).
31 Courcelles to Henri III, 31-i/10-ii-1587 (Bell, *Extract from the Dispatches of M. Courcelles*, p. 30): Elizabeth's regime maintained by violence 'and the blood of poor Catholics'; Elizabeth, in *CSP Scotland 1585–86*, p. 661; *1586–88*, p. 81.

3

A LETTER FROM THE QUEEN

I STEAL TWO SENTENCES FROM A MASTER-STORYTELLER: 'At this point a secret must be imparted. Pnin was on the wrong train.' On 10 February 1993 I took my own train to the British Library to check my supposition that an unattributed document described in the calendar of the Hatfield Manuscripts, and therefore from the papers of Lord Burghley, was in fact a piece referred to in a leaked letter from Castelnau to Mary. It was, or near enough.[1] While I was there, it seemed the moment to check up on some other pieces which looked as if they might be of interest. One of them was said in the Calendar to be a letter from a certain Walter Williams to Mary, written in London on 31 August 1583, about a letter she had sent to someone who did not believe that it was in her handwriting, and was very frightened of being found out.[2] It looked as if this was the trace of another item in Mary's secret correspondence, and that the terrified recipient was a potential recruit to her cause. If he was, he had reason to be scared, because Walter Williams was known to be a minor agent in Walsingham's intelligence operations. We find him in Conyers Read's list of people employed to spy on Catholics, sitting in the jail at Rye trying to extract treasonable information from a Catholic fellow-prisoner. A longish stay had not produced anything worthwhile, and he had left Rye in the February of 1583 with a comic reference from the anonymous Catholic commending his devotion to the holy bottle. As he was later to be found out, on a similar errand in Paris, through being plied with drink by Sir Edward Stafford, he had not been thought to be a very skilful practitioner of his craft.[3]

Nevertheless, to judge from the abstract in the Calendar, six months later he was still on the job, coaxing along one of Mary's correspondents in London. It emerged from the letter itself that Williams was not doing

1   *HMC Hatfield*, iii, 3 (no. 11); Cecil Papers 162, no. 105. Actually, Lord Henry Howard to Mary, 12/22-vi-1583. See below, p. 71.
2   *HMC Hatfield*, iii, p. 26; Cecil Papers, 162, no. 114; (Document (a)).
3   Read, *Walsingham* ii, 325–7, 420; it is a mistake, arising from the episode in the jail at Rye, that Williams had been a servant of Thomas Copley.

quite what one had supposed. It had no address, but had evidently not been written to Mary: nobody, in August 1583, was likely to write to her about the peace and quiet of her present state and kingdom. The 'sovereign lady' addressed was Elizabeth, and the person to whom the queen had written the letter it mentioned was or hoped to be serving her, not Mary. The letter to the unnamed 'party' must have been delivered by Williams himself, and he was reporting a conversation he had had with him after delivering it. The party, when he had read the letter, was not enthusiastic; he said it was not in the queen's handwriting, with which he was familiar. He was in a panic: the queen was asking him to do 'a thing wheron his life dependeth'. He was also very nervous that others than those originally acquainted with the matter had been let into the secret; he would not continue if anybody else was brought in.

Williams went on: 'He marvayleth why your Majestie should desire to knowe the messengers, who are allready knowen to be but too, assuring himself that if they should be apprehended, then were ther but one waye with him . . .' Messengers? That sounded familiar. '. . . but one waye with him [that is, he would have his throat cut], for he onely hath ben employed for this sixe yeares in writing all matters of importaunce, and now specially in the absence of Corsselles' – ! – 'who was accquaynted with the delivering of theym from tyme to time, yt can not be but he only must be suspected to be the revealer of secretts . . .' So this was a message from the horse's mouth, and the horse was not Courcelles, any more than it had been Arnault. A biter bit, I withdraw into the glimmer of the microfilm-reader and finish Williams's letter. 'What reward he maye attend, I leave to your heighnes' wisdome.' He asked the queen to take care of those who wished to do her faithful service, and to 'burne all his writinges which shall come unto your highnes, for he feareth greatly to be bewrayed'. He supported what the party had said about the danger to him of passing secret material at this particular time, and advised her not to lose 'so fitt an instrument' by pressing him too hard for a while. 'Tyme breadeth daylie newe matters and ripeing of the oulde, so a fitter tyme maye serve to take the practisers and dealers agaynst your highnes' state and quiet, with less suspition for your servantes discoverye, and greater confusion and shame to the trecherous and evell mynded agaynst your Majestie.' In other words: if you give the Catholics a little more time to mature their enterprises (say, by waiting until Courcelles comes back), the party will be able to give you more damning intelligence than he has so far provided, and will risk his skin much less into the bargain. Williams ended by asking the queen to burn his letter; happily for us, she passed it on to Burghley instead.

When we have answered some questions of fact, like 'Why Burghley?' (Walsingham was in Scotland) and 'Where was Courcelles?' (in France), we ask who the 'party' may be, and get a simple answer. Through Williams, he has told us himself. He is the embassy clerk, and has been for the past six years; he is one of the two people in the establishment who have access to the secret correspondence with Mary, the other being Courcelles. We have seen him doodling. He is, unless there had been a change in Castelnau's office personnel between August 1583 and April 1584, 'Laurent, who never leaves my chamber and writes everything in front of me and in my presence' (Laurent, qui ne bouge de ma chambre, qui escript tout devant moy et en ma presence). Laurent is a Christian name, and Castelnau used the Christian name for another upper servant, the butler and book-vendor Girault.[4] So: Laurent Who? There was a man in the household called Laurent Feron. He was mentioned five or six times between 1582 and the end of the embassy in 1585; his Christian name was generally used with his surname. In May 1582 he took packets for Mary from Salisbury Court to Walsingham and in January 1584 Fagot said that Castelnau had given him money at New Year; in August 1584 he took another letter to Walsingham, and acted as interpreter in disputes Castelnau was having with his neighbours; in September 1585 Châteauneuf, the incoming ambassador, told Fagot that people in France suspected Feron to be a spy.[5] He was, then, in a confidential position; his English was good; he was known to Walsingham, to whom he took packets of open letters to Mary. The last fact echoes what Fagot said about the ability of his friend the 'secretary' to slip extra things into an official packet for Mary after Walsingham had vetted it. I suppose opinions may differ as to whether this makes Laurent Feron Castelnau's clerk, Fagot's friend and Williams's contact; but mine is that it does. From Williams's description I take him to have filled that position from about 1577 to 1585. Anyone who finds the evidence insufficient is welcome to read 'X' where from now on I write 'Feron'.

We can find out more about him from the London tax rolls, which record him five times between 1564 and 1582. He was a French denizen, that is, naturalised English, who had lived in the country for thirty years

4   Above, p. 45; Castelnau to Mary, [22-iii/1-iv-1584] (Document (d)). The letter is one of the copies made by the clerk for Walsingham and sent in the parcel (below, chap. 6); it was written in haste. At first sight the name looks like 'aurant'. When the 'r' is placed correctly it becomes 'aurent'. But 'le' in the letter often looks like 'a' (as in f. 372ᵛ, l. 7), and I am satisfied that this is the case here; hence the strict reading is 'leurent'. But letters or parts of letters are often skipped over in this piece, especially when they involve repeated short upward strokes (in adjacent lines, 'treshum-blement', l. 6 up; 'chambre', l. 2 up; 'devant', last l.); and the writer has not got too much room at the end of his line. So, since all the other letters now seem clear, and since I doubt if 'Leurent' is an acceptable spelling even in the sixteenth century, I read 'Laurent'. We may remind ourselves that the writer was writing his own name and, even under stress as he was, would be unlikely to misspell it. For Girault, see *GB*, pp. 19, 196, 225f, 233f, 237.

5   *CSP Foreign 1582*, p. 11; *1584–85*, p. 11; *GB*, Texts nos. 9 & 15, pp. 211 & 235, and pp. 49–51.

in 1567; so I imagine he was born in London in 1537 or so. Hence his English. He was described as a merchant, no doubt trading to France; this is confirmed by a remark of Castelnau in the summer of 1584 about a dispute he was having with persons at Portsmouth. He lived somewhere about Mincing Lane, a desireable area of houses with gardens in the direction of Tower Hill, where the wealthiest foreign merchants lived. He was not one of them, but assessments of £3 or £4 suggest a reasonable competence. No sign of a wife or children here, but in 1568 he had a French servant.[6] London gives us one more piece of knowledge about him: on 15 February 1560 his son Thomas was baptised in the church of St Dunstan in the East, though his parish was given in 1564 as All Hallows Staining. He would then be 23 or so, and I take him to be married; he possibly had another son called Jacques.[7] It looks as if his wife had died before 1568, which perhaps had something to do with his change of profession. Given his date of birth or arrival, he cannot have been a Protestant émigré; he does not appear in the records of the French Reformed Church in London. He was therefore a Catholic or a conformist to the Church of England, more likely a mixture of both. I have found no trace of his dealings as a merchant where we might have expected them, as in the records of the Court of Admiralty; but there is one sign of him in April 1582, when the queen sent a letter to the Lord Mayor requiring him to take bonds of 'Laurence Farron of London, merchant stranger' not to go beyond seas, or to attempt anything prejudicial to the queen or the realm. A bond *ne exeat regnum* generally implies something political and I suppose it did here: perhaps Feron had been planning to take money over to English exiles in France. His bond was signed by four citizens of London.[8]

6 R. E. G. Kirk and E. F. Kirk, *Returns of Aliens dwelling in the City and Suburbs of London* (Proceedings of the Huguenot Society of London, x: 3 parts and index, 1900–8), i, 295 (1564), 341 (1567, with length of residence); iii, 385 (1568). PRO Exchequer, Lay Subsidy Rolls: E 179/145/252 (1577); E 179/251/16 (1582) – Tower Ward. I find no trace of him after this. *CSP Foreign 1584–85*, p. 11, and a (just) marginal note in Appendix, no. 15, f. 386, about Archibald Douglas: 'You are a knave'.

7 A. W. Hughes Clarke (ed.), *The Register of St Dunstan in the East, London, 1558–1654* (Harleian Society, lxix, 1939), p. 3; 'Thomas son of Lawrence Ferant baptised.' The register only gives fathers. St Dunstan is almost opposite the bottom of Mincing Lane, off Tower Street; All Hallows is near the top of it, on the corner of Fenchurch Street and Mark Lane, which is the next street east of Mincing Lane and west of Seething Lane. A Jacobus Feron, with wife, is in the tax registers for Copt Hale and Wapping in 1591 (*Returns of Aliens*, ii, 433); a Jacques Fearn was buried in St Mary Woolnoth in 1593 (Boyd's Burial Index, 1538–1855: Guildhall Library, London).

8 *CSP Domestic 1581–90*, p. 50 (PRO SP 12/153, no. 1); this was evidently the source of the difficulty mentioned by Castelnau shortly afterwards (*CSP Foreign 1582*, p. 11), in which he asked for Walsingham's help. Feron's co-signatories of the bond were John Keblewhyte, merchant tailor; William ?Achelley, grocer; John King, butcher; and Robert Chawnder, pewterer. We can take it from this, and from his subsidy assessment of the same year, that he kept up his house until at least 1582, and continued to live there at least some of the time.

Whatever this incident was about, it points us in the direction of another possible source of knowledge about Feron. It seems very likely that his father had come from Rouen in Normandy, where Feron was a common name and trading connections with England were strong. One Pierre Feron was, during the 1550s and 1560s, a rising foreign merchant in the city who had achieved a good deal of prosperity by the time Laurent was in the service of Castelnau. He had a daughter called Laurence, which is unusual and suggests that Laurent might have been a family name. If this is the right family, I should be inclined to suppose that Laurent's father was Pierre's brother, who had come to London as a merchant in the 1530s or so, married, and died before 1564. The family was Catholic, because one of Pierre's sons became a canon of Rouen cathedral and his daughter left her goods to a religious house.[9]

We may well have got the right place but the wrong family. Laurent cannot have been a very successful merchant, or he would have paid more tax and would hardly have accepted the position with Castelnau. If he was a Catholic, he does not sound like a zealot or, unless there was more than I imagine behind the bond *ne exeat regnum*, a friend to Catholic politics; his style looks more like Arnault's, in whose time he had been appointed to his job, than Courcelles'. He seems contented in his status as a naturalized subject, and as such he will of course have been vulnerable to the pressure he was now being put under by the queen. His house in Mincing Lane or thereabouts, if as it seems he continued to keep it up, would have been handy for passing documents to Walsingham's house in Seething Lane, two streets away; perhaps he had met Williams there.

Since we have now caught Feron in the act, the difficulties which arose when we attributed treachery to the absent Courcelles might appear to be solved. But this is hardly so: the reasons for the attribution had been serious, and Feron (or Williams) had now, if we reduced the charge against Courcelles from performing the treachery to conniving at it, added one more. Fagot had described the person to whom he had talked as Castelnau's secretary, who was Courcelles; the leaked documents appeared, from the hand itself and the distribution of hands in the products of Castelnau's

9   The details of the Ferons in Rouen are from Archives Départementales de la Seine-Maritime (Rouen), série E: Tabellionnages de Rouen: 1 meubles, 16-ii-1555, 22-vi-1589; 2 meubles 27-i-1587; 2 heritages, 5-iii-1585, 25-vi-1604, 31-i-1614, 17-v-1614; 2 EP 1/331 (7-xii-1565), 335 (3-vii-1567), 362 (7-i-1581): dates after 1583 new style. I am extremely grateful to Dr Gayle Brunelle, of the California State University at Fullerton, for communicating these references to me; and to my colleague Stuart Carroll for putting me in touch with her. There appear to be no traces here of a Laurent Feron trading with his family while in England, nor of his having gone there after September 1585, when we lose sight of him.

office, to be in Courcelles' handwriting; and Feron had said that Courcelles was 'acquainted with the delivering of [the documents, apparently] from time to time'.[10] It was true that the second and third of these reasons were incompatible: if Courcelles had deputed the actual work of the leakage to Feron, the documents would be in Feron's hand, not in his. Was this the case?

I record the results of reinvestigating the corpus of matter which was to be leaked from Castelnau's office between the spring of 1583 and the autumn of 1584. I have said that practically all the documents in question were in one of three hands, of which the first was Castelnau's own and the third certainly Feron's. The issue was whether the second hand (Hand II), which was the hand of the mole because it was the hand of the notes to Walsingham, was Courcelles' or not. A closer investigation was made possible by the survival of a number of pieces written by Courcelles in Scotland, and of others he had signed but not written. It emerged: (1) that the resemblance between Courcelles' own hand and Hand II was no stronger than that between Hand II and the pieces Courcelles had signed but not written: they were all in the same kind of hand, but not in the same version of it; and (2) that whereas, when in a hurry as he evidently often was, the hand of the mole (Hand II) became large, loopy and sprawly, when Courcelles was in a hurry his writing became almost invisibly small.[11]

The identification of Hand II as Courcelles' was therefore unreliable; meanwhile its identification as Feron's became more plausible. I know of no other pieces certainly written by Feron which are in Hand II; hence one had to depend on other indications than the handwriting itself. There was to start with the certainty, as one might think, that Feron, a professional scribe, would have had other hands than the formal hand he used for his fair copies. There was the whole character of the one sizeable bundle of papers which had been passed over to Walsingham, and seemed to amount to the contents of somebody's bottom drawer; on reflection it was fairly obvious that the somebody was a clerk, rather than a secretary. One found drafts of letters with handwriting practice in the margins and on the back; another, in Hand II, on the rest of a page left by an abandoned letter in Feron's best handwriting. One found a note in a top margin reminding the writer to make out a certificate for somebody of the date

10 Above, p. 45.
11 The first point is clear if we extend the comparison made above, p. 37, to include (1) PRO 78/15, f. 4 (Plate IV); (2) PRO SP 52/42, no. 51 (both Courcelles autographs); (3) BL Harleian 1582, f. 311ff (Hand II; Plate IV); and (4) PRO SP 52/42, no. 50 (signed by Courcelles but written by a clerk). (3) is no more like (1) and (2) than (4) is. For the second point, compare Plate IV and VI (Hand II) with Courcelles' Plate VII.

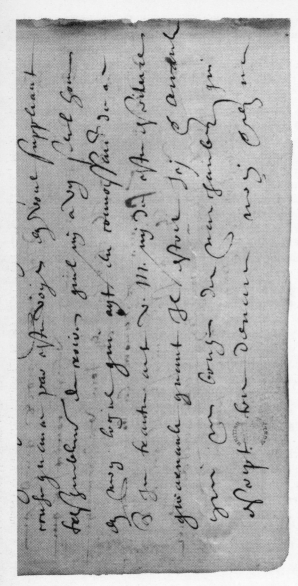

(continued overleaf)

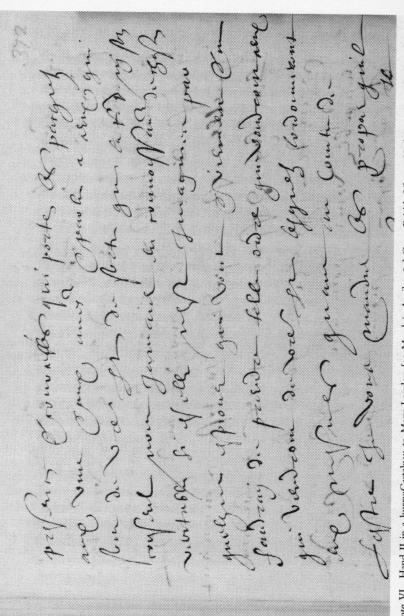

Plate VI Hand II in a hurry: Castelnau to Mary, London [22 March/1 April 1584] Copy. British Library, Harleian Ms. 1582, ff. 371v–372r. Appendix, no. 34: transcribed below, Document (d), p. 177.

Plate VII   Courcelles in a hurry. Draft, Edinburgh, September 1587. Public Record Office SP 52/42, f. 74r.

12 November 1583, which admittedly seemed to be in another handwriting altogether. One found a page of rather creditable attempts to copy the monogram of Elizabeth, which suggested what Feron had told Williams, that he knew her handwriting.[12] Then there were the two notes which the despatcher of the parcel had written to Walsingham, one with it and one later. The first expressed exactly the same feeling of panic that Feron had confided to Williams; the second had the writer rewriting a copy of a letter at Castelnau's instruction because the ambassador did not want the addressee to read some of the things that were in it.[13] The *envoi* to this note, which was indeed very like that of a letter written by Courcelles to Walsingham not much later, was perhaps no more individual than 'Yours faithfully'; and we might notice that the writer of it had prayed for 'the accomplishment of all [Walsingham's] desires', which Courcelles had not.

There can really be no doubt that the writer of Hand II, the copier, the leaker and the author of the notes to Walsingham was Laurent Feron. It is indeed a point that, in that case, there was nothing at all in the material passed from Salisbury Court which was in Courcelles' handwriting. This is certainly surprising, since we know from the contents of the parcel that Courcelles had written confidential letters, though he had had little or nothing to do with the ordinary products of the office.[14] We are to suppose that no trace of these had got to Feron's bottom drawer. In any case, when envisaging Courcelles as a 'secretary', we are to think of him more as a keeper of secrets than as a writer of letters.

Here we arrive at our other difficulties: that Fagot said he had talked to Castelnau's 'secretary'; and that Feron had said that Courcelles was *au fait* with the leakage. Now that we had got the handwriting straight, the natural interpretation of all the evidence was that Courcelles had done the deal with Walsingham, and left the work to Feron. But it did sound a little implausible. Does a mole in the Foreign Office pass the job, from the photocopying onwards, over to his typist? Does, in this case, Courcelles arrange to betray the secret correspondence, leave Feron to get on with it, and then go off on a long holiday? It sounds perfectly suicidal. And what were we to suppose that Walsingham had thought about it? Feron was not the only party to the affair who had views about letting new people into secret matters; connoisseurs of Master Secretary's mode of operation might well reject the story on this ground alone. We must enquire whether Fagot's 'segraitaire' had not been Feron in the first place. In favour of this idea

12 BL Harleian 1582, ff. 324f, 329f, 361f, 377f, 386, and *passim*.
13 BL Harleian 1582, f. 313ᵛ; BL Cottonian Nero B vi, ff. 371ᵛ–372ʳ; Labanoff, v, 429; vi, 26f.
14 BL Harleian 1582, f. 398; cf. *CSP Scotland 1581–83*, p. 654.

there is to be said that by this time the use of 'secretary' to mean 'somebody who writes someone else's letters' was already current, though probably not the principal use; that Feron's duties certainly included ciphering and deciphering, so that he was in a position to hand over Castelnau's cipher with Mary, as Fagot's contact had promised to do; and that we are to consider the experimental quality of Fagot's French.[15] He might have meant Feron; and Feron was perhaps a man he was more likely to have made 'friends' with, especially if he was Bruno, than the apparently *dévot* and uncommunicative Courcelles.

Then there was what Williams had said Feron had said about Courcelles. He had said that, if the 'messengers' were to be arrested he, Feron, would be the one to get the blame:

> for he onely hath ben employed for this sixe yeares in writing all matters of importaunce, and now specially in the absence of Corsselles, who was accquaynted with the delivering of theym from tyme to time, yt cannot be but he only must be suspected to be the revealer of secretts.[16]

It had been natural, since what I had been looking for was evidence about leaked letters, that I should have taken 'them' to mean 'matters of importance' or 'secrets', and 'delivering' to mean 'leaking'. On second thoughts, this does not seem so clear. Part of the vigour of Elizabethan English is the freedom of its construction (and Williams is reporting at second hand in it). I think it would have been virtually impossible for Queen Elizabeth or any of her contemporaries to have understood 'them' to mean 'secrets'; I am not even sure that it means 'matters of importance', as it ought to. It could just as well mean 'letters', not mentioned but understood from the context. In that case, and really even if 'them' does mean 'matters of importance', it becomes gratuitous to suppose that 'delivering' means 'leaking'. Delivering a letter in 1583 meant what it means nowadays: Feron surely meant that Courcelles, as Castelnau said, 'carr[ied] the packets to various people'; the contrast is between 'delivering' and writing, not between handing letters to their addressees and passing them to Walsingham. This is more particularly the contrast as 'from time to time' here means not 'occasionally' but 'all the time'; or 'whenever it happened'.[17] True, Feron/Williams did not say that Courcelles delivered the letters, but that he was acquainted with the delivery of them; but that need not hold

15 Above, pp. 35–6, and n. 23; *OED, secretary*, senses (1) and (2); Labanoff, vi, 26f; *GB*, pp. 16f.
16 Document (a).
17 Above, p. 31 and Document (d); *OED, deliver* (8), *time* (41).

us up. The point is that Courcelles knows all about the delivery of the letters written by Feron, so that, if they are betrayed, they must have been betrayed by one or other of them. Which is exactly what Castelnau was to tell Mary.

I cannot quite exclude that Feron meant to say that Courcelles was in the game; and we certainly cannot exclude the idea that Fagot meant Courcelles when he spoke of Castelnau's secretary. But I shall now proceed on the assumption that Fagot's friend, and the solitary mole in the house, was Feron, and that Courcelles had nothing to do with the matter at all. This assumption will save all the other phenomena known to us about Courcelles, except perhaps the castles in Spain. If anyone wants to make something of these, and to preserve the natural meaning of Fagot and the possible meaning of Feron, I should advise him to pursue the idea insinuated above that Courcelles launched a spurious leakage intended to muddy the waters and give Catholic conspiracy a chance. I shall not be taking this line myself.

After Feron and Courcelles we come to Williams, who has by courtesy of Lord Burghley entered our story like a torpedo hitting a battleship and looks as if he may now become a principal character in it. We need to know more about him: he does not now look quite the comic bungler described by Conyers Read. He came from Wales, perhaps Monmouthshire, and was probably now in his forties. He had some land, so was perhaps a gentleman; but Walsingham calls him 'Wat', so perhaps not. He wrote a good hand, though on principle he put pen to paper rarely. He spoke French (in French his name came out as 'Vatter Wilelhem') and perhaps other continental languages. He certainly had a reputation for drink, and was perhaps also a betting man, hence not one of the godly; according to a companion he 'never toucheth maid but from the knee upward'. Read thought him 'a fellow of no morals and of very little religion'.[18] That may be; but he served the godly Walsingham almost continuously for some fifteen years, which is a testimony to his competence and reliability.

He had been with Walsingham in his first post, as ambassador to France between 1571 and 1573; after Walsingham became secretary of state in December of that year, Williams spent some seven years carrying letters back and forth to the continent, taking a holiday in 1577–8 when he went

---

18 Read, *Walsingham*, ii, 325–7, 420; below, p. ••; BL Harleian 6035 (below, p. ••), f. 10ʳ; C. T. Martin (ed.), *Journal of Sir Francis Walsingham from December 1570 to April 1583* (Camden Society, 1st series, civ [1871: repr. 1968] part 3), pp. 8, 13; quotation from testimonial by 'Pasquinus Romanus', the prisoner at Rye (see next note), 1–ii–1583 (? style), cited from Read, ii, 326. *CSP Foreign 1581–82*, no. 249 (betting); *1586–88*, p. 108 (W. never writes while 'travelling'); BL Harleian 1582, f. 104 ('Vatter . . .').

to France with the young brothers of the Earl of Oxford and served briefly
as a soldier in the Netherlands. Perhaps he was doing some spying as well:
he was possibly already in Rye in April 1582 passing an agent into France,
and was certainly there in August and September, trying to get something out of the unnamed Catholic prisoner who wrote his very funny
testimonial. I think he returned to London shortly after this, and that
Walsingham now put him in charge of his London house in Seething
Lane: in December, when Archibald Douglas was under house arrest there,
Walsingham sent Williams a letter with news he was to pass on to Douglas.
'Your trustie servitor', Douglas described him to Walsingham, and drunk
or sober that is evidently what Williams was.[19] When Fagot passed the
word to Walsingham about Feron, Williams was the man to make contact.
We cannot be absolutely sure of this; but since Williams was Feron's contact
in August 1583, and Feron was unwilling to deal with new people, we can
fairly assume that Williams had been his contact from the start.

At Williams's meeting with Feron we come, at last, to the real beginning of our story. I think I can now produce a fairly circumstantial account
of how it happened; but before I do this we shall have to confront a prior
question which has become a matter of controversy: *When* did it happen?
The controversy has arisen because, although Fagot's letter is not dated, it
has been endorsed as of April 1583. It must have a connection with two
other pieces sent by Fagot on 19 and 24 April, which also report things
going on in Salisbury Court. In it he says that it is 'a long time' since he
wrote last. We cannot therefore date it between 25 and 30 April; if we
follow the endorsement we must date it before the 14th, and probably
some while before, since the other pieces do not follow it in any obvious
way; we must also conclude that Fagot had written to Walsingham before
this. In that case he cannot be identified with Bruno, since Bruno, who
came from Paris to live at Salisbury Court around this time, did not leave
Paris before about 28 March. The date of Fagot's letter matters a good deal
less for Feron's history than for Bruno's; but it matters to some extent.
Since we are now attempting to pin down the circumstances in which
our story begins, we need a proper date to start with. When I wrote Fagot's
and/or Bruno's story I offered a date between about 20 and 31 May. I was

---

19 Martin, above, n. 18; *CSP Domestic 1547–80*, p. 502; *CSP Foreign 1577–78*, nos. 22, 256, 447; *1578–79*,
    nos. 52, 573–74; *1579–80*, nos. 490, 451; possibly PRO SP12/153, no. 3. Williams at Rye: PRO SP
    12/155, nos. 29–31, 37, 45; 156, no. 7 – dated by Williams 15-xii-1582, but I think September;
    CSP Scotland 1581–83, pp. 664f (misdated to 1583), 248 (Douglas). The dates of the last two
    (1-xii-1582, ?12-i-1583, old style) make the previous date impossible, unless the man in the prison
    at Rye was somebody else: 'Pasquinus' does call him 'William Williams', and he only signs with
    a 'W'. He also seems to have to return to Rye before the beginning of February for Pasquinus'
    testimonial. But I agree with everyone else that he was Walter; it is a real pity we do not know
    who his witty victim was.

thus in dispute with the endorser of the letter, who has reasonably been thought to have known better what he was doing than I. I have now come to the conclusion that my date was a little early.

For reasons I explain at the end of the book,[20] I now suggest the following dates. If we take Fagot and Bruno to be the same person, they are either between about 5 and 7 June or between about 16 and 20 June 1583; if we keep Fagot and Bruno apart, any date between about the 5th and about the 20th will do.

A story of the circumstances of the leakage will begin just after Easter (March 31), when William Fowler has been haunting Salisbury Court for five months, Williams is directing him[21] and looking after Archibald Douglas in Seething Lane, and Fagot has not yet emerged. From Walsingham's point of view, things do not look good. True, the disaster of the Anjou marriage has been avoided, and the political–Catholic Duke of Lennox has been winkled out of Scotland. But Parma is rolling back the gospel in the Netherlands, where Anjou, who has been sent to resist him, is doing more harm than good: he is possibly going to join the other side. What side the King of France is on is anybody's guess; but he is no longer, if he ever was, material for a vigorous collaboration against Spain, and the forces of popery are creeping up on him. The next step on the Roman agenda, as every Protestant knows, will be an assault on England, besought by Mary and her friends, prepared by a tribe of Jesuits and seminaries, and surely to be launched through Scotland. There, King James is entertaining as ambassador a confidant of the Duke of Guise; his relations with his mother, and what his mother may be up to in general, are unknown. It has been decided to attempt an agreement with her which will keep her out of mischief;[22] but, mischief being the air she breathes, this is a dangerous venture, and it is not at all clear that the remedy will not be worse than the disease.

All that being so, and Castelnau apparently adrift on the Catholic tide, the need for intelligence from Salisbury Court was pressing, and Walsingham must have wondered whether Fowler, for all his diligence,

---

20 *GB*, Text no. 4, pp. 195–8, also pp. 13–21, and Texts nos. 2 & 3; review by Jill Kraye, *Heythrop Journal*, xxxiii (1992), 324–7; see below, 'A Note on the Date of Fagot's Letter'. The *terminus ante quem* of Text no. 4, if it was written in April, is the 14th/24th because that is the date of the first event mentioned in Text no. 2.

21 For Fowler, see above, p. 34f. I take it that Williams was 'your [Walsingham's] servant', who took Fowler to Douglas on, probably, 16/26 April, and by whom Fowler received Walsingham's instructions on 5/15 June (*CSP Scotland 1581–83*, pp. 376f, 379f, 490). In a letter of 29 May/8 June (PRO SP 52/32, no. 51; a passage omitted in *Calendar*, p. 473) Fowler told Walsingham that he would have sent it sooner 'if that your honour his servant had been present or in town to whom I might have delivered my letters'.

22 Read, *Walsingham*, ii, 199f, 391–5.

was actually providing it. The search for a more penetrating alternative occupied the next three months, until Fowler was finally relieved of his task and sent off to Scotland in July 1583. The first idea was to replace him by Douglas, a person of much higher standing, intelligence and influence whom Castelnau thought he had won over to Mary's side the year before: whence his house arrest. In the middle of April Williams, presumably, took Fowler to see him at Seething Lane, and Fowler made him an offer of liberty and employment as a double agent with Castelnau; when, immediately after this, Fowler was seen by Fagot at Salisbury Court, he was perhaps selling Douglas to Castelnau. It was Douglas rather than Castelnau who made difficulties: perhaps he thought that Walsingham was double-crossing him; but in the end, freed and pensioned, Douglas came to a satisfactory arrangement with Castelnau at a meeting in Fowler's lodgings some time in June. For the next two years he was constantly in and out of Salisbury Court; I am not convinced that, all told, he was really better value than Fowler. Since Scottish affairs turn out not to be central to our story, Douglas will be a passenger in it; but while we have him in our sights it would be mean not to report a tale he told to Robert Beale about Queen Mary's reaction to the blowing-up of her second husband Henry, Earl of Darnley, at Kirk o'Field in 1567. Douglas ought to have known, because he had been one of the engineers of the explosion: it was alleged that his slippers were found, intact, on the scene of the crime. He said that when she knew her husband was dead she sent for a number of 'light ladies and women' to come to Holyrood House and participate, stark naked, in a ball; then they had cut off their pubic hair and had it put in puddings to be eaten by the male guests, who were sick. If Douglas's conversation was often of this calibre we can see why he appealed to Walsingham, to whom he also expounded Protestant political theory, and even more to Castelnau. Balancing as he did between the two of them, he probably had equally interesting aperçus to offer about the story that follows. Alas, he did not record them.[23]

Early in May, while Douglas was arguing, another possibility came and went. A potential Scottish defector called John Smallet turned up from Paris with an offer from the Duke of Lennox to come over to Elizabeth. Smallet talked a lot to Fowler, to somebody from the embassy, Courcelles or Feron, and to Douglas; Walsingham thought he might be used to break into Mary's correspondence. But nothing came of the offer, which was

23   *CSP Scotland 1581–83*, pp. 376f, 369f, 432f, 440, 444; BL Harleian 1582, ff. 402f; Chéruel, p. 255f; *GB*, Text no. 2, pp. 187, 192; story in BL Addnl. 48027 (Yelverton Mss., 31), f. 780. Read, *Walsingham*, ii, 219 (political theory). The *DNB* is thin on Douglas.

probably spurious, and he was packed off back to France: it looks as if Walsingham told Williams to get rid of him.[24] Then there was a lull during the Whitsun entertainments (Whit Sunday being 19 May in 1583), which included a tournament at Whitehall probably attended by most of our cast.

Meanwhile Feron was writing his letters, and his friendship with Fagot was maturing. It is surprising that nobody except Fagot seems to have thought he was vulnerable. We can think that his position as a naturalised English subject was an issue; that it had been raised by his little brush with the crown, whatever it had been about, the year before; and that the progress of Castelnau's or Courcelles' relations with Mary and the Catholics had stirred a conflict of loyalties. We can also think that he had observed Walsingham's willingness to spend money around Salisbury Court on people like Fowler who knew a great deal less than he did. It looks to me as if he had benevolently provided Fagot with much of the information in his April messages by letting him read confidential letters from the Catholic side; but he can hardly then have been aware that Fagot was writing to Walsingham. I wonder which of them was the first to see through the other; it would be nice to think of instantaneous recognition, followed by giggles.

If we agree to date Feron's betrayal to June 1583, we have enough evidence about doings at Salisbury Court to reconstruct, without much recourse to imagination, the circumstances in which he decided on it. We cannot read his mind, but we can see business at the embassy going on around him, much of it to do with the uncertain future of the Duke of Anjou, which might have influenced him. He and Fagot, we may suppose, were turning over the bad things happening in the house, such as the import of popish books by the downstairs mafia, of which Feron, a merchant by trade, would know the ways and means. On 3 June, a Monday, Feron wrote fair a long letter from Castelnau to Henri III. This was mostly an account of Castelnau's day at the Whitsun tournament: managing a chilly interview between Elizabeth and an envoy of Anjou called Chartier; snubbing a Polish visitor, the Palatine Laski, with whom Bruno was about to go to Oxford; complimenting the riders. Elizabeth had told Chartier that she was informed (?by Fagot) of his master's plan to change sides, and knew more of what was going on in the world than people thought.[25]

24 Read, *Walsingham*, ii, 192–4; *CSP Foreign 1583*, no. 288; *CSP Scotland 1581–83*, pp. 446, 450–2, 464 (conversation between 'Mauvissière's servant' and Smallett), 473; BL Harleian 6035, f. 10ʳ.
25 *GB*, Text no. 4; Chéruel, pp. 258–64; on the background to Chartier's visit, see 'A Note on the Date' pp. 165–7.

On Tuesday Feron (probably) took a letter from Castelnau to Walsingham asking him for help to get money out of some Italian bankers, and lamenting Chartier's capture by the enemy on his way back to Anjou at Dunkirk;[26] Fowler appeared at Salisbury Court with the news of the Duke of Lennox's death in Paris.[27] On Wednesday Fowler came again, and found Castelnau writing another letter home; we get a snapshot of the scene in Castelnau's chamber. I imagine he was writing the letter himself; but Feron (again probably) was in the room, because he said, when Castelnau was telling Fowler about the money problem he had sent to Walsingham to get sorted out, that Walsingham had not been very helpful when he had talked to him about it. As Fowler was leaving, he took a quick look at another letter, which Feron was probably writing or preparing to seal up: what Fowler saw was about the fatal consequences of Anjou's attempt at a *coup d'état* in Antwerp in January.[28] If Fowler and Feron had any time on their own, Feron kept his thoughts to himself: he knew that Fowler was working for Walsingham but thought he was two-timing him.[29] Or so he said; perhaps he just wanted Fowler out of his way.

This intimate but ordinary scene, as from a Dutch interior of some decades later, took place on 5 June 1583 (or on the 4th if Fowler wrote it up next day). Then or in the next few days something more dramatic happened: the Spanish ambassador, Don Bernardino de Mendoza, came in person to see Castelnau. Mendoza is famous as an 'ambassador of ill-will', a relentless enemy of Protestants and their sympathisers, and of Elizabeth herself. He had been a rabid opponent of Anjou's marriage to her, and had not spoken to Castelnau for a very long time. Since April he had been putting out feelers, which had been picked up by Fagot. Now he evidently thought that the winds of change were blowing through Salisbury Court, and came to talk about fixing up a marriage between Anjou and an Infanta. Everybody knew that the marriage to Elizabeth was now dead: Castelnau had talked about the consequences with Chartier, and was about to go and talk about them with two of the oldest supporters of the mar-

---

26   *CSP Foreign 1583*, no. 350 (p. 386); for Feron, below, n. 28.

27   *CSP Scotland 1581–83*, pp. 489, 490.

28   *CSP Scotland 1581–83*, p. 490 (no. 507); PRO SP 52/32, no. 61: 'He has written in another letter, which in closing I did see by a glance and view, that etc. . . . As concerning his particular, he doth esteem your honour to favour too much Baiamonte [the Italian merchant above] and his man was showing him that your honour had small regard to that which he spake in his part to your lordship [*sic*].' I take 'his man' to be Feron, since the whole scene is of Castelnau writing or dictating letters, and the 'man' appears to be connected with the letter Fowler saw 'by a glance and view'; if so, it was Feron who had taken Castelnau's letter to Walsingham the previous day. Courcelles seems to me an unlikely, Bruno a possible alternative.

29   *GB*, Text no. 4, p. 197: 'Donnez vous bien de garde s'il vous plaist d'ung escosoys dont son nom est foulain car il est fort traistre. Car le segraittaire de mondit seigneur l'ambassadeur vous le mande de par moy.'

riage, Sir Edward Stafford and Lord Henry Howard.[30] Some time after Mendoza's visit Feron decided to jump, and Fagot passed his offer on to Walsingham. It will have been about 7 June or, if Feron had to wait for Fagot to get back from Oxford, about the 17th.

30 *GB*, Text no. 4, p. 197; G. Mattingly, *Renaissance Diplomacy* (London, 1955), pp. 204f; 'A Note on the Date', below, pp. 166f; Castelnau to Mary, c. 3/13–vii–1583 (Appendix, no. 1); below, pp. 67 and 71f. In the 'Note', I date Mendoza's visit between 4/14 and 12/22 June; Castelnau's discussion with Stafford and Howard took place before 12/22 June.

PART II
A Mole and his Masters

Sir Francis Walsingham; by John de Critz, the elder. National Portrait Gallery, London.

4

PROOF

THE INTELLIGENCE OPERATION launched at Williams's meeting with Feron lasted for something over a year, and went through three phases, divided by events in November 1583 and April and May 1584. The first ended with the arrest of Francis Throckmorton and others early in November, and the authorities gave a succinct account of it six months later:

> The cause of [Throckmorton's] apprehension grewe first upon secret intelligence given to the Queen's Majestie, [read, to Walsingham] that he was a privy conveiour and receivour of letters, to and from the Scottish Queene: upon which information, neverthelesse, divers moneths were suffered to passe on, before he was called to answer the matter; to the end there might some proofe more apparant be had to charge him therewith directly; which shortly after fell out.[1]

This was perfectly accurate so far as it went; but it isolated one aspect of an action which in conception had had various objectives. Walsingham, and Elizabeth, certainly wanted to discover the mechanics of Castelnau's clandestine correspondence: the who and the how, the where and the when. But they also wanted reliable political intelligence about Mary: what kind of a party she had, and what they and their continental friends might be going to do, principally in Scotland, secondarily in England. This intelligence was not only needed to pre-empt an attack on the realm: Elizabeth at least wanted it to judge whether Mary was genuinely interested in the discussions about releasing her from captivity in return for adequate assurances about her future conduct which had been formally launched at Sheffield at the beginning of June 1583. Then they wanted to shed some light on the enigma of Castelnau himself, whom Elizabeth had now put down as no longer the reliable friend of two or three years ago, and on the larger enigma of Henri III and France. Whose side were they

---

1 *A Discoverie of the Treasons practised and attempted . . . by Francis Throckmorton* (1584: *Harleian Miscellany* [10 vols, London, 1808–13], iii, 190–200), at p. 192.

now on? This was the point of knowing what Anjou was up to, and what Castelnau was talking to Mendoza about. One thing they do not seem to have been looking for was information about a Catholic enterprise to be launched in the near future in or against England; all their concern at this time seems to have been about Scotland, and it remained fixed there for another five months. In that respect the replacement of Fowler by Feron had not done them all the service it might have done.

If we still have all the letters that Feron passed, which I think we have, there were forty-odd of them altogether. That sounds a lot, but the total includes plenty of dead wood, as we shall see. There are eight letters from Mary to Castelnau, and at least eight in the opposite direction. Seven of these (four and three respectively) were passed before November 1583; all are copies in Feron's hand (Hand II), and appear to have been passed one at a time.[2] There are also two other items to be considered: the first copied in Hand II, but not written to Mary; the second to Mary, not in a copy by Feron but in a decipher by Thomas Phelippes, Walsingham's well-known decipherer.[3] Taken as a whole, this corpus of items is not very impressive; there are some nuggets in it, but not many. This is not because Feron was holding things back, though he was keener to perform at some times than at others. It is partly because Castelnau was not fully in Mary's confidence, any more than he was now in Elizabeth's: Mary always regarded him as a fairly tepid ally compared with Mendoza, to whom she wrote freely.[4] It is also because Feron did not put everything down on paper. He was very scared of being found out: we may take seriously the death or dishonour he thought would happen to him if he was.

We can take it from Williams and from the official account just quoted,[5] that one item passed orally by Feron, presumably to Williams himself, was the names of the 'messengers', Throckmorton and the actual postman, one George More. He no doubt gave them on the undertaking that Walsingham gave them to nobody else; as I fancy he always did in such matters, Walsingham kept his word, and must have irritated Elizabeth royally by not telling her. I should think Feron gave Williams the names at their first meeting, and that on the same occasion he also handed over the cipher he had promised via Fagot, which it only seems to have been necessary

---

2 See 'Appendix: Letters passed from Salisbury Court', section (i), where they are listed and so far as possible dated. I refer to them hereafter by number.

3 Below, p. 79; *CSP Scotland 1581–83*, pp. 380–3, 654–6.

4 *CSP Spanish 1580–86*, pp. 446f, 475, 491 (Mary to Mendoza, 28-ii/10-iii-1583, 5/15-vi-1583, 13/23-vii-1583).

5 Above, p. 45 ('the messengers, who are already known to be but too'); above, p. 65. The reference here must be to Feron rather than to Fagot, since Fagot did not say, and probably did not know, anything about Throckmorton and the correspondence.

to use once. Since Williams will surely have asked Feron what he had on Henry Howard, Feron may have told him that Howard was receiving letters from Mary, as he confirmed later. Howard was actually questioned about something early in July 1583,[6] but we do not know about what, and I should be a little surprised to find Walsingham using this information so soon after it had been given him.

We already know what was in the first letter from Castelnau to Mary that Feron leaked, written on 3 July or very near it.[7] It reported Castelnau's recent discussions with Chartier and Mendoza about Anjou changing sides and how Mary might help the scheme along; it recorded that he had accepted Walsingham's gambit with Archibald Douglas, and was recommending him to Mary. There may have been more sensitive material in the letter that Feron did not copy; as it stands it did not tell Walsingham much he did not already know from Fowler and Fagot.

The second leaked letter was Mary's reply to this or an earlier letter on the same subject, written on 14 July. She had written to Mendoza a good deal more confidentially the day before, and both letters were no doubt carried to their destinations by George More.[8] Most of Castelnau's letter was of fairly moderate interest. Mary had always detested Anjou: her line about him was that he had the pox, which he had got from his mother, her own mother-in-law, Catherine de Medici.[9] She had just told Mendoza that she did not believe what Castelnau had told her about the prospects of an agreement between Anjou and Philip II, and visibly hoped that he would stew in his own juice. She thought that Douglas might do some good, and encouraged him to keep hobnobbing with Walsingham so as to find out where he stood about the treaty negotiations with Elizabeth, of which she sent Castelnau an account.

There was something more worthwhile than this in the letter, but before we come to it we have an awkward obstacle to get over. There exist two versions of it, which is not the case, so far as I know, of any other letter in the series. We have Feron's; and we have another copy made by a scribe in Paris two years later for the benefit of M. d'Esneval, Courcelles' superior in Scotland.[10] I shall call this the Paris version. The two are different,

---

6 BL Harleian 6035, f. 20ᵛ; for Howard, see *GB*, index.

7 No. 1; 'A Note', p. 167.

8 No. 2; *CSP Spanish 1580–86*, p. 491; for More, below, pp. 80f.

9 Labanoff, v, 108; Teulet, *Relations politiques*, iii, 57 (Mary to Castelnau, November–December 1579). It seems pretty clear that this is what Mary had said.

10 Part of the D'Esneval Ms., a copy of letters of Castelnau and others, many of which do not otherwise survive, made in France between Castelnau's return in October 1585 and D'Esneval's departure for Scotland in December; printed in Labanoff, v, 348–52. The Ms. belongs to the de Broglie family, and there is a microfilm of it in the Archives Départementales de la Seine-Maritime (1 Mi 1386).

and not simply because the second writer was very careless, or because of difficulties in decipherment. The text which was copied in Paris differed from the letter as Feron sent it to Walsingham: either Mary had sent it in two versions, or Feron had changed what was in front of him, and left some of it out.

The important thing Feron may have left out was a sentence at the end where Mary mentioned, in cipher, one of the people who was carrying her letters: 'I shall write to you at greater length in three days, when [blank] will be returning' (Je vous escripray plus amplement dedans trois jours que retournera [ ].)[11] This is in the Paris version, but not in Feron's. Otherwise there are three passages where Feron's version is different: he is always crisper and shorter, but it is not easy to see that he is concealing anything, and he adds some things. In one case Mary refers to the fall of Dunkirk to the Spaniards, and briskly voices English suspicion that this has been due to sabotage by Anjou and the French: Feron then has Mary asking in reply to Castelnau, as she does not in the Paris version, how the reconciliation between Anjou and Philip is getting on, and what has become of Chartier.[12] The passage about Archibald Douglas leaves out the reason why Elizabeth will not agree to his going to Scotland ('because she is afraid of him'), and suggests that he accept a pension from England rather than, as the long version has it, from France.[13] These are trivia; the third passage, which comes first in the letter, is something else. Mary enclosed an account of her negotiations at Sheffield in June; as she had promised them not to pass on anything about their discussions, Castelnau was to keep the knowledge under his hat. Feron's version goes on: 'Ce neantmoins vous en pourrez faire part a mon frère pour lequel est la lettre cy encloze, luy envoyant d'avec icelle la bague dont a mon grand regret il a este trouve faulte entre vous et luy.' (Nevertheless you may pass it on to my brother, for whom this letter is here enclosed, sending him with it the ring which I am very sorry to see has gone missing between you and him.)[14]

Mary had no brother: if she had had, she would not have been where she was. 'Mon/votre frère' was the term used between Mary and Castelnau for Lord Henry Howard, on the grounds that she had intended to marry his brother the Duke of Norfolk. Castelnau was to tell Howard

11   Labanoff, v, 352.
12   No. 2(a), f. 320ᵛ: 'Faictes moy scavoir quelle response vous avez dudit Sr. duc pour sa reconsiliation avec le Roy Catholicque et ce qui a esté faict de Chartier son secretaire'; cf. Labanoff, v, 352.
13   No. 2(a), f. 320ʳ; Labanoff, v, 351.
14   No. 2(a), f. 320ʳ.

about her negotiations with Elizabeth, send him a letter enclosed, and with it a ring which, it would appear, he ought to have sent him already but Howard had not received. The Paris copyist left a gap at 'mon frère', no doubt because he had an undeciphered symbol in front of him; he made a mess of the following phrase, which does not however seem to have said anything more than what Feron wrote except that the letter was 'marked I'; after 'envoyant', he read 'dans' instead of 'd'avec', meaning that Castelnau was to send the ring in, not with, the letter, which I am sure was a mistake. The phrase attributing the non-delivery of the ring to Castelnau is replaced by another apparently saying that she had meant to send it in her last letter but had forgotten.[15]

Had Feron tinkered with Mary's letter? Walsingham is alleged to have done this, and we shall find Feron doing it later under instructions from Castelnau.[16] I do not think he did it on this occasion. True, if he had the sentence about the messenger in front of him, he left it out; but he did not leave out the equally confidential information about Howard, and he had probably told Williams the names of the messengers anyway. The passages about Douglas and Anjou are not more or less confidential, just different. Feron did not send Walsingham a letter emasculated either by Castelnau or by his own nervousness. In that case Mary must have sent two versions of it, and Feron copied the earlier or shorter one. I think this would be quite exceptional, and a needless risk; but there is a just possible account of why and how she may have done it. The why would be that she sent a copy to Mendoza, to show him that she had nothing up her sleeve in her dealings with Elizabeth and Castelnau; the how would be that she sent it by the travelling political Jesuit Henri de Samerie, who managed to pay her a brief visit incognito at more or less exactly this time, and saw Mendoza in London on his way back to France.[17] He would be

---

15 Interrogation of Henry Howard, December 1583 (PRO SP 12/163, f. 93 [no. 39]), questions 10 and 11. Labanoff, v, 350: 'Ce neanmoings vous en pourrez faire part à . . . comme verrez qu'il sera [prêt] de partir [avec] mes lettres cy encloses marqué I, luy envoiant dans icelle la bague dont à mon grand regret il a este trouve faulte, pour l'avoir obmise dernièrement.' Labanoff evidently thought the blank referred to the messenger, and made the additions to make sense of the sentence. But it must mean Howard, and I presume the scribe had misread 'de partir' for 'départi(es)', meaning distributed or conveyed: the original will have read: 'comme verrez qu'il sera départi(es) mes lettres, etc.' Cf. p. 351, line 7 up: 'de me départir votre bon conseil'.

16 Below, p. 130.

17 *CSP Spanish 1580–86*, p. 499, using Samerie's alias 'La Rue'. Mendoza reported seeing Samerie in a letter of 9/19 August, and he cannot have left Paris very long before 23 June/3 July, since his general Acquaviva wrote to him as in Paris on that date: A. Lynn Martin, *Henry III and the Jesuit Politicians* (Geneva, 1973), p. 111f, and see index under *Samier*. Hence 17/27 July or somewhat later would be a good date for him to have left Sheffield. He had accompanied two new waiting-women sent to Mary from France to replace Mary Seton and Mlle. de Courcelles, but cannot have gone back with them, since they arrived in London on 26 August/5 September (*HMC Bath*, v, 46).

the unknown party who would be 'returning' in three days' time when
the first version of the letter (the Paris version) was written, and he would
have carried the second version (Feron's).[18] Since Samerie had come to
tell Mary and Mendoza that the invasion scheme was now off the ground,
which was music to the ears of both of them, Mary might well have felt
that this gesture of complicity with Mendoza was in order. The objection
to this interesting hypothesis is that it requires Mendoza, having received
his copy from Mary, then to have passed it on to Castelnau. It seems insu-
perable: whoever took Feron's version took it to Salisbury Court.

We have not got much out of pursuing this tiresomely inscrutable
problem, but we have got something. We seem to have found that Feron
was an honest mole. If the unidentified party was indeed Samerie, which
I think rather likely, then he was someone for whom Mary and
Castelnau had a coded symbol, which would show us that Castelnau had
been sailing nearer the wind than one had supposed.[19] But most of what
we have found is about Howard: he was a party to Mary's clandestine correspondence, and she had sent him a token of fidelity. Among other points
arising out of this passage, Howard was asked at his interrogation about
the letter in December: 'To whom the ring that was lost should have been
delivered if it had come into his hands?' He denied all knowledge of a
ring, and the only letter he would admit to was an anonymous one which
he had been given in St James's park around Whitsun (19 May 1583). The
messenger had told him that it came from Castelnau; he had gone to
Salisbury Court to enquire, and Castelnau had denied it 'par le sang
Dieu'.[20] Most of this was evidently untrue, but the interrogators were not
allowed to squeeze Howard, and all that resulted was a set of Chinese whis-
pers about the ring. Howard was going to marry Mary, had married her,
was to 'be elected King of England by the English Catholics', to be installed
by the pope. Protected by Elizabeth, Howard was in a position to scoff at
all this as a 'pretty fancy'.[21]

18   Above, p. 67: understanding 'retournera' to mean 'going back to London' rather than 'coming
     back here'. If he, or whoever it was, carried Feron's version of the letter on this occasion, the
     sentence would of course have been left out of it; which is a point in favour of Feron's honesty.
19   Samerie visited Castelnau after another visit to Mary a year later (*CSP Foreign 1583–84*, p. 592),
     but we do not know that he did so on this occasion.
20   Interrogation of Howard (above, n. 15, and below, p. 83); the question about the ring was added
     to the original series (?by Walsingham). Answers in *CSP Scotland 1581–83*, pp. 675f; *1584–85*, pp.
     21f. H. Nicolas, *Life and Times of Sir Christopher Hatton* (London, 1847), p. 368; Howard to Sir
     Philip Sidney, 27-viii/6-ix-1584 (Durham University Library, Howard Mss. 5, f. 40), saying he
     could not tell who the letter was from.
21   PRO SP12/168, f. 30 (no. 14): query (12/22-ii-1584) whether Howard should not 'be more straitly
     examined' about a letter from Mary via George More, which he denies receiving: the queen to
     be asked. The rumour about the marriage began with one of Herle's reports from Salisbury Court
     (*GB*, Text no. 5, p. 200), was taken up by Thomas Norton, who perhaps made the enquiry above

Howard remained in the picture in Feron's next offering, a letter from Castelnau written about 20 July 1583, which Feron may well have sent before Mary's.[22] Castelnau, it appeared, had been quite excited by contacts with the Protestant party which indicated that they were in favour of an agreement between Mary and Elizabeth. This was probably disinformation; the interesting thing about it was that those to whom the benevolent view was attributed included not only the inevitable Walsingham and Leicester, but Philip Sidney as well. Sidney, 'the most capable young man' in the kingdom, Castelnau said, was showing himself sympathetic to Mary, keen to advance her case with his friends, and not irreducibly hostile to popery. He was about to confirm his standing as a future leader of the Protestant interest by marrying Walsingham's daughter, as he did in September. In the past Castelnau's relations with him had been extremely distant because of Sidney's public hostility to the Anjou marriage; but this was now perhaps an advantage. We do not have to think that Sidney was a closet Catholic, though he had difficulties about predestination:[23] he was either being polite or doing a job for Walsingham. The report may have come via Douglas, who was close to Sidney's best friend, Fulke Greville, or via Bruno, who during the trip to Oxford in June had discovered a passion for Sidney which lasted through his stay in England.[24] But the evidence is that it came from, of all sources, Henry Howard. Howard had been at enmity with Sidney for a long time, and in Bruno's book, and for English Protestant opinion, they were emblematic figures of the alternative destinies facing the nation.[25] But this was not the tune of Castelnau's letter. Immediately after mentioning Sidney, he told Mary that 'votre frère' was as firm as ever on her side, and enclosed a short letter from him. We know what was in it, or at least we know what Howard said was in it: he had written it at Castelnau's prompting a month before (12 June 1583) after a conversation with Castelnau at dinner at Sir Edward Stafford's house in Highgate. The three of them had been energetic supporters of the Anjou

(M. A. R. Graves, *Thomas Norton* [Oxford/Cambridge, Mass., 1994]. p. 269), and found its way into William Camden, *The Historie of . . . Elizabeth* (London, 1630), book iii, p. 41. Howard, in Nicolas, *Hatton*, pp. 376f – 'prety fancies', private whisperings. Camden attributed it to 'Hart, a priest', presumably John Hart, then in the Tower.

22 No. 4. This is at Hatfield, which may suggest a later date; but it is certainly before 8/18 August.

23 Katherine Duncan-Jones, *Sir Philip Sidney* (London, 1991), pp. 124–7 & elsewhere; 'Sir Philip Sidney's Debt to Edmund Campion', in T. McCoog (ed.), *The Reckoned Expense: Edmund Campion and the Early English Jesuits* (Woodbridge, Suff., 1996), pp. 85–102; *GB*, p. 150, and 'Postfazione' to the Italian edition, *Giordano Bruno e il mistero dell'ambasciata* (Milan, 1992), pp. 341f; R. A. Rebholz, *Life of Fulke Greville* (Oxford, 1971), pp. 24ff. And now Blair Worden, *The Sound of Virtue* (New Haven/London, 1996), pp. 32–7, 95–6.

24 Rebholz, *Life of Greville*, pp. 33, 53, 68, 75f; *GB*, pp. 23 f.

25 *GB*, pp. 113–25, etc.

marriage; Castelnau now said that since that project was dead the best way to preserve the friendship of France and England and to serve the interests of English Catholics was to encourage the negotiations between Elizabeth and Mary. Howard wrote to Mary that he understood from Castelnau that she and Elizabeth were likely to come to an agreement, 'forgetting all discontentments or discords past'; he suggested that she help things along by 'bestow[ing] some favourable message' on Walsingham, and also on Sidney, 'a man though likely through his kindred to be carried to some other course, yet pretending [claiming] to me to wish you no misfortune.'[26] Primed with his knowledge of the ring, Walsingham assumed that Howard's letter contained something more sinister than this. He may well have been right, though the concordance between Castelnau's letter and what Howard says he said in his own is a point on the other side.

Walsingham's suspicions will have been confirmed by the next item of information in Castelnau's letter, which was that a courtier called William Cornwallis had approached him with an offer of service to Mary. He said that he had decided to withdraw from Court, and would do so unless Mary instructed him otherwise. Castelnau suggested that Mary send him a cipher for correspondence, which she did in her next letter but one, enclosed in a 'message of trust and favour'.[27] Cornwallis had certainly changed sides. This was a piece of news for Walsingham to reflect upon. Cornwallis, Castelnau said, was a 'rich, honourable and wise Catholic gentleman' who was brother-in-law both to the Earl of Northumberland and to Lord Burghley's phlegmatic elder son, Sir Thomas Cecil. He was eventually to put his wisdom into a set of *Essayes* published at the same time as Francis Bacon's, in which he wrote about the moral dangers of the political life, from which he had by then been exempted.[28] This was not so in the summer of 1583. He was the elder son of Sir Thomas Cornwallis, a client of the Howards and pillar of mid-Tudor government who had been Queen Mary Tudor's Comptroller of the Household, in which role he had protected Princess Elizabeth from persecution by her enemies. This service secured him a quiet life during Elizabeth's reign, which he

---

26   *HMC Hatfield*, iii, 3; Cecil Papers, 162, f. 105. The account of the conversation and the letter, which Howard says he is remembering, are in a plain secretary hand, not Howard's, and do not identify him; but it is obvious who is writing. I do not know on what occasion Howard was questioned about it.

27   No. 7; for the 'message', of which I see no sign in this letter, Cornwallis to Burghley, [ ]-xi-1588 (*HMC Hatfield*, iii, 376).

28   L. B. Smith, *Treason in Tudor England: Politics and Paranoia* (London, 1986), pp. 47, 145: the *Essayes* (1597) were edited by Don Cameron Allen (Baltimore, 1946). Also Charles Nicholl, *The Reckoning: the Murder of Christopher Marlowe* (London, 1992), pp. 188ff (Cornwallis and Thomas Watson).

lived through; he was devout, and during the reign dithered between con-
forming Catholicism and recusancy without forfeiting Elizabeth's good
opinion. William was therefore the effective head of a considerable estate,
and had an influential set of connections at court and in the network of
Catholic families among the nobility and richer gentry. With Henry
Howard and others, he had agitated for the Anjou marriage. He married
one of four joint heiresses. Marriages were in his line, and he had recently
been trying to arrange one between Northumberland's son and heir, Lord
Percy, and a Catholic niece of his. No Counter-Reformation enthusiast,
he was in good standing, not only with the queen and her more conser-
vative advisers like Burghley and Pallavicino, but also, as Castelnau said,
with Walsingham. If so sensitive a barometer of the political weather was
signalling change, it was time for Protestants to be worried.[29]

William said later that he had made the move in 'a foolish fit of discontent',[30] but the folly was an afterthought, and it is more than likely that
the discontent was not his alone. Howard was close to the family, and may
have inspired his venture; but more probably, and more dangerously, it was
his brother-in-law Northumberland. Immediately before his approach to
Castelnau, Cornwallis had been at Northumberland's house at Petworth
in Sussex writing to Walsingham in terms which suggest that he was acting
as the earl's right-hand man, and that he was not sure on which side his
bread was buttered.[31] If he had now made up his mind, Walsingham will
have concluded, Northumberland must have made his mind up too; which
was no light matter. Henry Percy, eighth earl, was a potential dissident from
the Elizabethan regime. His brother the seventh earl had been executed,
as a leader of the Northern Rising of 1569, not long before the execution of Henry Howard's brother the Duke of Norfolk. He put on a posture
of stoic retirement, but this disguised a good deal of frustration at his exclu-
sion from power, and he was the most politically capable of the Catholic
peerage. Three years earlier, at the height of her crisis with the Protestants
about the Anjou marriage, Elizabeth is said to have considered appoint-
ing him a privy councillor. Now he made little effort to conceal his connections with the circle of Mary's servants in Paris: when he sent his

29 *DNB*, Cornwallis, Sir Thomas; Diarmaid MacCulloch, *Suffolk and the Tudors* (Oxford, 1986), pp.
244f and see index; P. McGrath and J. Rowe, 'The Recusancy of Sir Thomas Cornwallis', *Proceedings of Suffolk Institute of Archaeology*, xxviii (1961), 226–71; Stone, *Palavicino*, p. 12; Ann Weikel,
'Sins of the Fathers? The Marriage of Mary Cornwallis', *Recusant History*, xxiii (1996), 16–26;
Lord Paget to Northumberland, 22-ii/4-iii-1583 (PRO SP 12/159, no. 8). There is a lot of
relevant material about the family in the Paget Papers at Staffordshire Record Office, which I
hope will soon be made public by David Crankshaw of Robinson College, Cambridge.

30 Above, n. 27.

31 MacCulloch, *Suffolk and the Tudors*, p. 245; Cornwallis to Walsingham, 20/30-vi-1583 (PRO SP
12/161, no. 15).

son and heir there to learn the ways of the world, he entrusted him to
the care of his and Thomas Morgan's friend, Charles Paget.[32] At home,
Charles's brother Thomas, Lord Paget, was very close to him, and he sat
in the middle of a web of Catholics and sympathisers which touched on
the Howards and Throckmorton at one end and the queen's councillors
Sir Christopher Hatton and Sir James Croft at the other. Out of government, the musical appetites of the circle were met by William Byrd and
its spiritual ones at this time apparently by the Jesuit Jasper Heywood, who
is said to have reconciled Northumberland to the Roman Church around
Christmas 1582.[33] Now, via Cornwallis, Mary seemed to have gained access
to, and perhaps the allegiance of, this pivotal group. Cornwallis's plan to
unite the clan by marriage, and his approach to Mary via Castelnau, look
like two aspects of a programme, which he probably had the talent to carry
through: as a party organiser he would have been more dangerous than
Throckmorton and more single-minded than Howard. Elizabeth did not
forgive him for his fit of discontent; nor did she forgive Northumberland.

The last of these letters of July 1583, written by Mary at about the same
time as Castelnau's, contained nothing really confidential, but conveyed
her response to the excellent news, for her, that James had escaped from
the junta of Protestant nobles who were keeping him under surveillance
in his castle at Falkland, and had fled to more congenial company at St
Andrews. She told Castelnau to try to push Henri III into sending troops
to Scotland to support her son; no doubt she knew that the king would
not do this on his own account, but she also knew, from Samerie and
otherwise, that her cousin the Duke of Guise was getting ready to inter-
vene with or without the king's authority. Clearly she now thought everything was going her way, and had no patience for Castelnau's treaty. She
suggested, I should think out of pure malice, that he should get Douglas
to write her a letter explaining how much she was beholden to Walsingham for his good offices on her behalf, send it by the ordinary post so
that he and others would read it, and see what happened then. She claimed
that she would like to make friends with him, 'l'estimant homme rond et
plain [sic]'.[34] Walsingham, who had been floated this bait already, must have

32   DNB, Percy, Henry, 8th Earl of Northumberland; L. Stone, *The Crisis of the Aristocracy* (Oxford,
     1965), pp. 655ff; my 'English Catholics and the French Marriage', *Recusant History*, v (1959), 7;
     CSP Foreign 1581–82, nos. 573, 607; BL Cottonian Otho E iv, ff. 128ᵛ, 132.

33   *HMC Bath*, v, 24 (from Thomas Baldwin, on whom see below, pp. 92ff); Northumberland to
     Burghley, 28-ii-1579 (BL Landsowne 29, no. 38), re Byrd; D. Flynn, 'The English Mission of Jasper
     Heywood', *Archivum Historicum Societatis Iesu*, liv (1985), 45–76.

34   Appendix, no. 3: there appear also to have been two versions of this, differently dated (see note
     there); *CSP Spanish 1580–86*, pp. 463, 475, 491; Mary's description of Walsingham is repeated in
     CSP Scotland 1581–83, p. 505.

read it as a poisoned gift designed to get him into trouble with Elizabeth, and a satirical comment on Castelnau's dream of a reconciliation of parties behind the agreement between the two queens.

This was in any case a sickly creature, and Elizabeth now did her best to kill it by counter-attacking sharply against James's bid for freedom: early in August she decided to send Walsingham himself with a large official embassy to the king intended to bully him back into line. Castelnau, who had been assuming that progress on the treaty would be completed by a joint mission to Scotland of the two of them together, was furious with Walsingham, and his anger may have influenced his conduct during the next few months. But it was hardly Walsingham's fault, since a trip to Scotland was the last thing he fancied. Publicly he said he detested the country, which he did, and was ill, which he was; privately, I take it that he thought the key to England's security was his intelligence from Salisbury Court, and despaired at the idea of leaving his arrangements in the hands of Burghley and Elizabeth.[35]

If this was his attitude, we have seen that it was warranted. Elizabeth, perhaps from a reading of the leaked letters, concluded that Feron was not earning his money and sent him the stiff letter we know about from Williams, requiring him to do better and in particular to tell her the names of the 'messengers'. Williams, obviously most unhappy about the new arrangements, took the letter, retailed with sympathy Feron's nervous reply, and no doubt advised him to keep his head down until Walsingham got back.[36] This seems to be what Feron did: from the wording of Williams's letter, it looks as though neither of them told Elizabeth about the messengers, and the letters he passed were even more anodyne than usual. After the last letter mentioned, which probably came to Walsingham but has ended up, like Williams's, in Burghley's papers, little real intelligence came out of Salisbury Court for three months.

Hence nothing was known on the government side of the sharp movement among the enemy forces which happened in August, after a new meeting in Paris of the promoters of the English enterprise.[37] Perhaps

---

35 Walsingham's visit is described in Read, *Walsingham*, ii, 202–24; Castelnau to Walsingham, 8/18-viii-1583 (*CSP Scotland 1581–83*, p. 579).

36 Above, chap. 3, *passim*.

37 On which the authority is L. Hicks (ed.), *Letters and Memorials of Robert Persons*, i (CRS xxxix, 1942), pp. lviii, 171ff; also now Martin, *Henry III and the Jesuit Politicians*, 105–15, and my 'The Heart of Robert Persons', in McCoog, *The Reckoned Expense*, pp. 141–58. Simon Adams has found various signs of a scare in the Council, early in September (old style), about an impending Catholic rising with help from France (e.g. a letter to the Earl of Leicester from one of his secretaries, 17/27-ix-1583: BL Cottonian Caligula C. ix, ff. 99–100). I do not think this can mean any knowledge of the actual scheme proposed. Hicks's evidence (*An Elizabethan Problem*, p. 34 n. 92) for government foreknowledge of the scheme refers to an expedition to Scotland, so is

Feron did not know about it; if he did know, he did not pass his knowledge on. The relevant part of the scheme was that Guise would lead in person a small force of some 5,000 men to land in the vicinity of Arundel in Sussex. It was the more practicable part of a grandiose conception, which included a landing of twenty thousand Spanish troops in Lancashire intended to raise the allegedly Catholic north of England: between the two of them they were to liberate Mary, defeat Elizabeth's forces, and overthrow her. As a whole this piece of grand strategy looks amateurish: thought up by enthusiasts in Paris, it did not cut much ice in Spain. But the Sussex venture itself was a relatively modest and precise idea, and if a Catholic rising in the region could be expected not altogether unpromising. Whether the rising could be expected depended very much on the attitude of the Earl of Northumberland, and it may be that some kind of encouragement had been received, or was thought to have been received, from that quarter. In any case, Charles Paget paid a visit to Sussex early in September 1583, probably via the house of one William Shelley at Rustington by the sea, and talked to the earl, and to others who included Charles's brother Lord Paget, at Petworth. Castelnau's wife had by then returned to Salisbury Court, perhaps bringing with her Francis Throckmorton's brother Thomas; Thomas may have brought a message to his brother telling him to get in touch with Mendoza and explore the prospects of support from the rest of the country.[38] This Francis did, and during the next two months, while he continued to run the secret correspondence, he saw a great deal of Mendoza and probably not much of Castelnau; but it seems clear that he saw something of him, and that Castelnau was not wholly in the dark about what he was now doing.[39] I have no doubt that Courcelles knew all about it, and presume that he discussed it with Guise on his trips to France.

These moves give the venture an air of seriousness which is not, I think, altogether illusory. It was not destined to get off the ground: Philip II

---

not relevant. Stuart Carroll's masterly exposition of the Guise, and Norman, side of the scheme(s) in *Noble Power during the French Wars of Religion: the Guise Affinity and the Catholic Cause in Normandy* (Cambridge, 1998), pp. 188–92, shows that it was not a myth; and see M. J. Rodriguez-Salgado 'The Anglo-Spanish War, in her own and Simon Adams's (eds), *England, Spain and the Gran Armada, 1585–1604* (Edinburgh, 1991), p. 5.

38 *A Discoverie of the Treasons*, pp. 191bis–192bis (the manuscript version, PRO SP 12/171, no. 86 has Paget talking not to 'some principal persons', but to Northumberland), 199; J. H. Pollen and W. MacMahon (ed.), *Philip Howard, Earl of Arundel* (CRS xxi, 1919), pp. 120ff, 127f; *CSP Foreign 1583–84*, p. 23 (Mme. de Mauvissière, cf. *1581–82*, no. 347); Examination of Sylvanus Scory, 14/24-ii-1585 (PRO SP 12/176, no. 53). Hicks, *An Elizabethan Problem*, pp. 21–9 and Fraser, *Mary Queen of Scots*, pp. 552–3 claim that Paget, when he came over, discouraged the invasion plan; but the evidence is from Parsons, and not reliable.

39 Below, chaps. 5 and 6.

said at first that he was not willing to support it, and Throckmorton himself told Mendoza that he did not see how the enterprise could come off.[40] But I sense a fairly widespread feeling, and not only on the other side of the Channel, that there was now an opportunity which would not last for very long; Guise persuaded Philip to change his mind, and to offer money and troops for the raid into Sussex. He also got preparations under way on the Norman coast. There turned out to be no time for more, and just as well we may think; but it was a fairly near thing.

Feron passed three more letters in August and September. The first, written by Castelnau about 12 August in a bad temper after he had heard that Walsingham was to go to Scotland, was probably sent between Walsingham's departure and the writing of Elizabeth's letter to Feron. As copied by Feron, it was mostly about the implications of the mission and various wheezes thought up by Archibald Douglas for sabotaging it. It showed Castelnau still trying to get Mary to make friends with Leicester and Sidney; and it recorded an acid interview with Elizabeth, when she said that she had heard 'from a good source' that what was keeping him so long in London was the hope of pulling off some kind of a coup on Mary's behalf. If she had by now read Howard's account of his letter to Mary, she was perhaps thinking of that.[41] Castelnau's letter had nothing about Mary's English contacts at all, and it would not surprise me if a reading of it inspired Elizabeth's intervention with Feron. The two letters from Mary which were sent after this, one of them a reply to the above, do not suggest that the intervention did much good. The only thing of interest in them was that Mary sent a cipher for correspondence with William Cornwallis and I suppose, though she did not mention it, her 'message of trust and favour'. Comically, since Mary told Castelnau that he was not to let Douglas into the secret of their correspondence, this letter appears to have been brought to Burghley by Douglas himself.[42]

On 14 October Walsingham was back on the job, with what reflections on how it had been conducted in his absence we do not know. Nothing now happened on the intelligence front for three weeks: we can presume that Walsingham was waiting for his 'proof more apparent' about Throckmorton to emerge,[43] and he had perhaps told Feron to send nothing more until he could provide it. Meanwhile the wires of the Catholic

---

40 *A Discoverie of the Treasons*, p. 198.
41 No. 5.
42 Nos. 6 and 7, and note on no. 7.
43 *CSP Foreign 1583–84*, p. 171, which might mean the 14th or the 21st; from the Diary of Arthur Throckmorton (Canterbury Cathedral Archives Ms. U.85), ii, f. 17[r] it is fairly clear that the date was the 14th. Above, p. 65.

network were buzzing. Thomas Throckmorton left the country with the help of the Countess of Arundel at Arundel Castle. Francis had gone down to Worcestershire for a while, but by the end of October he was back in London putting together for Mendoza a list of Catholic gentlemen who might be relied upon to support the enterprise, and of places where an invasion force could land. This kind of thing was not his forte, and it was Mendoza, not he, who had the grandiose ideas; but he had the sense to point to Sussex, where the Earl of Arundel headed his list, and to Lancashire.[44] The Catholic aristocracy, or those of them who frequented Lord Paget's house in Fleet Street, appear to have been in a state of euphoria. At the end of the month a Catholic gentleman from Warwickshire called John Somerville, whose connections included the Throckmortons and William Shakespeare, was arrested for announcing his intention to go down to London and shoot the queen.[45]

Courcelles arrived back from France about 1 November with some presents for Mary from Mary Seton and probably with a packet of letters for her from Morgan.[46] Except for Mendoza's dealings with Throckmorton, we are very short of knowledge about what either he or Castelnau had been doing: the correspondence of both of them during this autumn has disappeared, and not I think by accident. But we do know that they had kept in touch since their contacts of the early summer, because a hanger-on of Castelnau called Sylvanus Scory said that he got to know Mendoza through the latter's visits to Salisbury Court 'after the coming over of Madame Mauvissière'. The two ambassadors, along with a Florentine called Tommaso Sassetti satirised by Bruno for something wrong with his teeth, settled a dispute between Scory and another Florentine about money won at the card-table.[47]

Unwilling to pass the time at cards, and still sick, Walsingham waited patiently for his proof to turn up. The official account of the investigation said that this 'shortly after fell out', though it did not say shortly after what; I doubt if the weeks after his return to London seemed very short to him.

---

44 *A Discoverie of the Treasons*, pp. 198ff; Pollen and MacMahon, *Philip Howard*, p. 52; interrogations in PRO SP 12/163, no. 8 and 164, no. 9. Wallace MacCaffrey, *Queen Elizabeth and the Making of Policy, 1572–1588* (Princeton, NJ, 1981), pp. 326ff thinks that Mendoza tried to hold back the conspiracy.

45 Pollen and MacMahon, *Philip Howard*, pp. 42, 132 (Somerville); S. Schoenbaum, *William Shakespeare: a Compact Documentary Life* (Oxford, 1978), pp. 15, 19; confession of William Ward, Lord Paget's secretary, PRO SP 12/164, no. 26, but cf. Pollen and MacMahon, p. 294, where Lord Paget tells Throckmorton a landing in Sussex is no good.

46 *CSP Scotland 1581–83*, p. 656; *HMC Shrewsbury and Talbot Papers*, i, 123; and below, pp. 92f.

47 Examination of Scory, above n. 38; *GB*, pp. 34, 105–8; Giordano Bruno, *Dialoghi italiani*, i, 23, on Sassetti. Scory was the son of John Scory, Bishop of Hereford; Castelnau wrote to Walsingham on his behalf in the summer of 1585 (*DNB*, Scory, John; *CSP Foreign 1584–85*, pp. 547, 584, 589).

His vigil ended on the night of 5 November 1583, or perhaps the night after, with the arrest of Throckmorton at his London house at Paul's Wharf, followed by that of Lord Henry Howard, but of nobody else for the time being. What 'fell out' seems clear: a letter from Castelnau to Mary, written on that day and with a postscript by Courcelles, which exists only in a decipher copy made by Thomas Phelippes.[48] The substance of the letter was even less compromising than many of those already in Walsingham's and Burghley's hands. It reported an interview Courcelles had had with Walsingham a couple of days before: Walsingham had complained that Mary, perhaps meaning Castelnau and Douglas, had wrecked his mission to Scotland by spreading lies about him among the Scots; but he had spoken favourably of an agreement with her again. In consequence, Douglas had been shuttling back and forth between Walsingham and Castelnau, mainly I should think to keep Castelnau's mind off the leakage of his correspondence.

This was no great news; what was new was the beginning of the letter, which put down in black and white what had not figured in any of the leaked correspondence so far. He was writing a quick letter now, Castelnau said, so as to catch the 'Sieur de la Tour', who had sent to him to say that he had a man ready to leave London that evening, whom he could not keep any longer. 'Sieur de la Tour', as we may suppose Walsingham already knew, was the alias used by Mary and Castelnau for Throckmorton; we may presume that the man waiting was George More. Since his return to London Throckmorton had been dealing, so far as we know, only with Mendoza: what he probably wanted from Salisbury Court was the current packet for Mary from Morgan in Paris brought over, I guess, by Courcelles. He did not get it. He got instead only this letter, which he must have had on or with him when two gentlemen 'of no mean credit and reputation' (which appears to mean the tough Protestants Henry Killegrew and Thomas Norton; Norton would be Throckmorton's interrogator) arrived at his house that night to arrest him. They caught him in the act of ciphering a letter of his own to Mary, which however he managed somehow to get out of the house under their noses; and they found an indeterminate number of other compromising papers.[49] It was

---

48 PRO SP 53/12, no. 62: *CSP Scotland 1581–83*, p. 654 – the translation is exceptionally inaccurate.
49 *A Discoverie of the Treasons*, pp. 192, 194; the 'gentlemen' are so named by Arthur Throckmorton (Diary, ii, f. 7ᵛ, under the date Tuesday, 7-xi-83); the *Discoverie*, p. 194, read with the ms. version in PRO SP 12/171, no. 86, implies that one of the 'gentlemen' was the equally Protestant Thomas Randolph, to whose house in St Peter's Hill, round the corner, Throckmorton was taken. Perhaps Randolph had been sent to Throckmorton's mother's house in Lewisham; or perhaps Arthur had got it wrong. In *GB*, pp. 28–31, I made the serious mistake of dating the arrest between 16 and 20 November, supposing that Phelippes's endorsement of the letter above n. 48 as of the 15th was an old style date, which it was not. The date of 5th/15th seems

not the rich haul Walsingham was surely hoping for, but it would just about do.

There must have been a tip-off, and there are only two possible sources for it: Feron, of course, and the second messenger, George More. Courcelles, if anyone still suspects him, can be excluded because he did not give Throckmorton what Walsingham most wanted to catch him with, the packet from Thomas Morgan; he was soon to find, and perhaps had up his sleeve already, another messenger by whom he sent it later. He would also, if he had tipped Walsingham off, have told him where Throckmorton was to be found; but Walsingham did not know this, or he would not have sent a posse to Throckmorton's own house and another to his mother's at Lewisham in Kent.[50] Feron is the obvious favourite. He was presumably sitting in Castelnau's chamber while the letter was being written and, though I doubt if he wrote any of it himself, he probably ciphered it. He had asked for no arrest to be made while Courcelles was away, and Courcelles was back;[51] the letter contained, more or less, the 'proof' of Throckmorton's dealings as a messenger that Walsingham was looking for, and Feron may well have thought that the packet from Paris would go with it. He had not had time to copy the letter or to wait for a contact; I guess that he sent Williams a message by someone who was instantly available, and why not Fagot? Feron knew that Phelippes could read the cipher, and probably did not know exactly where Throckmorton was.

This is almost certainly the right story; but we need to consider More, who was waiting that evening, somewhere in the city, to pick up his packet from Throckmorton. We can take it from Williams that Walsingham had known him to be a messenger for months. We know that he brought letters from Mary to Mendoza and Castelnau around the end of September 1583; after that, nothing of his whereabouts until 5 November, and nothing about his arrest or surrender until about the 14th, when Williams was sent to do something about him. His real confession, for which articles were drawn up about the 20th, does not survive, and what we have is a limp interrogation dating from a month later which was evidently only done for show: he was allowed to get away with the claim that he had never

---

to be established on the authority of Thomas Wilkes, probably the author of *A Discoverie* (Hicks, *An Elizabethan Problem*, p. 30 n. 88, from BL Egerton Mss. 2074); the attorney-general, John Popham, thought it was 'about' the 4th/14th (PRO SP 12/171, no. 79); Arthur Throckmorton's date of the 7th is undermined by his describing the day as a Tuesday, which would mean the 5th. Mendoza reported the arrests on the 8th/18th (*CSP Spanish 1580–86*, p. 510), and Howard was being questioned on the 9th/19th (PRO SP 12/163, no. 59). According to Arthur Throckmorton, Howard was arrested by Sir Thomas Leighton.

50 No. 14, and below, p. 93; *A Discoverie of the Treasons*, p. 192.
51 Above, p. 54.

met Throckmorton. He was put in the Tower, but his name was kept out of Throckmorton's trial and the publicity connected with it; he must have been let out quietly soon afterwards, and disappeared, probably abroad. He had certainly done something to earn his liberty, and the tip-off may well have been it.[52]

But it seems to me far more likely that More got off by co-operating freely with the investigation after Throckmorton's arrest. I think the best thing we can do, now that we know that Walter Williams was Walsingham's fieldworker in the siege of Salisbury Court, is to enquire how he would have seen the matter. Williams had dealt with Feron since June; he dealt with More from at least the middle of November. If More had been nobbled before 5 November it would have been Williams who nobbled him. From Williams's letter of August we can suppose that he would have been hostile to this new departure: he had faith in Feron, and shared his dislike of complications; he had undertaken that the messengers would not be arrested while Courcelles was away; More was an unknown quantity, and I think Williams would have feared that a move in his direction might easily go wrong, and blow the gaff. If Walsingham had considered picking up More, I am sure he would have gone along with these reasons for rejecting the idea. Perhaps Williams had indeed been deputed to deal with More some time before 14 November, but I see no good reason to suppose that the contact predated Throckmorton's arrest. That being so, we may settle for Feron as the source of the tip-off; no doubt in his usual state of fear and trembling, he fulfilled his undertakings to Walsingham and Elizabeth.

52　Read, *Walsingham*, ii, 388f; More's confession, 20/30-xii-1583 (PRO SP 12/164, no. 44); SP 12/168, no. 14; BL Harleian 6035, ff. 35ᵛ, 39ʳ, 43ᵛ, 49ʳ; More to James I, Bordeaux, 19/29-iv-1603 (PRO SP 14/1/55), on false and malicious reports against him; and below, p. 90.

5

DATES IN A DIARY

i

THE ARRESTS OF THROCKMORTON AND HOWARD were presented to the nation as the successful result of a patient intelligence operation lasting several months, and there is no need to quarrel with the description. But the success was actually limited. Elizabeth and Walsingham had been looking for three things: a description of the mechanics of the correspondence; political intelligence about Mary and her party; and light upon the larger political scene, and in particular on the frame of mind of Castelnau and Henri III. They had done well on the first count, but not too well on the second and third. In the long run Walsingham's (and Williams's) Fabian policy would be vindicated; but it is not clear that it had been vindicated by anything that happened up to 5 November. Feron had solved the question about the 'messengers', but he had only provided a modest budget of information about Mary's other contacts; Walsingham and Elizabeth had not got access to the correspondence between Mary and Paris which had been passing through Salisbury Court, nor to that between Mary and Mendoza. They knew nothing about the invasion scheme, or about the canvassing of Catholic support for it which had been going on for three months. Since they did not know about it, they were in no position to judge the attitude to it of the Catholic powers; they were really no closer to fathoming Castelnau's attitude than they had been when their sources were Fowler and Fagot. The arrest of Howard indicates that they were barking up the wrong tree.

They certainly added to their knowledge from the papers taken on or with Throckmorton, though what they discovered was more alarming than informative. According to the published account, he had under the bed in his chamber a green casket, probably full of correspondence with Mary and Morgan, when the officials knocked on the door; but they failed to lay their hands on it. A quick-witted housemaid and a priest called John Meredith got it out of the house and away to Mendoza. The letter he was ciphering to Mary also disappeared. What was found was some odd papers which for some reason or other were not in the casket but lying about in the house. Two were mentioned by the government: a list of Catholic noblemen and gentlemen around the country, written some time ago; and an improved version of this which Throckmorton was in the middle of doing for Mendoza. This 'paper of havens', as it came to be called, added to the list notes of harbours convenient to the gentlemen's estates, and suggestions about how an invading force might proceed. Without the correspondence it was hard to know whether it signified immediate danger or not. Other pieces were found which were not mentioned in the published account: one or more notes from Courcelles to Throckmorton which had accompanied packets he had sent him, kept by Throckmorton to Castelnau's extreme irritation; presumably Castelnau's letter to Mary which had been the occasion of the arrest; half a letter to Throckmorton from his mother about ways of getting his brother Thomas, and perhaps himself, out of the country, and a two-year-old note from Castelnau about some money paid to Thomas in Paris.[1] That seems to be all. The one thing that mattered was the paper of havens, which was news out of the blue and came as a terrific shock, perhaps even more to Elizabeth than to her councillors. Castelnau reported, to Mary but without much exaggeration, Elizabeth's frame of mind during the next few months: 'She has never been so suspicious of everybody or so nervous for her estate as she is at present, now fearing the king of Spain, now the king [of France], sometimes both together.'[2]

The collection of intelligence could not now go on at the same leisurely pace; the principals, so far as they could be got hold of, had to be persuaded to reveal what they knew. Throckmorton was now in the house of Thomas Randolph, Howard in that of Sir Ralph Sadler.[3] Polite questioning elicited no result. Howard probably did not know anything to speak of, and since there was no real evidence against him Elizabeth refused to allow him to be tortured. Throckmorton, who was in a heroic mood but had the paper of havens to explain away, claimed that it was not in his handwriting; that it had been 'foisted in' on him by the searchers, or left by a former servant who was now abroad. No one can have believed any of this, and he was sent to the Tower on 13 November. He must have taken a pack of cards with him, because he managed to get messages out by buzzing some of them out of the window to his youngest brother George,

---

1 *A Discoverie of the Treasons*, pp. 192, 195, 200; No. 15 and Document: (b) '. . . et qu'il a gardé des petits morceaux de papier où Courcelles luy mandoit qu'il luy envoyoit des pacquetz'; PRO SP 12/163, no. 8; *CSP Foreign 1581–82*, no. 347.

2 No. 34.

3 Above, chap. 4; Pollen and MacMahon, *Philip Howard*, p. 338.

who had been let into the precincts by the Lieutenant of the Tower's romantic daughter Cecily Hopton.[4]

The tribulations of Francis's next and last eight months will be a motor of our story, and it is high time to give some account of him and of how he had come to be where he was. He was a young man, now twenty-nine, who had recently come into a large inheritance. He had the usual Elizabethan sense of honour, it seems in a particularly interior and unaggressive form. He was allowed by everyone to be a very agreeable acquaintance; he had charm, possibly the charm of shyness, and had certainly charmed Castelnau. He was close to his brothers, and good friends with his Protestant cousin Arthur. Along with his property, which included a large house in Worcestershire, he had inherited the Catholicism which, with the exception of his distinguished uncle the Protestant statesman Sir Nicholas, his family had maintained since the days of Henry VIII. Such families did not necessarily do badly in the reign of Queen Elizabeth, and Francis's father, Sir John, who had been Queen Mary Tudor's lawyer, had continued to rise in his profession until he had been appointed vice-president of the Council of Wales. But in July 1579 he had been dismissed for corruption; a flexible charge which I presume was a disguise for dismissing him for Catholic recusancy. Both he and Francis were sent to learn a better lesson from the Dean of St Paul's, the eminent theologian and catechist Alexander Nowell; but Nowell did not succeed in converting them and, when his father died shortly after, Francis emerged into maturity with a black mark against his name.

He was no intellectual, but he had been sent for his education to a hotbed of papists, Hart Hall in Oxford, and thence to the Inner Temple, where he had pursued the study of the common law to some purpose: but for the recusancy he might have had a career as one of the Catholics, like Edmund Plowden, who adorned the Elizabethan legal profession. This was now out of the question: after his studies he took a trip abroad to the Catholic Netherlands, or more exactly, since at the time the Netherlands properly speaking were no place for a Catholic Englishman, to the Bishopric of Liège; there he had met various Catholic émigrés, among them Sir Francis Englefield, another member of Mary Tudor's establishment now

---

4 *A Discoverie of the Treasons*, pp. 192–1bis; the 'Tower Diary' of John Hart, a priest who was imprisoned there from 1580 to 1585, published in Edward Rishton's edn of Nicholas Sanders, *De Schismate Anglicano* (Rome, 1586: the diary is added at the end without pagination), gives the date of Throckmorton's arrival in the Tower. The card incident must have happened on the 14th/24th or 15th/25th, because Hart says that Throckmorton spent his first day in the Tower in the dungeon called 'Little-Ease', and Mendoza reported receiving the card [*sic*] on the 16th/26th (*CSP Spanish 1580–86*, p. 510). For Cecily Hopton and George Throckmorton, *CSP Domestic 1581–90*, pp. 136, 160, 178.

serving her ex-husband Philip of Spain. It was to be alleged, indeed to be alleged by Francis himself, that they had persuaded him to work for a Catholic invasion when he returned to England; but for reasons to be explained we can dismiss this idea as a fiction. He was at this time on the devout-establishment rather than the aggressive political side of the still amorphous English Catholic body, and perhaps always remained so. Hence the recusancy, and if we follow Robert Parsons the zealous response of himself and his brothers to the arrival in England of Edmund Campion as a champion of the Catholic faith. But since Elizabeth did not smile on him he was surely looking for an alternative career, and this was offered to him via Castelnau.

We do not know whether he had made contact with Castelnau during the time of the French marriage: I very much doubt if he was in favour of it, since the position was generally incompatible with recusancy and an admiration for Jesuits. But by the autumn of 1581, when Campion had been arrested and was awaiting execution, he had been hooked. Castelnau had two hooks to employ. One was his very Catholic wife, who had her own contacts in English Catholic circles and became friendly with Francis's younger brother Thomas: perhaps only in Paris, where he and she were living at the time. The other was Courcelles, who was looking for agents among people of Throckmorton's kind. It looks as if Francis approached Castelnau in order to arrange for money to be paid to Thomas in Paris by his wife; and that he was then invited to dinner at Salisbury Court, where Castelnau personally, or Courcelles on his behalf, persuaded him to use his connections in the Catholic scene to set up a network for communication with Mary at Sheffield. This he did successfully, and without arousing suspicion, between the Christmas of 1581 and the spring of 1583. He kept his head down to such effect that we know nothing about him until after Christmas 1582, when he turns up having a conversation about Scotland in the gallery at Salisbury Court. From this point, certainly, he was at Castelnau's a good deal, and going to Mass there; he was also in touch with at least three Catholic eminences, Lord Henry Howard, the Earl of Northumberland and Lord Paget.

All this sounds rather incautious, and rather political, and he had of course now been revealed to Walsingham by Fagot as Mary's *facteur* or agent. But he had not evidently, as yet, done anything treasonable, and he will have known how to keep his doings at least formally within the law. Pressure from Paris during the summer, and probably instructions from Mary, not any initiative of his own, had carried him well over the line; it is an indication of his unease about this that at the time he was arrested he was thinking seriously of leaving the country. I think his sense of honour would have forbidden him to do this without telling Mary:

which was perhaps what he was doing in the unfinished letter he was ciphering when the knock on the door came. Now, inside the Tower, he was awaiting an ordeal he will have known he could not pass with honour.[5]

As we work out what happened next we have the help of a source of knowledge which has appeared briefly already, and will figure quite a lot from now on. Sir Francis Walsingham was a vigorous rather than a tidy man, but he and the clerks in his office in Whitehall kept a desk diary. The surviving volume, which like Feron's leakages is in the Harleian Manuscripts in the British Library (Ms. 6035), spans almost exactly the period of our story (April 1583–December 1584); quite accidentally, I am sure. Like all such notebooks, its function was to tell the head of the department what he had to do; it was designed for use not beauty, to remind not to explain. If there is anyone who still thinks that all historical documents are rhetorical texts he ought to have a look at it. The entries are short jottings, sometimes by Walsingham himself and sometimes by one of his clerks like Laurence Tomson or Nicholas Faunt. As such things will, these tend to accumulate into lists: long lists of things for Walsingham to attend to himself, like writing letters, seeing people or preparing matters for the Council; shorter, and tidier, lists of things for him to bring up with the queen.[6] Most of the lists in the earlier part of the book are headed by a date, few in the later part. It has some long gaps: the longest of these covers the two months of Walsingham's trip to Scotland, and during the others I imagine that he was with the queen, at Barn Elms, or sick or otherwise out of touch with his office.

It was not a new source, since Read, Pollen and Hicks had looked at it.[7] But (if I may say so) they had looked at it rather shyly, and had not shown the determination which so cryptic a document required. Nor had I: a first examination seemed to add no more than marginal details to the story. This was not entirely our fault: it was also a tribute to the standard of security prevailing in Walsingham's operations. I had no key which

---

5   I have put this sketch together from the (sparse) materials in *DNB*, where he is said, probably by mistake for his brother Thomas, to have been out of the country between 1580 and the beginning of 1583; A. L. Rowse, *Raleigh and the Throckmortons* (London, 1962); the references above, chap. 2, nn. 8, 11, 13; PRO SP 12/164, nos. 22, 26; and *A Discoverie of the Treasons*, which is surprisingly informative, e.g. in the introductory letter from 'Q.Z.': 'You know how well I have always loved the man, and delighted to converse with him, in respecte of the good partes, wherewith he was endued, and of the pleasant humour that for the moste part did possess him when hee came into the companie of friendes.' It seems typical that he was married (and had children), but nobody seems to know to whom.

6   See Robert Beale's description in Read, *Walsingham*, i, 437; the memos for the queen are divided into 'public' and 'private', as Beale says, but not systematically.

7   Read, *Walsingham*, i, 271 rightly says that it is important, and ought to be edited and published; I refer to it hereafter as 'Diary'.

would open a door into the diary, since I had not read Walter Williams's letter to the queen; and when I had read it, it took me a year to realise that this was what it was. It was not Williams's fault that the key was lying about, nor the fault of Walsingham's other servants nor of their master: it was the consequence of a gaffe committed by Elizabeth and Burghley. Williams did not figure in the diary very often; but to go through it again with him and his doings in mind was to discover that I had been a very inadequate reader the first time round.

As I say, the diary hibernated while Walsingham was in Scotland, and there seems nothing in it for us for some time after he got back in October. At the beginning of November 1583 the office was preoccupied with the arrest of John Somerville and his friends; the 5th of the month passed without any indication in the diary that anybody had given Walsingham a tip-off about Throckmorton, or that he and Howard had been arrested. There was nothing about their early questioning or about Throckmorton being taken to the Tower. At last, in a list of memoranda dated the same day (13 November), something turns up:

'A warrant for secret money . . .

'To app[rehend] G[eorge] Throck[morton] . . .' There is a trefoil against this, meaning that the queen is to be told. Then, in the list of things to bring up with her:

'3. Secreat Advertysementes'.[8]

In the reign of Queen Elizabeth the collection of information by 'secret advertisements' from third parties and its extraction by interrogating the suspects under torture were different kinds of operation, done by different people under different conditions. Resort to the third degree was an indication that spying had only partially done its work, and still, in 1583, a serious step from which Elizabeth flinched. She was extremely loth to be known to her subjects, to foreign princes, and to Christendom at large as a torturer. I am sure she was especially loth as 17 November came up, which was her accession day and a festival celebrating the sacred bonds which bound her and her people. It was surely on account of her reluctance that Throckmorton's interrogation under torture was delayed for ten days. She does not appear to have regarded Throckmorton's paper of havens, however alarming, as in itself sufficient evidence for torturing him. She wanted Burghley and Walsingham to find out what it meant; and they themselves needed to find out more precisely what they should be questioning Throckmorton about, so as not to lay themselves open to the charge of torturing 'at adventure upon uncertainties'. In the end it turned out to be exactly on the eve of Accession Day (Saturday, 16 November) that he was put on the rack,[9] and what we catch in the diary is a glimpse of how the previous two or three days had been spent.

To begin with George: there is conflicting evidence as to the fate of his brother's playing card or cards, and this affects what we may think Walsingham meant by bringing him to the queen's attention. Either he picked the cards up and got them to Mendoza or, as the government said, they were 'intercepted' by the beefeaters. The message explained what Francis had said about the paper of havens, and asked Mendoza to tell those Catholic friends who had been communicating with Mary through him that he would die 'a thousand deaths' rather than expose them. Mendoza passed the message on, at least to Castelnau.[10] If the message had been intercepted, its fairly damning contents would be what Walsingham would have wanted to tell the queen, and I should think they would have been enough to persuade her to authorise torture. But I do not think it can have been intercepted, otherwise Mendoza would not have got it; hence Walsingham could only have told Elizabeth that George had been found to have been lurking on the premises of the Tower, which would not have done the trick.

The 'warrant for secret money' looks like an alternative to the warrant for torture. Some of the money, I suppose, must have gone by way of Williams to Feron, and some of it to two new missions. When Walsingham noted that he was to speak to the queen about 'secret advertisements' he may have meant that he had some to give her, but at this point I see no sign that he had. I think he was – exceptionally and because she had in this case instructed him to do so – to tell her what he was proposing to do to get hold of the information she wanted, and to get her consent.

9   Read, *Walsingham*, ii, 382 for Walsingham's famous letter to Thomas Wilkes of 18/28-xi-1583. The date of the first torture is given as 'about the 16th' in the draft of *A Discoverie* (PRO SP 12/171, no. 86); the printed version omits the date but gives us three days before the second torture, which was certainly on the 19th/29th. See *The Execution of Justice* (below, n. 28), pp. 48f on *precise* questioning.

10 *CSP Spanish 1580–86*, p. 510; *A Discoverie of the Treasons*, p. 192; No. 13, where Castelnau repeats Throckmorton's message to Mendoza that he would die 'a thousand deaths' before confessing. But Castelnau says that Throckmorton sent him this message before being moved to the Tower, so it looks as if it was not, as Mendoza implies, on the playing card, but conveyed either to both of them, or to Castelnau and thence to Mendoza, before the 13th/23rd. Walsingham's note to arrest George dates from the 13th/23rd (Diary, p. 33'), that is, before the incident of the playing card(s), but he was not put in the Tower until the 17th/27th (Hart's diary, under date). He was probably arrested on the 15th/25th: Herle, writing on that day, was told that 'Throckmorton's brother' (whom I now take to be George, not Thomas) was planning to leave the country (*GB*, p. 201).

After this, and I suppose as a result of it, two steps were taken. One was to get in touch with Salisbury Court by means of William Herle, a person of middling importance on the Elizabethan diplomatic scene, and a long-herm *habitué* of the house. He has more to do with Fagot's story than with Feron's, and it was probably Fagot whom he now contacted: Feron was surely anxious to lie low, and in any case Elizabeth may have thought Fagot better value. Herle had a job on that would provide an excuse for drifting towards Salisbury Court; he was Burghley's man, and would be reporting to Burghley, hence less visible than Williams and perhaps more apt to persuade the queen that she was not being deluded by the godly party. Herle does not appear, at this point, in Walsingham's diary, but we have his report to Burghley dated Friday 15 November.[11] He said that there was indeed a Catholic enterprise afoot, designed to overthrow and kill the queen. It was being organised by the Duke of Guise, who would bring in foreign troops to support a widespread Catholic rebellion. The pope would confer the crown of England on a person unknown who would be married to Mary.[12] Herle went out of his way to add a lot of hostile information about Henry Howard, such as that (probably) his nephew the Earl of Arundel was harbouring (probably) the Jesuit Heywood; he only had a little about Throckmorton, with whom Fagot cannot have had much to do at the time. He thought that George was planning to leave the country; if George had now been arrested, Herle did not know about it. Most of this was simply the gossip of Salisbury Court, but there was probably enough meat in it finally to persuade Elizabeth to authorise the torture of Throckmorton, which began the next day at the hands of the many-talented Thomas Norton. Walsingham recorded the success in the diary, soberly enough: 'To appoynte a newe examination of Throgmorton'.[13]

I doubt if there was time for his other initiative to affect the issue. Walter Williams had been kept away from Salisbury Court, but he turns up in the diary, probably on the day after Walsingham's discussion with the queen about secret advertisements, Thursday 14 November 1583. 'Wa. Will.' appears in the margin of a note to send for one Master John Bodley. Bodley was a substantial citizen of London, father of the founder of the Bodleian Library and printer of the Geneva Bible. A reliable man, certainly, who did jobs for the Council in London, and was I take it being asked to do

---

11 *GB*, Text no. 5, and *Ibid.* pp. 25–31, for Herle, and add the biography (by Nicola Sutherland) in P. W. Hasler (ed.), *The History of Parliament: the House of Commons, 1558–1603*, ii (London, 1981), 302–4.

12 Above, p. 70, n. 21.

13 Diary, p. 35ᵛ, probably 15/25-xi-1583. Heywood had been arrested by early December (*Ibid.* f. 40ᵛ).

one now. One of the clerks elaborated the jotting into a note to send for Williams followed, in a bracket of things for him to do, by 'Trees/Moore/Bodley'. It is nice to think that in the middle of this crisis Walsingham was telling Willliams to do something about his garden; Moore is certainly George More. Bodley proves hard to raise, and is sent for again next day.[14] My guess is that he is being asked to keep More quietly in his house until further notice; where More has been, and how he has turned up, we do not know, but Williams is to see to him. He will not, officially at least, be questioned until after Throckmorton has broken down; he must have had a good deal to offer, and it looks as if he offered it with a will, but that is about all we can say.

After 16 November everyone's attention shifted to the Tower, where the passion of Francis Throckmorton took place and his confessions were made. This is not exactly our subject, and the facts are in any case difficult to untangle because all but a snippet of his original confessions have, for reasons I shall be considering, disappeared. Walsingham's diary sheds a good deal of light, but also raises problems. The rough story is that Throckmorton resisted his first torture on the 16th, keeping up a front of 'Roman resolution' that Walsingham diagnosed as skin-deep. The second time, on the 19th, he caved in at once; he could not, he said in a message he got to Castelnau, bear the pain.[15] Or at least he appeared to cave in, because he tried to put his interrogators off the scent with a long fabricated tale about the paper of havens which incriminated only Mendoza and others who were out of harm's way, and was meant to protect himself by showing that the treasons had been committed a long time ago.[16] This tale seems to have occupied a session or two, but as soon as the interrogators (the rack standing menacingly by) tackled him on the recent past, Throckmorton had to come clean with the real story about Mary, the Duke of Guise and Charles Paget's visit to Sussex; he said that the Earl of Northumberland and Lord Paget were in the know and sympathetic; and he gave

---

14   *Ibid.* ff. 33ᵛ–35ʳ, probably 14/24-xi-1583; above, pp. 80. Simon Adams suggests that the contact with Bodley was about a loan from London to Geneva, so nothing to do with More; in that case, More would probably have been kept in the house in Seething Lane.

15   *A Discoverie of the Treasons,* p. 191ᵇⁱˢ; Castelnau to Mary, c. 14/24-xii-1583 (No. 15 and Document (b)): 'Je ne puis porter de [*sic*] peine.' This assumes the accuracy of the *Discoverie*; Hart's diary says he was racked on both 23-xi/3-xii and 2/12-xii, and Castelnau, above, says he has been racked four times. I imagine the confusion arises from his being questioned in the presence of the rack.

16   *A Discoverie of the Treasons,* p. 191ᵇⁱˢ (the 'historical narration'), 197; and below, chap. 6. The nearest thing to an account of the original state of his next confessions is Thomas Norton's 'The Plott of the Treasons intended . . .', which underlines the complicity of the Earl of Northumberland and Lord Paget and was severely bowdlerised in the *Discoverie,* p. 192ᵇⁱˢ (BL Addnl Mss. 48029, ff. 64–69; Graves, *Thomas Norton,* pp. 266, 269). Norton used Herle's reports from Salisbury Court in his interrogation, because he quotes the items about Mary's marriage (to Howard, as he claimed) and about the 'triumphs' in Spain on the supposed news of Elizabeth's assassination (*GB,* Texts nos. 5 and 7).

a fairly accurate account of his dealings with Mendoza since August. These revelations drew attention away from the secret correspondence; but early in December, when Walsingham had arranged more agreeable conditions for him to talk in, Castelnau's part in facilitating the arrangements, and the contents of the correspondence he had been forwarding, began to come out.[17] Throckmorton probably said more about Castelnau than we have evidence for. As his pile of confessions mounted, numerous people, including the Earls of Northumberland and Arundel, William Byrd and a variety of small fry, were arrested and/or questioned; some of them were tortured. Henry Howard survived relatively unscathed, to the irritation of Thomas Norton and of many others; and William Cornwallis, either due to his family connection with Burghley or so as to protect Feron, was left alone, though in deep disgrace. While the hunt was going on Throckmorton seems to have collaborated willingly; having confessed pretty well all he knew and perhaps, as Castelnau said, more than he knew,[18] he put himself on the queen's mercy and must have expected to save his skin. Later, in a state of self-laceration, he changed his mind.

The state of affairs at Salisbury Court after 5 November 1583 is a cause for wonder and speculation. One may see the household, as in a late novel by Henry James, sitting (or waiting) at the dinner table asking themselves who had done what, who knew who had done what, and who knew who knew who had done what. Castelnau's own feelings appear to have been simple: if we can judge by what he told Mary, he did not suspect treachery under his roof but was shattered by Throckmorton's arrest because he had become very fond of him. He followed his tribulations in a state of anguish, and not mainly, I think, because they threatened to put him on the spot himself.[19] He was facing trouble with Elizabeth, which he probably thought he could manage, and trouble at home, which would be more of a problem: it appears to have taken him some time to tell Henri III what had happened.[20] The zealous majority in the house, includ-

---

17 *A Discoverie*, p. 193; the draft (above, n. 9) shows that this occurred after the confessions already mentioned. No. 15: 'Il a confessé avoir intelligence avec Votre Majesté mais que cela estoit venu par mon moyen . . .'. This will have occurred at one or more of the interrogations on 2/12 (Hart), 4/14, 9/19 (*CSP Scotland 1586–88*, p. 64: an abstract of some of the confessions) and 12/22-xii-1583. The last is shown by the only surviving fragment of the autograph confessions (PRO SP 12/64, no. 22), of that date, which describes a meeting at Salisbury Court with the Duke of Lennox's secretary Cavaillon. I take this to be the tip of an iceberg which has disappeared. On 20/30-xii-1583 Philip Sidney wrote to the Earl of Rutland about 'the ambassadors of Spain and France' being 'noted for great practisers'; Duncan-Jones, *Sir Philip Sidney*, p. 256.

18 Pollen and MacMahon, *Philip Howard*, pp. 40–53; *HMC Bath*, v, 47 (Leicester on Northumberland); for Byrd, Diary, ff. 56ᵛ, 61ʳ, and below, p. 97; Castelnau, No. 15 and Document (b) – 'ce qu'il scavoit et ce qu'il ne scavoit pas'.

19 Nos 31 (Document (c)), 34 (Document (d)) and 35; below, pp. 105, 107, 109.

20 His first surviving mention of it is in a letter to Henri III, 9/19-xii-1583 (No. 11), and then as told to him by Elizabeth, and without mentioning Throckmorton; but Henri III to Castelnau, 7/17-xii-1583 (BN fr 3308, f. 79ʳ), records his reporting it in an earlier letter.

ing his wife and Courcelles, will have been looking for traitors among the less zealous minority, including Feron, Florio and Bruno; unless Fagot (in Bruno's shoes or not) was successfully posing as a zealot, they must have wondered about him. He will surely have thrived on the situation, Feron not so much. But if there was any sort of enquiry, Feron must have come out of it successfully: Courcelles's suspicions seem to have fallen on Douglas.

Our only hard knowledge of things in the house comes from a second report of Herle's dating from 23 November and presumably the result of a further conversation with Fagot.[21] According to Herle's source, who may have got the wrong end of the stick, Castelnau and Courcelles thought that Walsingham had intercepted a letter of Mary's on the way towards them, and read and resealed it before sending it along. They had sent secretly for Douglas and grilled him about it in Castelnau's chamber. I see no sign of any such letter, and wonder if they were not asking him what he had been doing on the night of the 5th, or at least whether he had heard anything about it from Walsingham. After he left, Fagot (if it was Fagot) told Herle, Castelnau and Courcelles 'debated of the matter and manner how to deal with her Majesty touching audience; desirous by some course of terrification to withdraw her Majesty from proceeding too far in examining those actions that are broken forth and the deciphering of their greater friends not yet discovered.' The question was whether Castelnau was in a position to demand from Elizabeth a halt to the torture of Throckmorton by threatening some kind of drastic breach with France if it continued; their conclusion, certainly, was that he was not. Elizabeth will have known what to make of that, and Throckmorton's confessions will shortly have added fuel to her fire. For the time being there was nothing for Castelnau to do but to keep his head down; after Christmas, when the household must have needed cheering up, he recovered his nerve sufficiently to wine and dine virtually the entire English political establishment.[22] If there were gaps in the conversation, Bruno will have filled them.

Courcelles got on with his job. We have seen that, even before the arrest, he may have become nervous about the security of Throckmorton's arrangements; he did not take long to find a replacement. This was Thomas Baldwin, the Earl of Shrewsbury's London agent. He lived at the earl's house by the river near London Bridge, and ran a carriage service between London and Sheffield, which had no doubt already been used to send Mary things too big to be put in the official letter packets. Courcelles had

21   GB, Text no. 7.
22   Castelnau to Henri III, 22-xii-1583/1-i-1584 (No. 18).

brought back from France a box of presents for Mary from Mary Seton, now in Reims. It was a short trip down the river from Salisbury Court to Shrewsbury House, and ten days after Throckmorton's arrest Baldwin told the earl that Courcelles had brought him the box, and that he was sending it with some stuff for Sheffield and Worksop; Courcelles had said, piously, that they ought to be searched. Then or shortly after he must have persuaded Baldwin to take a packet of letters, and Baldwin seems to have made no difficulty.[23] No doubt he was offered a good deal of money, for this was an extraordinarily dangerous time for him to take on the job. But he refused to take money from Mary, and he may simply have been one of the numerous servants of Shrewsbury sympathetic towards her. The venomous feud now raging between the earl and his wife Elizabeth Cavendish, who had accused him of adultery with Mary, may very well have had something to do with it.[24] Courcelles's packet, sent just before Christmas or perhaps taken by Baldwin in person, was a fat one and extremely confidential: it contained the letters from Paris which Courcelles had held back from Throckmorton, four letters from Castelnau and himself recounting the arrest and its aftermath, and who knows what else. In the last of his letters Castelnau said he was in a panic because of a rumour that there was a warrant out for Baldwin's arrest; but there seems to have been nothing in it, and the packet got to Mary undetected.[25] Two or three more appear to have got through by the end of March 1584, and although in January Baldwin said that the surveillance of Salisbury Court made a return of post too dangerous, Mary got packets back in both March and April.[26] No sign of betrayal from Courcelles here; and for the time being no sign of life from Feron. Between Christmas and Easter (19 April), while Mendoza was escorted out of the country, Bruno enjoyed his Ash Wednesday supper, and interrogation ground out the doings of Northumberland and his friends, no intelligence came from anyone in Salisbury Court except a few more messages, of varying credibility, from Fagot.[27] One of them was that Castelnau had given Feron his New Year's bonus, which will have gratified Walsingham on more than one account.

23 *HMC Shrewsbury and Talbot Papers, passim* (i, 123 for Courcelles); *HMC Bath*, v, 24, 29, 44, 46; Castelnau, No. 15 and Document (b) – 'J'ay escript dernierement à Votre Majesté par Baudouin et luy ay envoyé tous les pacquetz que vous pensoit envoyer le Sieur de la Tour lorsqu'il fut pris prisonnier.'

24 Labanoff, v, 479f (assuming that 'Renous Banque' is Baldwin), and vols v and vi *passim* for the feud with the Countess.

25 Castelnau, No. 15.

26 Labanoff, v, 424. Letters from Castelnau: Nos. 24, 27 and perhaps 34, which was acknowledged by Mary in No. 38; packets from Mary, Nos. 22 and 31 received by Castelnau on 18/28-iii (so No. 34), Nos. 32, 33 and probably another of 2/12-iii (Labanoff, v, 431: not in parcel) must have been received in April, before the sending of the parcel.

27 *GB*, Texts no. 9–11a.

ii

If we have been led to think of Queen Elizabeth's conduct towards neigh-
bouring powers as dominated by caution and dither, we shall be surprised
by the vigour and indeed recklessness she showed in this case. Confronted
with the seeming revelation of an aggressive coalition of Catholic Europe
to overthrow her, promoted by both ambassadors resident in London, she
came out of her corner spoiling for a fight with all and sundry. She had
recently had to digest the collapse of the politics of her person which for
four years had linked the fortunes of England to those of the Duke of
Anjou. It may be that, now she had paid off the mortgage on that policy,
she felt a free woman; if she anticipated, as I suspect she did, that the end
of her Anjou adventure was very likely to inspire a closing of Catholic
ranks against her, she will only have been surprised by the speed with
which it seemed to have happened. Both she and her councillors were
shaken by Throckmorton's revelations, but what was a nightmare to them
was a stimulus to her. She reacted in anger, as to a string of personal
betrayals, hanging the consequences; Walsingham of all people had the
job of restraining her.

Burghley was perhaps a little compromised by Cornwallis, and preferred
to attend to the domestic side of things; his only contribution to the international situation was to write and publish a propaganda piece, which
would become famous, called *The Execution of Justice in England.*[28] Written
in mid-December, in the light of Throckmorton's main confessions but
not actually mentioning him or them, the piece was designed mainly for
consumption in France; its object was to cut away French support for
English émigrés and priests by explaining that all of them were engaged
on an enterprise of political treason and diligently preparing the ground
for an invasion of their homeland. I suppose he meant it as a help to
keeping Henri III out of the Catholic crusade, and if possible as an incen-
tive to him to crack down on English Catholic institutions, publications
and political activity in France; in fact its obvious partiality had the oppo-

28 A good edition by R. M. Kingdon (ed.), *The Execution of Justice in England, by William Cecil and
    A True, Sincere and Modest Defense of English Catholics, by William Allen* (Ithaca, N.Y., 1965). The
    only flaw in it is that Kingdon, like Hughes, *Reformation in England,* iii, 298 n and 344ff, Conyers
    Read, *Lord Burghley and Queen Elizabeth* (London, 1960), pp. 251–4 and MacCaffrey, *Queen Eliz-
    abeth and the Making of Policy,* pp. 136ff, treats it as a general and representative statement of English
    policy towards Catholics; which makes no sense of the date ('xvii. Decemb. 1583') carefully
    stated on the title page. When we look at it closely we find that it is mainly concerned with
    English émigrés, and fits very snugly into the immediate situation. Two points of some impor-
    tance follow: (1) it is an occasional work, designed for a particular purpose: if Burghley had
    been making a considered statement on the subject he would have been more cautious; (2) for
    the reason stated in the text, it does not necessarily express Burghley's own opinion. Cf. below,
    n. 30.

site effect. It also, by hinting at revelations to come, gave Elizabeth a broad platform for displaying her wrath in future, and I should think she had instructed Burghley to write it.

She briskly disposed of the Spanish connection, though not quite so briskly as she would have liked. Immediately after Throckmorton's first confession, probably on 20 November, Walsingham's diary has a note 'to send to Mendoza', I imagine with a demand for the surrender of the green casket which naturally did not come off. After that Elizabeth seems to have been determined to put him on trial, and over Christmas Walsingham had to send to Oxford to his friend the Italian émigré Alberico Gentili, connoisseur of the law of nations, to tell her that this could really not be done. She fell back on summoning him to a sort of court martial before the Council on 9 January 1584, when Walsingham led for the prosecution and Mendoza was told to get out of the country within fourteen days. Breathing fire, and after a heart-to-heart talk with Castelnau about the need to get rid of Protestantism once and for all (I imagine Bruno nodding sagely), he made the deadline. Elizabeth had already sent off to Spain one of the clerks of the Council, William Waad, in the hope of getting an expression of regret from King Philip for his ambassador's conduct.[29]

That left Castelnau to take his medicine, which at the risk of precipitating simultaneous crises with France and Spain Elizabeth evidently meant to be nasty. From the start she had been champing to write to Paris, preferably one of her scorchers to Henri III personally, to demand the extradition of everyone connected with Throckmorton's scheme and to complain about Castelnau's 'extraordinary dealing'.[30] I do not think the enquiry to Gentili about the privileges of an ambassador was directed against Mendoza alone. In January, when she saw Castelnau, she told him to stop intriguing with her subjects, and said she was going to write to his king to tell him to keep out of Mary's affairs. They both got extremely angry, so much so that Elizabeth later apologised: the Council must have begged her to calm down, at least until Mendoza was out of the way.[31] On 7–8 February, balked again of her letter to Henri III, she finally got

---

29 Diary, ff. 39ʳ, 45ᵛ (about mid-December: 'To sende for Mr. Attorney[-General Popham]. The privileages of an Imb[assador].') and 50ʳ; *CSP Spanish 1580–86*, pp. 512–15; *CSP Foreign 1583–84*, pp. 318, 397; Nos. 25, 26, 28; *DNB*, Gentili, Alberico, and his *De legationibus libri tres* (London, 1585), pp. 77ff; Garrett Mattingly, *Renaissance Diplomacy* (London, 1955), pp. 238f; Read, *Walsingham*, iii, 438f.

30 Diary, f. 39ʳ, about 20/30-xi-1583: 'To cause a letter to be wryten to the French kinge for the delivering of B.C. [?Thomas Throckmorton]'; 46ʳ, about 16/26-xii-1583: the queen to write to Stafford: 'extraordinary dealing; delivery of Fug[itives]'. Neither of these was sent, so far as I can see, if written; and since Burghley's *Execution of Justice* is dated the 17th/27th, it looks as if it was an alternative to the second.

31 Castelnau to Henri III, Nos. 20, 23, and see notes for dates.

Walsingham to write to Stafford asking the king to cut off all dealings between Castelnau and Mary. She had wanted to add a demand for the surrender of her 'rebels and traitors' like Thomas Morgan and Charles Paget, whom she would have accused (rightly as it turned out) of conspiracy against her 'life and person' as well as against her state: Walsingham told Stafford he had fended her off with a promise to get the ambassador to find out what Henri III would do if such a demand were made.

He was, he told Stafford, desperate to persuade Elizabeth, 'now that the King of Spain seems so maliciously bent against her, to entertain the amity of France'; but this was not her frame of mind, and she refused the modest courtesies Walsingham recommended.[32] She still seems to have thought that she could get an apology out of Philip, and the immediate object of her wrath was Castelnau. Walsingham's resistance was weakened by one of his regular attacks of severe illness, something to do with his kidneys or his bladder, which sent him home to Barn Elms and kept him away from court for at least a month.[33] This, and some prudent temporising by Stafford in Paris, held things up for some time; meanwhile something occurred which is obviously germane to our story, but how germane is difficult to say. Considering Walsingham's condition, and his intense anxiety to avoid stirring up trouble with France, I am inclined to suppose that the initiative for it came from Elizabeth herself; in which case it would be another of her adventures in intelligence conducted while the cat was away.

It featured Dr William Parry, yet another Welshman in our story: a figure of modest fame in the annals of Elizabethan intelligence, and a puzzle to generations of historians.[34] He had just come back to England after a trip to France and Italy during which he had turned Catholic. Parry's letters home, and the number of times Walsingham's diary reminded him to write to Parry, suggest that he was acting under direction; but this is not at all clear, and I agree with the usual view that there was something genuine about his conversion. The climax of his trip, which occurred in Paris around the Christmas just past, was a ceremony in the chapel of the Jesuit college during which, apparently under the eye of two cardinals, he received communion as the seal of a vow to assassinate Elizabeth, inter-

---

32   *CSP Foreign 1583–84*, nos. 408–10: in the first of these Walsingham talks about the delivery of plotting subjects being in accordance with 'the law of nations', no doubt from Gentili; also no. 466, and Diary, f. 55ᵛ.

33   *CSP Foreign 1583–84*, pp. 345, 377, 387; Diary, f. 60ᵛ; Read, *Walsingham*, ii, 114.

34   Various views of Parry in J. H. Pollen, 'Dr Parry', *The Month*, cix (1907), 356–65; Read, *Walsingham*, ii, 399–406; L. Hicks, 'The Strange Case of Dr William Parry', *Studies* (Dublin), xxxvii (1948), 343–62; Hasler, *The House of Commons, 1558–1603*, iii, 180–4; L. B. Smith, *Treason in Tudor England*, pp. 11–19. Behind all these, W. Cobbett (ed.), *State Trials* (2 vols, London, 1809), i, coll. 1095–112; and *Holinshed's Chronicles* (6 vols, London, 1807–8), iv, 561–87.

preted as a deed of piety and devotion. He had perhaps done this with Thomas Morgan; in any event he and Morgan had become friends, Welshness assisting, and Morgan had warmly encouraged him. After the vow, the two of them had written to the pope's Secretary of State, Cardinal Gallio, asking for the pope's blessing on a (not precisely specified) venture of which they had good reason to think he would approve: Parry, so he said, wanted to be sure that if the enterprise failed he would be known as a martyr to the faith. When he arrived in England he reported, via Walsingham or otherwise, to the queen; he apparently saw her on 1 February, and Elizabeth possibly wanted to make use of the story in the rude letter to France of the 7th which Walsingham persuaded her to water down. While waiting for his own letter from Cardinal Gallio to arrive, Parry remained in discreet favour at Court, socialising with the Catholics but escaping the hue and cry to which they were being subjected.[35] In the meantime he paid a visit, probably two visits, to Salisbury Court.

There was nothing unusual about this, since he had been known there for a long time: before his trip abroad, he had been an intermediary between Castelnau and Burghley in the days when they were friends; he also knew Courcelles.[36] But he had not just come on a social visit, but to attend to his correspondence. Not long after he had seen Elizabeth, Parry received, via and probably in Salisbury Court, letters from Morgan and Charles Paget in Paris. We do not have their letters, but we have his replies, dated 12 February 1584 (actually 22 February, new style, Parry being or wishing to be taken as a Catholic).[37] He was, naturally, not being very explicit, but it did not take much reading between the lines of his letters to see that Morgan and Paget had been party to acts of treason, and that their correspondence with Parry dealt with such acts. In effect, he told Paget that Throckmorton had confessed his, Paget's, part in the invasion scheme and that he was therefore thought responsible for the 'trouble' of the Earls of Northumberland and Arundel; he also mentioned that Paget's friend and teacher William Byrd had just been examined by the Council: it may be that Paget had written to Parry under cover of a letter to Byrd.[38]

35　Diary, ff. 14ʳ, 17ᵛ, 35ᵛ; *State Trials*, i, 1097; Walsingham to Stafford, 7/17-ii-1584 (above, n. 32), talks about the 'maintenance of the safety of the life and person of [the queen]'; Anne Lady Lee to Charles Paget, her brother, probably 29-i/8-ii-1584 (PRO SP 12/167, no. 51): Parry known to be a spy.

36　Parry to Burghley, 11-ix-1580 (BL Lansdowne 31, no. 13); *CSP Foreign 1584–85*, p. 261; and below, p. 134.

37　Parry to Paget and to Morgan, 12/22-ii-1584 (assuming new style: PRO SP 12/168, no. 23; SP 15/28, no. 61 = *CSP Domestic Addenda 1580–1625*, p. 113).

38　Parry to Paget (above, n. 37): 'It was strange to me to see your letters and some others to me enclosed and sent in any other man's packet. Direct mine to myself hereafter . . . Mr Byrd is at liberty and hath been very honorably intreated by my Lords of the Council.' Byrd and Paget had

He explained to Morgan why he had not so far fulfilled his vow to assassinate Elizabeth: a priest whom he had consulted had ruled against it. In both letters he took pains to indicate how they had come to him ('so honorable a hand', or 'means'); he deprecated the despatch of quantities of assorted mail to England by this exceptional route. He and Castelnau had sat together, presumably in Castelnau's chamber, putting two months' worth of it on the fire.[39] I suppose that it was on this occasion that Parry had received his letters from Morgan and Paget, and that they were then burned: this must have been before 12 February, when Parry wrote his replies. What happened to them then we do not know, except that they ended up in Walsingham's papers.

I can think of three accounts of this sequence of events. The plainest is that they were bona fide letters of a conspirator to his fellow-conspirators, discovered and handed over by unknown means. But Parry came fresh from telling his story to Elizabeth; he was not arrested when the letters came into government hands; so far as I know they were never used in evidence against Parry or anyone else. The plain account does not hold water. The alternative accounts bring Parry's doings sharply within our story of intelligence; they presuppose that the letters were inspired, a plant intended to show that Castelnau was conveying treasonable correspondence through Salisbury Court. In that case we can guess that the idea came from Elizabeth, since Walsingham was out of action and was in any case against doing anything to incriminate Castelnau. One version of what then occurred is complicated, the other simple. The complicated story is that Parry took the letters to Salisbury Court on or shortly after 12 February; that Castelnau accepted and, presumably, Courcelles despatched them; and that they were then intercepted by some means no doubt involving Fagot or Feron. This is not impossible: a letter home from Girault the aggressive butler, written three weeks earlier, was now or had been intercepted, and like Parry's ended up in Walsingham's papers: Fagot, who shows signs of knowing what was in it, may very well have been responsible.[40] May he not also have been responsible for the interception

remained very friendly, as David Crankshaw will show from the Paget Papers in Staffordshire Record Office; the letter from W. B. to Paget, 17/27-xi-1583 (PRO SP 12/164, no. 37, a copy) is presumably from Byrd, and part of a continuing correspondence through Salisbury Court. This must have been what the Council questioned him about.

39   Parry to Morgan (above, no. 37): 'Myselfe and thelder gentleman to whose hands the last packets were delyvered [i.e. Castelnau, not Courcelles] dyd burne all the letters . . .' The *Calendar* version has 'the gentleman', but I am confident that the correct reading is as above.

40   Girault de la Chassaigne to his wife, Katherine des Champs, London, 24-i/3-ii-1584 (PRO SP 12/168, no. 5): endorsed 'Febr[uary] 1583/ Fr[ench] l[etter] intercepted'. Part of it is about worsted hose which Girault had sent to his wife to sell in France, a trade Fagot mentions as one of

of Parry's letters? I doubt it: unlike Girault's, Parry's were not endorsed as having been intercepted; they were extremely confidential, and if sent off from Salisbury Court would have been sent in the diplomatic bag; if one of Castelnau's official packets had been seized or tampered with we should have heard about it. I think this story requires too many unsupported assumptions, and so plump for the simpler version: Parry wrote his letters under instruction, and took them to Salisbury Court; Castelnau, who was diligently keeping his head down, refused to accept them; Parry handed his now useless letters to Walsingham, if Walsingham was at work; to Elizabeth; or to whoever finally deposited them in Walsingham's archives. In that case, Parry's letters, like Walter Williams's letter to Elizabeth of August 1583, were the residue of a failed essay in intelligence by an inexperienced hand.[41] This is the story I prefer. I do not wish to play down Walsingham's own interest in Parry; but I suppose that what he wanted from him was Cardinal Gallio's letter encouraging his enterprise, which would not turn up if Parry was exposed at this point, and might not be much use if Parry was exposed at all.

At the beginning of March 1584, when Walsingham was starting to pick up the threads, he was back harping on the theme that the security of the country depended on keeping up 'jealousy' between France and Spain, and hence not upsetting the French by an open attack on Castelnau.[42] Elizabeth was no more persuaded than before: she was no doubt waiting for the return of William Waad, who was having the hard time in Spain that everybody had predicted, and was unable to communicate.[43] On 10 March she told Walsingham testily to get on to Stafford and find out what he had been doing about his instructions of a month before to tell Henri III about Castelnau's disgraceful use of the secret correspondence and enquire whether he would surrender Morgan and her other traitors. When Stafford's report finally arrived, some time after the 20th, and showed that he had been both dilatory and unenthusiastic in pursuing the matter, she blew up.[44] It looks as if she demanded a new interrogation of

Girault's activities in February 1585 (*GB*, Text no. 13, p. 225). Both Pollen, 'Dr Parry', p. 362, n. 1 and Read, *Walsingham*, ii, 403 thought that Parry's letters might have been intercepted, and the biographer in Hasler, *House of Commons*, states it as a fact. Pollen also thought (p. 364, n. 2), more shrewdly in my view, that Parry's letter to Morgan might have been written 'with the connivance of Elizabeth's government'.

41 Above, p. 75.

42 Diary, f. 60ʳ, 2/12 March; *CSP Foreign 1583–84*, p. 388 (9/19 March).

43 *CSP Foreign 1583–84*, pp. 391–99, 446; cf. above, p. 95.

44 *CSP Foreign 1583–84*, pp. 390, 413, 478f (Stafford's 'slack dealing'); Diary, f. 63ʳ, probably 10/20-iii-1584.

Throckmorton about his dealings with Castelnau, and that this occurred on the 25th or just before.[45] The consequences of it appear in the diary, probably on the 26th: they show that everyone was now in deep water.

> To sende unto the Sollycytor [-General Thomas Egerton] the
> examinations of Throg[morton]
> To send for Moodye
> To gather the particularytes against Movesier [Castelnau] for secreat
> dealing with the Scot[tish] Q[ueen]
> Mislike Seaton
> Privat opinion. Q[ueen']s disposition.[46]

These notes are connected: Throckmorton having presumably been persuaded to confess what was asked of him, his case was to be prepared for trial; Walsingham was to put together a detailed case against Castelnau; and a letter was to be written to Stafford in strong terms. Michael Moody was a servant of Stafford's who had probably brought his unsatisfactory letter, and was no doubt to take back the reply;[47] Lord Seton was a Scottish Catholic who had been sent to Paris by James VI to try to persuade Henri III to support him against English machinations. In Walsingham's letter, which he wrote on 27 March, he passed on the queen's rebuke to Stafford for paying Seton a visit, adding that he had tried to persuade her that it had been perfectly in order, but had failed.[48] This was not the only point where his 'private opinion' and Elizabeth's 'disposition' were at odds. Concerning Castelnau's 'intermeddling to convey secret letters to the Queen of Scots' Stafford was to get his finger out and tell Henri III 'that the parties themselves whom the ambassador did use as instruments for the conveying of the said letters [hence both More and Throckmorton] have plainly confessed the same, which may seem to be proof sufficient to convict the said ambassador therein'. That was not all the parties had confessed, and one can hear Elizabeth's tone rising as she told Walsingham that he was to '[add] besides that this very day one of the said parties has confessed that the ambassador has had secret conference with him touching means how the Queen of Scots is to be set at liberty, and enquired particularly of the state of the country, convenience of

45   Below, p. 102.
46   Diary, f. 65ʳ, dated by letter below, n. 48.
47   Moody had brought a letter from Stafford to Walsingham of 2/12-ii-1584 (*CSP Foreign 1583–84*, no. 415), and may have brought that of 16/26-iii (*Ibid.* no. 486); he was back in Paris before 14/24-iv (*Ibid.*, no. 536).
48   *Ibid.* no. 509.

landing-places, strength of the forts, and disposition of the subjects; which cannot proceed from any good meaning'. No indeed! But, as on the previous occasion, Elizabeth was foiled of her pleasure by her ministers, and presumably by Walsingham himself; when the letter was sent off the extra passage had been removed, though it may well be that Moody was instructed to pass it on to Stafford by word of mouth.

Elizabeth was willing, once again, to tone down a ferocious complaint to Henri III about Castelnau; she was not willing to softpedal her own campaign against him. Walsingham was to assemble Throckmorton's relevant confessions, go through his archives, and launch his customary gambits on the intelligence board: to 'gather the particularities' against Castelnau. We do not know what, immediately, he did about this: he will certainly have refused to allow anything from Feron or Fagot to appear in the public eye (and surely Parry's evidence as well, though Parry's letter of indulgence from Cardinal Gallio arrived very pat, no doubt via Courcelles, on 31 March).[49] If he had put his cards on the table, a weighty case against Castelnau could have been constructed; it may be that something in that direction was done, since there is an entry in the diary six months later to send his servant Faunt to Sir Walter Mildmay, to help him with a big speech he was to make to Parliament about the security of the nation, with 'the booke of secreat advertysements and letters decyphred'.[50]

But sources of this kind did not contribute much to the actual list of charges which I assume to have been put together, under pressure from Elizabeth, early in April 1584. Historians have not noticed it, and forgivably: it is an undated document which has had to be retrieved from a remote place in the State Papers and the *Scottish Calendar*, whose editor dated it ten years earlier.[51] It is entitled, and has been endorsed by Tomson, 'Principall matters wherewith the French Ambassador is to be charged'. It contains seven of them:

[1.] That he hath had secreat intelligence with the Scottish Queen aswell by letter as by message.

49 *State Trials*, i, 1097, 1102, 1105.

50 Diary, f. 100ᵛ; J. E. Neale, *Elizabeth I and her Parliaments, 1584–1601* (London, 1957), pp. 28–31. Nicholas Faunt in his 'Discourse' (below, pp. 144, 147), describes the making of such books.

51 PRO SP 53/9, no. 40; *CSP Scotland 1574–81*, p. 72. I ignore a set of charges about Castelnau's Scottish doings in 1582, when he was alleged with the help of Archibald Douglas to have foiled an English coup against the Duke of Lennox; these were probably prepared two years before, and have nothing to contribute to our story (*CSP Scotland 1581–83*, p. 425). Actually the two are connected by Tomson's addition to his endorsement, after 'charged' of 'against Engl[and]'.

[2.]   That he hath sought to understand howe the Catholikes of this Realme stand affected in case any forraine Prince should seeke to invade this Realme.

[3.]   That there hath been plottes delivered unto him to that purpose.

[4.]   That he hath sought to drawe the affectiones of her Majestie's subiectes unto the Scottish Queen.

[5.]   That he hath daily intelligence and is a cherisher of such of her Majestie's subiectes as are traiterously affected towardes her and her estate, aswell such as are beyond the seas as others in England.

[6.]   That he receaveth letters daily from Thomas Morgan, Thomas Throgmorton and other practising Traitors in France: doth conveye their packettes and letters to the Scottish Queen and hers to them.

[7.]   That he hath had inward and secreat intelligence with Francis Throgmorton and of his trayterous purposes and hath employed him as a minister in practising of treason against her Majestie.

While digesting the depth and venom of these accusations, we can consider what evidence might have been brought in their support. Charges 1 and 4, having had secret intelligence with Mary and sought to win the queen's subjects to her cause, were minor in themselves: they imply some use of Feron's material, but could probably have been established otherwise. Charges 5 and 6, communicating with and 'cherishing' of traitors in England and overseas, receiving letters from Morgan and others, and passing their correspondence with Mary back and forth, come much nearer the bone. They are the only things Castelnau is said to be still doing, and seem to me to depend on the evidence of Parry: I cannot think what other traitorous subjects still at liberty in England the composer might have had in mind. Charges 2, 3 and 7 are sensational, since they amount to attributing to Castelnau what at Throckmorton's trial was to be attributed to Mendoza. He has been spying out the land for a Catholic invasion; has received Throckmorton's papers of havens and gentlemen; has been hand in glove with him and his schemes and 'employed him as a minister in practising of treason'. The evidence here will have been Throckmorton's confessions, especially the most recent, assuming that it had occurred.

This set of charges can only have been put together as grounds for expelling the ambassador, or for something even more humiliating: Stafford, on the receiving end of a string of angry letters from her which immediately followed, told Henri III that Elizabeth 'would be fain to use [her] own authority to restrain [Castelnau]', and that she '[had] the sword in her own hand, and must do [herself] reason'.[52] We are to conclude that around the beginning of April 1584 Elizabeth was proposing to proceed against Castelnau on these lines; that the confrontation would have accompanied the trial of Throckmorton, whose indictment was now being prepared; and that that indictment would have substantially implicated Castelnau as well as Mendoza. We are also to conclude from the story of the past three months that this was an outcome to which Elizabeth's councillors were unanimously opposed. It was not what happened, but it seems to me to have provided the principal context to what actually did happen, which is a large event in our story of intelligence. There is no immediate evidence of what provoked it, and I can but record what seems relevant, and otherwise resort to conjecture.

Through April Elizabeth continued to have normal dealings with Castelnau, and indeed went out of her way to be civil to him. By the 16th of the month they had met twice: on the first occasion she told him that his dealings with Mary had not been so disgraceful as she had supposed and, or so Castelnau said, giggled with him over her complaints to Henri III about the secret correspondence; on the second, she was particularly complimentary to the king. She thought of giving him the Garter for his friendship.[53] But when he sent over the secretary of his courtier the Duke of Joyeuse with the brief of going to see Mary about a land transaction, Elizabeth was most unwilling to let him go, and finally sent him to Sheffield with William Waad as minder on a very short and very supervised visit; Waad took the opportunity to vent on the French some of the anti-popish bile he had been obliged to bottle up in Madrid.[54] Castelnau told Henri III that Elizabeth and the Council assumed that after the death of Anjou, which everybody now expected very soon, he and King Philip would get together again; and that they were accordingly fortifying the coasts, which was true.[55] In view of what Elizabeth was writing to Stafford at just this time, her polite remarks to Castelnau must have been intended to put him off the scent; she had not forgotten the explosive list of charges against him which she had up her sleeve. Uninformed, he himself awaited events with apprehension.[56]

---

52 Stafford to Elizabeth, 2/12-v-1584 (*CSP Foreign 1583–84*, pp. 478–9).

53 Chéruel, pp. 292, 297; Diary, f. 70ᵛ; Labanoff, v, 463f.

54 *HMC Bath*, v, 49 (Marion, the secretary, leaves London on 19/29-iv-1584); Diary, f. 69ᵛ; Labanoff, v, 454f, 457f, 469; Chéruel, p. 302.

55 No. 37, about 20/30-iv-1584; the version in *HMC Hatfield*, iii, 81 needs to be corrected, to the effect that the English 'ne doubtent nullement' that the death of Anjou will mean a rapprochement between Henri III and Philip II, the opposite of what the *Calendar* says; cf. *CSP Domestic 1581–90*, pp. 163f, 169f (fortifications). For the history of this letter, see below, pp. 118f.

56 Below, p. 113.

This is the only explicit context we have for the extraordinary call on Feron's services which was now made: the step must have been taken around 25 April, perhaps a few days before, certainly not more than a few days after. In reconstructing the reasons for the decision, we have no help from the diary; but a certain number of things are either clear or reasonably so. What is clear is that the charges against Castelnau were not brought, at least not brought in public, either directly or at Throckmorton's trial. What seems reasonably clear is that they were not brought because the Council was against bringing them. At least two things now happened to exacerbate their already settled conviction that a public confrontation with Castelnau would be a disastrous step. By about 9 April they knew from Waad that Philip had responded with extreme intransigence to the expulsion of Mendoza, and must have told the queen that they had always known that this would happen: her scheme, if that was what it was, of balancing an attack on Castelnau against a truce with Philip had proved a fiasco. While Parma gobbled up the formerly Protestant-run cities of the Netherlands, and re-established Spanish power on the coast of Flanders, Philip had no need to offer conciliation. By the 16th of the month they had learned that a coup intended to restore English control over the policies of James VI, which had been brewing since Walsingham's visit to Scotland in the autumn, had proved a fiasco, leaving James unsupervised and indignant in their rear.[57] It would now be suicidal to provoke a crisis with the king of France: if Elizabeth wanted to ensure a universal Catholic crusade against her, that was the way to go about it. Elizabeth, I take it, was abashed and alarmed by the reception of her mission to Philip, and had surely to give her councillors best on that score; I doubt if she cared one way or the other about the coup in Scotland. But, if they jibbed at creating a crisis with France, what did they suggest she do about Castelnau and Throckmorton, who had conspired against her? Nothing? At this point, I imagine Walsingham saying something to this effect: we cannot deal with Throckmorton until we have dealt with Castelnau; and we cannot deal with Castelnau until we know what he has actually done, which at the moment we do not. As they stand, the serious charges against him depend, at best, on a recent confession by Throckmorton which may very well turn out to be spurious. Let us find out, says Walsingham (or perhaps: find out then, says Elizabeth) whether they are true or not.

The way out of their dilemma would then be a sort of Watergate operation, a raid on Castelnau's files. They would not need plumbers, since they had Feron sitting inside. If he had been doing his job properly

---

57 MacCaffrey, *Queen Elizabeth and the Making of Policy*, pp. 419–20; CSP *Foreign 1583–84*, p. 448; Castelnau to Henri III, 16/26-iv-1584 (Chéruel, pp. 296ff).

during the past five months, when nothing had been asked of him, he ought to have the evidence: let him earn his money by producing it. Our imaginary conversation ends with an agreement between Elizabeth and Walsingham that the next move is to burgle Salisbury Court; and that is what actually happened. We cannot be quite sure which of them the idea came from, which would be good to know because it would make a difference to what the precise object of the break-in was. To judge by their performance so far, Elizabeth was looking for evidence of Castelnau's guilt, and Walsingham, in order to restrain her, for something like innocence. This is not what is expected from spymasters in general or from Walsingham in particular, and it may seem a comic suggestion, but in my judgment it is likely to be true. What may have come from Elizabeth, if only because of the economy entailed, was the idea that Feron should provide the documentation, not only for Castelnau's dealings with Throckmorton and Mary, but also for what, if anything, Henri III had been told about them and what, if he had, his attitude had been. Where Stafford had flinched, Feron should step in, though in that case he would be taking on a job more extensive than anything he had done so far. In a nutshell, he was being asked to hand over the substance of four months of his master's correspondence, and to avoid being found out while doing it. This bold operation agreed, it was Walsingham's business to set it up, and he will undoubtedly have hastened to send for Walter Williams.

We may assume that Williams and Feron made contact about 25 April.[58] Williams made his extraordinary request, and offered a decent reward; Feron gulped but complied. Back at Salisbury Court, he looked at his piles of drafts, decipher copies, and odds and ends; he looked rather particularly at his decipher of a letter from Mary, dated 25 February 1584, in which she told Castelnau that everybody knew he had a mole in his house. He had already written the soothing reply in which Castelnau explained his office arrangements and expressed his confidence in their security; but I doubt if that will have convinced him that he was not under suspicion, any more than it convinced Mary.[59] While Castelnau was out or asleep he found time to make new copies of these two and of one earlier letter from Mary. The rest, Castelnau's letters to Mary and to France, he had in front of him in the form of Castelnau's drafts or his own; of his own, he picked up a wodge of miscellaneous matter which he did not stop to sort out. The last piece to go in, Castelnau's draft of a newsletter to Guise about Scotland, is dated 24 April, and Feron must have written it fair in the last

58 This follows from assuming that the last letter in Feron's parcel is No. 36.
59 Nos. 31 & 34; Documents (c) and (d).

day or two: it will hardly have needed ciphering.[60] He put on top of the
pile the alarming letter from Mary about him, wrote a note to Walsingham at the end of it, wrapped the parcel up and slipped out of the house
to his rendezvous with Williams. This is what he had written (see Plate
IV):

> Je vous supplie bien humblement Monsieur de tenir tout cy' [whence
> we can infer the size of the parcel] 'de tenir tout cy le plus secret qu'il
> sera possible, affin que Monsieur l'Ambassadeur ne s'en apercoive en
> aucune sorte, comme Je say que vous scaurez tresbien faire. Car Je ne
> voudrois pour tout l'or du monde estre descouvert, pour la honte que
> Je scay que je receverois, non seullement la honte mais aussi la vye y
> penderoit, de laquelle je ne me soucie point tant que de ladite honte
> que je pourrois recevoir. Car tousiours me fault-il mourir.[61]

> [I beg you very humbly, Monsieur, to keep all this as secret as you pos-
> sibly can, so that Monsieur the ambassador absolutely does not realise;
> which I know you will be very well able to do. I should not want to
> be found out for all the gold in the world, because of the dishonour I
> know I should suffer, and not just dishonour but death; though I do
> not care so much about that as I do about the dishonour, for I shall
> have to die some time.]

His faith in Walsingham's discretion sounds genuine; but his fate did indeed
depend on it. All the money in the world would not make up for the dishonour of being found out, nor for a knife in his back from the Catholic
mafia in the house or outside. Jumpy as he was, it was his face and not his
back that worried him; or so he said.

Feron was making the most of his brief appearance before the foot-
lights, but we need not be wholly sceptical about his honour. We do not
defend him if we show that he may actually have been doing Castlenau
a favour; but unlike Fagot he did not enjoy his work, and unlike Fagot he
had an excuse. I prefer his simple funk about being found out to the chic
apology for dissimulation which we may find in a work of Bruno (and
so, we may think, of Fagot) written shortly after.[62] All the same, he took
his thirty pieces of silver, as Walsingham's diary recorded a fortnight later:
'To remember to deliver to Walter Williams certain money.'[63]

60   No. 36.
61   No. 31, postscript, f. 312ᵛ; Labanoff, v, 429: reading 'la vye y penderoit', where Labanoff reads mis-
     takenly 'la vye y perdrois', and correcting a few other trivial errors.
62   *GB*, pp. 125–7, from *Spaccio della bestia trionfante*, pp. 707–8.
63   Diary, f. 73ᵛ.

6

FROM A VIEW TO A DEATH

WHAT WALSINGHAM FOUND when he opened Feron's parcel around 30 April 1584 was twenty-seven or twenty-eight letters: eight from Castelnau to Mary (dated between about 10 December and about 7 April); four from Mary to Castelnau or Courcelles (of between 5 January and 22 March); fifteen from Castelnau to Henri III (8), the Queen Mother (4), Anjou (2) and Guise (1); and an uninteresting letter from Henri III to Mary.[1] Whatever he was expecting to find, he will surely have been looking forward to one of the great pleasures of his life, listening as it were to a tape of the unguarded thoughts of the friend and enemy with whom he had been dealing for virtually the whole of his public career; perhaps we may imagine him sitting down after dinner in front of a good fire, with a rare bottle to celebrate the event. When he had read Feron's note with sympathy, he will have turned to the letters between Castelnau and Mary, of which Feron had sent most of those that had passed since November;[2] they recorded Castelnau's reactions to Throckmorton's arrest and its aftermath, Mary's response to his news, and Castelnau's rejoinder to Mary's response. He will have read Mary's first,[3] since Feron had put them on top, and as soon as he had read the one to which Feron's note was attached, of 25 February, he will have realised that Mary was not going to reveal any secrets to be passed on by the mole in Castelnau's house.[4] Apart from a good deal about the security of the correspondence, she did little more than express grief and despair at the arrests and the sufferings of those arrested, in particular of Throckmorton and his family, of Howard, and of George More's uncle Edward, who had been interrogated under torture in January.[5] She spoke of them all as being of her 'party', and as being

---

1 They are listed in the Appendix, section (ii), and I cite them by number.
2 He did not send Mary's of 2/12-iii-1584 (Labanoff, v, 431–33), which was nevertheless in the office because it was copied into the D'Esneval Ms. (above, p. 67); nor two of Castelnau's acknowledged by Mary on 30 April/10 May (notes to Nos. 34 and 35).
3 Nos. 22, 31, 32, 33.
4 No. 31 (Document (c)); above, p. 105.
5 Nos. 32, 33; Diary, f. 47ᵛ, about 1/11-i-1584.

persecuted on that account. She denied having had any communication with Northumberland, but did not mention Cornwallis; by implication she admitted corresponding with Howard and Throckmorton, whom she or more probably Feron identified as 'Monsieur de la Tour'.[6] She asked Castelnau to do what he could to help them, express her thanks to them if possible, tell her how they got on, and promise that she would reward them 'one day'. She indicated that she was willing, as she later said more explicitly, to offer some quid pro quo for the sparing of Throckmorton's life.[7] In February she sent a packet for Morgan, which Castelnau promptly despatched.[8] Except for the first item (about the mole) and the last, Walsingham can have found nothing much to thrill him here; he made no marks.

After this disappointment, perhaps anticipated, he got on to Castelnau; few of the drafts were dated, and hence he may not have realised at first that it had taken Castelnau or Courcelles a month to find their new messenger, whoever he was. Then there were four letters, all sent in the middle of the previous December, though the first of them had probably been started nearer to the event. They were certainly more fun than Mary's, and their respective contents were as follows.[9]

(1)   Arrests of Somerville, Howard ('votre frère') and Throckmorton ('Sieur de la Tour'). Throckmorton's removal to the Tower, his first two interrogations and the arrest of his brother George. He resists. The paper of havens discovered, books, 'some papers and ciphers'. Before being sent to the Tower, Throckmorton had sent to him to say that he would die a thousand deaths ('mille morts') rather than confess anything (actually he seems to have sent this to Mendoza, who had passed it on).[10] He has resisted torture twice. The only thing against him is the papers and ciphers. 'Je l'en avais assez averty . . .'; he had told him often enough not to keep papers. Castelnau still on good terms with Elizabeth, who thinks there is a vast conspiracy against her. Arrests and fugitives, including Lord Paget, who has fled via Arundel. Vague rumours that Mary and Spain are involved. Porter, not identified, in a hurry to go.

(2)   A postscript to the above, with the ominous news that one of the pieces Throckmorton had left lying around was a letter from Courcelles saying that he was sending him, for Mary, some packets and a letter from Douglas. Castelnau has given the porter the packets (from Paris) that

---

6   No. 31.

7   No. 32; cf. Mary to Castelnau, 22-v/1-vi & 31-v/10-vi-1584 (Labanoff, v, 472, 475).

8   No. 34: Castelnau, 22-iii-/1-iv-1584. Castelnau has received Nos. 22 & 31, 'ensemble cele du Sr. de Morgan, que je luy ay incontinant envoyée'.

9   Nos. 13, 14, 15, 16.

10   Above, p. 88.

Throckmorton should have taken, and Mary's 'camayeux d'agatte' (evidently a cameo or medallion used as a token).

(3)   Dictated by Courcelles to Feron with a postscript by Castelnau.[11] The porter is Thomas Baldwin ('Baudouin'); rumour of warrant for his arrest; if arrested to say that Walsingham told him to take letters for money. Breakdown of Throckmorton after fourth torture, because 'I cannot bear the pain', has put Castelnau in trouble. Throckmorton has confessed that Castelnau put him in touch with Mary. Castelnau further implicated by pile of papers discovered, which includes 'little pieces of paper' from Courcelles accompanying Mary's packets, and the paper of havens; 'I had warned them often enough about this, and about everything that has happened to them'. Outline of the plan now emerging: Guise running it through Morgan and Throckmorton; troops to come from Spain. Expects Throckmorton to be tried and executed next week. Of all this 'j' . . . ay tant de regret que j'en meurs sous le pied' (Castelnau in a state of utter misery and chagrin).

(4)   A brief note reporting previous letters. Fears that George More and other of your servants arrested. Earl of Northumberland put under house arrest yesterday. No news from 'votre frère'.

Three months later, in March and April, Castelnau was still keeping Mary's correspondence with Paris going back and forth: in his most recent letter, apparently of 7 April, he sent a new packet from Morgan which had probably come with Cardinal Gallio's encouraging letter to William Parry.[12] Otherwise, nothing much to report. Sad state of Throckmorton 'que j'ayme comme moymesme' (Walsingham puts a trefoil mark in the margin, reminding himself to bring this to Elizabeth's attention),[13] of his brother George, and of More, all incommunicado in the Tower (Walsingham underlines, happy that nothing about his dealings with Throckmorton and More has got out). Likewise the Earl of Northumberland. More optimistic news of Henry Howard, and of the Earl of Arundel whose house arrest has just been lifted. Castelnau repudiates Mary's allegation that the plot had been exposed by treachery in his household; blames it on Throckmorton's and More's visible frequentation of Mendoza, on Throckmorton's insecure procedures, and on his confessions: which have

---

11   See No. 16: Castelnau has just sent two letters, and told Courcelles 'de vous deduire plus particulierement la confession du Sr. de la Tour et ce qu'il avoit trouvé moyen de nous en mander, et des tourmens qu'il avoit enduré – which obviously means the present letter (No. 15; Document (b)). But we should not therefore suppose that the 'I' of this letter is Courcelles, not Castelnau; and the postscript, which includes the last phrase I quote from it, was dictated by Castelnau himself.

12   No. 35; cf. above, pp. 97, 101. What follows is from Nos. 34 and 35. No. 34 (Document (d)) contains the passage about Castelnau's office arrangements quoted above, pp. 29, 46, and elsewhere.

13   No. 35.

included a complete account of the secret correspondence and Castelnau's part in it. Finally, to cheer Mary up, he passes on a prognostication he has just received from the great Monsieur Bodin, who has seen in the stars a grand revolution in English affairs shortly to happen in her favour.[14]

Walsingham, underlining, chuckles at Bodin's change of sides, and considers Castelnau. If he had purloined the parcel to prove to Elizabeth Castelnau's innocence, he had not got an open and shut case. She had not been wrong to sense that Castelnau had changed sides too. He had been devoted to Throckmorton, and spoken with uniform friendliness of Catholics traitorous or not. Admittedly, this was to Mary; but deeds had followed from his feelings. He had made, and was still making, his facilities for communication available to her and her most dangerous followers; he had been perfectly well aware that Throckmorton was up to something more than the consolation of a lonely queen, and his only advice had been to make sure he left no evidence of what it was. He had corrupted Baldwin, who might keep open the lines between Mary and the Earl of Shrewsbury as readily as Cornwallis might have done between her and Northumberland; he knew how Lord Paget had got out of the country, and probably how Thomas Throckmorton had got in as well as out; through Courcelles he was in touch with the Catholic underground; he had been in frequent and amiable communication with Mendoza before Mendoza had been expelled, and had probably picked up Mendoza's contacts since.

There would be no difficulty in constructing an impressive case against Castelnau if that was what was wanted, and in any event he would have to be prevented from going on like this in future. But it was perfectly evident that the major charges, in the list which had been compiled against him, were not true. Castelnau had certainly not *directed* Throckmorton's treasonable doings, and could not even be certainly shown to have known about them; it did not appear that he had had anything to do with the paper of havens before he got wind of it through Throckmorton's confessions; he had not heard of Throckmorton's green casket, and his information about the papers seized at Throckmorton House was perhaps garbled (Walsingham will have known whether it was garbled, but made

14   No. 34: 'Monsieur Bodin qui est un grand personnage et astrologue et mathematissien m'a souvent escript comme il a fait encores depuis deux jours que vous estes presques sur le point de voir la fin de voz malheurs . . . ce qu'i[l] me prie de vous faire entendre comme à sa seule maistresse . . .' Compare *CSP Foreign 1583*, p. 84 (Bodin to Walsingham, 20/30-i-1583); my 'English Catholics and the French Marriage', *Recusant History*, v (1959), 10 and n. 40; Summerfield Baldwin, 'Jean Bodin and the League', *Catholic Historical Review*, xxiii (1937), 160–84. Bodin was prophesying Elizabeth's death at the time of the Babington plot (*CSP Foreign 1586–88*, p. 94).

no recoverable comment).[15] He appeared to have known nothing about Charles Paget's trip to see the Earl of Northumberland, though it was common currency in the correspondence he forwarded; he had had no direct relations with the earl. He had not tried to marry Mary to Lord Henry Howard, and he had not smuggled Lord Paget out of the country. In so far as the case for expelling him depended on his active participation in treason, it did not stand up, whatever Throckmorton had confessed. If I have got Walsingham right, he finished his reading of Castelnau's correspondence with Mary in a state of palpable relief, and presented his findings to Elizabeth with some satisfaction.

Without having to read them so carefully, he could come to an equally satisfactory conclusion from the remaining letters in Feron's parcel, an assortment of Castelnau's letters to France between Throckmorton's arrest and the middle of February: after that, either Feron's cupboard had been bare, or more probably he had kept in it enough to disguise the theft of what had been underneath. Walsingham, now no doubt ready for bed, could read of Castelnau's interviews with Elizabeth, which he knew about already, but find almost nothing about his relations with Catholics.[16] He had failed to mention the name of Throckmorton, still less what he had told him to do with his papers, or what he had confessed; nor had he mentioned Howard. He gave the impression that since the failure of the Anjou marriage he had done nothing about the Catholics in England except to bewail their lot, and that anything else was the work of Mendoza and the Jesuits. He shrugged off the secret correspondence as a trivial matter dealing with the affairs of Mary's property in France and with negotiations for the treaty with Elizabeth;[17] the name of Thomas Morgan was another that did not appear, let alone that of William Parry. If he had written nothing more confidential than this it was plain that, whatever he had been up to with Mary and the Catholics, he had not been telling Henri III about it. Nor, if he had been liaising with Mendoza via Throckmorton or otherwise, had he been doing this on Henri III's instructions. If he read hard, Walsingham could work out that Mendoza had visited Castelnau at least three times between Throckmorton's arrest and his own expulsion; he would learn that Mendoza was trying to give the impression that the two of them had some kind of understanding. Castelnau

---

15 No. 15 and Document (b): 'Ilz [apparently Francis and George] ont esté trouvez plaines de lettres chiffres et autres choses escriptes de leurs mains' as well as the paper of havens and Courcelles's notes. If this were true, it would imply that the story about Throckmorton getting his papers away to Mendoza in the green casket (*A Discoverie of the Treasons*, pp. 194f) was an invention; but I think not. Throckmorton acknowledged the existence of the casket (*Ibid.* pp. 194f, 200).

16 Unless No. 37 formed part of the parcel, which I am virtually certain it did not; below, pp. 118f.

17 No. 25 for both points.

claimed that there was nothing in it, though a letter to Anjou showed that they were still talking of a Spanish marriage for him.[18] To judge by Walsingham's annotations, almost the only interesting thing Castelnau actually had told Henri III was that he had been talking to a Scot called Patrick Adamson, a former follower of the Duke of Lennox whom King James, striking a blow against the ministers of his Church, had appointed Archbishop of St Andrews. James had sent Adamson to England in November, and he represented himself to Elizabeth as a champion of Protestant episcopacy in his country; in what he had been saying to Castelnau at the same time Walsingham found matter which might help to persuade her that episcopacy in Scotland was but a step on the path to Rome.[19] However, the fate of Scotland was not the immediate preoccupation; otherwise he could now reassure the queen that Henri III had not been involved in any activity against her,[20] and that a fairly restrained rap on Castelnau's knuckles would go down quite well with his king.

From Feron's parcel, then, it emerged that Castelnau was not only roughly speaking innocent; he was also extremely vulnerable. A few judicious leakages in Paris ought to ensure that his position was undermined from the rear while, in suitable privacy, they were demolishing it at the front. He was also vulnerable because he did not know, or would not admit, that Feron was betraying him; he did not know that More had turned queen's evidence, or exactly what Throckmorton was now confessing. His one recent success, the recruitment of Thomas Baldwin, would have to be attended to; but Walsingham made no mark to tell Elizabeth, and I think he kept the news to himself. It would only revive her dampened anger, and put Feron in danger: their position was now so strong that Baldwin could be left to run for the time being.

Walsingham must have been in a position to present his findings to Elizabeth on 1 or 2 May. I presume that he did so, and that Elizabeth was relatively pacified, for on the 3rd he sent a reasonable letter to Stafford by the returning secretary Marion conveying her request to Henri III that he expel from France five of her traitors, who were named, but not that he extradite them to England; he said nothing about Castelnau or his letters, though it is true that Stafford was by now making a great fuss about them, and threatening to produce extracts from the confessions.[21] Castelnau knew enough to be nervous. On the 4th he sent a note to Walsing-

18   Nos. 10, 25, 28; Mendoza, in *CSP Spanish 1580–86*, p. 515.

19   Nos. 16, 18; on Adamson's trip, Read, *Walsingham*, ii, 225f.

20   Cf. Walsingham to Sir Ralph Sadler, 16/26–ix–1584 (A. Clifford (ed.), *The State Papers and Letters of Sir Ralph Sadler* (2 vols, Edinburgh, 1809), ii, 399): 'We find in all the plottes and discoveryes that have come to our handes anie tyme these two or three yeares the French King hath no way been a party in them.'

21   *CSP Foreign 1583–84*, p. 483 (cf. pp. 478f, nos. 566, 611, 613, 615); probably referred to in Diary, f. 71ʳ.

ham about some bloodhounds which he hoped Leicester would be able to get for the Duke of Lorraine, and so calm down animosities with the family: for his part, he said, he wanted to do nothing but good, but 'si l'on veult tout mal je suys celluy qui le crains le moins' (if what people want is the worst, I am the one who has least to fear); which I doubt. He suggested that they take a ride together in the evening to talk things over.[22] I should be surprised if Walsingham responded, because just about then he put down a note 'to confer with the L[ords of the Council] about the directions for the French Imb[assador]'.[23] It is perhaps making too fine a point to argue from the word 'directions' that the major decision had already been taken not to provoke Castelnau's expulsion, but to impose a stiff set of conditions on his continued residence in London. On my account this was what the Council wanted, and their position will have been confirmed by what Walsingham told them of the contents of Feron's parcel; he must also have given them some assurance that the queen had come, or was coming, round to their view. The confusion which now ensued indicates that the question was not quite settled, and indeed that we should not be too confident that we know exactly what the question was.[24]

The Council's decision was put into a written *mémoire* with which Walsingham sent Archibald Douglas (who else?) round to Salisbury Court next morning (5 May). We can only infer what was in it from Castelnau's response. We can take it that it rehearsed all but the gravest charges which had been floated against him: running the secret correspondence with Mary, and cultivating her friends to the subversion of the queen's estate. He was probably also accused of collusion with Mendoza. In view of this unfriendly conduct he would have to renounce that part of his duties which required him to represent Mary's interests, and stop the secret correspondence; in future he was to show Walsingham all letters to and from Mary, if there were any, and apparently his letters home as well. It was perhaps intimated to him that he should submit his contacts in London and at Court to some kind of supervision by the Earl of Leicester.[25] It is an open question whether, in

---

22 PRO SP 78/11, f. 202; *CSP Foreign 1583–84*, p. 483, no. 572. I think the endorsement, by which it has been dated, says '2nd', not '4th' May.

23 Diary, f. 71ᵛ.

24 Remember Stafford's letter to Elizabeth of 2/12 May (above, p. ••) about her having the sword in her own hand; this must have expressed what he thought were the queen's feelings at the time he wrote it.

25 Castelnau to Walsingham, 5/15-v-1584 (PRO SP 78/11, f. 205; *CSP Foreign 1583–84*, p. 489; Document (e)). For the letters, see n. 26; for Mendoza, *Ibid.* p. 593; for Leicester, *Ibid.* p. 557, and PRO SP 12/177, no. 41, where the Earl of Lincoln complains to Burghley, in March 1585, that Leicester has told him to keep away from Castelnau, whom he wanted to take to a dog race. See Simon Adams (ed.), *Household Accounts and Disbursement Books of Robert Dudley, Earl of Leicester* (Camden Society, 5th Series, vi, Cambridge, 1995), pp. 182, 226, 249, 261, 305, for social civilities between Leicester and Castelnau, October 1584–September 1585.

the *mémoire*, threats were made of action against him if he did not comply. Perhaps they did not need to be specified; or perhaps the Council and the queen were still not agreed how threatening they should be.

Castelnau acknowledged Douglas's delivery of the *mémoire*, and said that he had 'written several letters in accordance with it' (fidellement sur le memoire), whatever he meant by that; then Douglas turned up again and, he complained, told him the opposite of what he had said before. Baffled, he went to see Elizabeth next day: she confirmed the substance of the *mémoire*, but it is not clear that she solved the contradiction, whatever it was, between Douglas's two messages. Castelnau said that he would do what he was told, although 'it will be doing things by halves and leaving a source of embarrassment still' (ce sera fere les choses a demy et laisser tousiours une difficulté), and although it would take away half the honour of his charge; there were people in France who would interpret it in the worst sense. He had always done his best, but since they did not trust his goodwill he would not stand in the way of an arrangement satisfactory to them, provided that there was reciprocity on their side. He would now rewrite his letters to Henri III and Mary, and send them along in the evening: which may mean that he had written stiff letters to both 'sur le memoire' and would now tone them down. He commended himself to the Earl of Leicester, whom he may now have viewed as the only friend in sight.[26]

Castelnau was being so wilfully obscure that it is impossible to be sure what the muddle was: from the remark about reciprocity ('provided that there is evidence of a will to behave amicably on both sides'; pourveu qu'il y ait resollution et aparence de bien fere de tous coustez), we might deduce that it had resolved itself into a discussion about what concessions were to be made to Castelnau in return for his compliance with the 'directions'. The great thing he had always wanted was to be allowed to make a journey to Scotland in the company of one of Elizabeth's servants, on the pretext of reconciling the parties, and with the purpose of recapturing a foothold for the crown of France in a country from which Elizabeth had fairly successfully excluded it; for this reason she had always turned the idea down. Now that Castelnau's bona fides was to some extent re-established, and the Council's coup in Scotland had misfired, she became less hostile towards it, or more willing to appear so. The Council, in accordance with its general policy of being nice to Henri III, would seem to have advised her that it would be a worthwhile trade-off for Castelnau's acceptance of

---

26 Castelnau to Walsingham, 7/17-v-1584 (PRO SP 78/11, f. 207; *CSP Foreign 1583–84*, p. 485).

the 'directions'; presumably on their recommendation, the gesture of
sending the king the Garter was now made a firm proposal.[27] In a climate
of such public togetherness, Castelnau might look for two further concessions, one explicit and one implied. The explicit concession was that
the supervision of his correspondence home should be balanced or disguised by allowing him to see Walsingham's letters to Stafford, a piece of
sham generosity to which Walsingham appears to have made no objection.[28] The other concession, which I do not suppose was openly talked
about but must have been rather prominent in everybody's mind, was
that his name would be kept out of Throckmorton's trial. While mulling
all this over, Elizabeth herself perhaps made the helpful gesture of calling
a halt to the trial of the Jesuit Jasper Heywood, which was begun on 6
May, the day she saw Castelnau, and was abandoned for no obvious
reason.[29]

Thereafter we know that they were on reasonable terms, since a day
or two later she took him down to Greenwich with her.[30] But there are
two good reasons for supposing that all was not yet settled between them.
One is that Castelnau was, during these very days, still pursuing the secret
correspondence, presumably via Baldwin whom Walsingham had left
at liberty. He had a letter from Mary on the 7th, duly passed by Feron,
and wrote back on the 10th, sending her two new packets from Morgan
and a pile of old ones: he was, as we can imagine, glad to get them off
his hands.[31] The other reason is that we have a string of diary entries,
written not earlier than 13 May and probably on the 14th and 15th, which
must record the completion of the concordat with Castelnau. Here
Walsingham's list of things to put to the queen runs:

1. Resolution F[rench] Imb[assador]
2. Herle . . . [three other items]
    Proceadings Throgmorton.

Then, after a pile of things to remember which included the note about
Williams and the money,

27 Below, p. 116; Diary, f. 90^r; Labanoff, v, 464 (No. 38).
28 I find nothing about this at the time, but Stafford was complaining about it in September–October
    (*CSP Foreign 1584–85*, pp. 69, 78, 104, 120).
29 Dennis Flynn, 'The English Mission of Jasper Heywood', *Archivum Historicum Societatis Iesu*, liv
    (1985), p. 62; a note in Walsingham's diary (f. 71^v) about distinguishing between Jesuits of state
    and Jesuits of religion may well be relevant: its date is between 3/13 and 13/23 May.
30 Le Laboureur, *Mémoires*, iii, 595.
31 *Ibid.* 594–7; he had received No. 38, of 30-iv/10-v-1584.

H. Tayler Batersey   Throg.
    [?]Inquis
To advertyse Master At[torney-General Popham] of her Ma[jesty]'s dys-
posytyon that the arraygnement

The note ends here, at the side of the page.[32] The resolution referred
to was, I suppose, to allow Castelnau to go to Scotland, but it covered a
multitude, as we gather from the letter from Walsingham to Stafford in
which it was recorded. It was a letter Elizabeth might have been expected
to write herself, and that she did not is rather strong evidence that she
was not at all happy about the volte-face, not to say perjury, it entailed.
On her behalf Walsingham announced the sending of the Garter, which
she had had in mind for a long time but 'for some considerations' put off
until now, when she had found the king's friendship confirmed 'by sundry
effects'. She had also now changed her mind about the mission to Scotland, which she had turned down in February, and was sure that Castelnau would behave himself on the trip, having no reason to doubt 'the
gentleman's own plain meaning and sincere disposition to do any good
offices for the weal and quietness of both realms'.[33] Castelnau's disposition being as described, he could obviously not have had anything to do
with Throckmorton. The first note about the trial ('Proceadings Throgmorton') may mean that it was not until now that the date for it had been
fixed, though it occurred no more than a week later, on 21 May; it looks
as if somebody was going to have to do something rather rapidly about
it. If this was part of the queen's 'resolution', as I suppose, Herle's job was
perhaps to take the good news to Castelnau, as Douglas had brought the
bad. The handing over of Feron's money indicates that his job was now
finished, and hence that Castelnau had promised to give up the secret correspondence and that Walsingham at least thought he could be made to
keep his word.

It is a pity that the note to explain to Popham the queen's 'disposition'
about Throckmorton's indictment has been left unfinished; but I do not
think there can be much doubt that it was going to say that anything to
do with Castelnau should be kept out of it. The signs are that this required
a good deal of hasty work from the law officers. One of the signs is the
mysterious preceding note. Who the devil, we may ask, is H. Tayler of
Battersea, who is something to do with Throckmorton, and for whom

---

32 Diary, f. 72ᵛ, 74ʳ; the date is fixed by a note on f. 72ʳ, about a passport for a Scot recommended
    by Castelnau on the 13th/23rd.
33 *CSP Foreign 1583–84*, p. 506; this is undated, but can hardly be later than the 16th/26th, since
    Stafford had acted on it and replied on 23-v-/2-vi (*Ibid.* p. 512).

apparently a hue and cry is to be set up? We can actually find him in a draft of the official account of Throckmorton's treason, from the published version of which he was dropped. Or rather, we find 'one [blank] a tailor in Battersea', who can be brought as a witness to treasonable correspondence between Throckmorton and Sir Francis Englefield, which he has carried or forwarded. Englefield was the best known and longest serving English servant of Philip II, a former councillor of Queen Mary Tudor who was now living in Spain and advising the king on English matters. According to Throckmorton's first confessions, he had corresponded with Englefield for several years, and had compiled the paper of havens for his benefit; this confession provided the substance of the case against him at his trial.[34] Tayler, if that was his name rather than his profession, was it seems at this very late hour to be searched for. He was not found, and I doubt if he existed. But his appearance in the diary at this point must mean that it had already, and perhaps hastily, been decided that Throckmorton's indictment would take the form it did: treasonable communication with Spain by means of Englefield and then of Mendoza, and nothing about Castelnau. This would leave the law officers with a nasty problem, which it looks as if Elizabeth was entitled to blame on her councillors.

Castelnau had saved his face; or should we not say that his face had been saved for him? He had even, I think in Elizabeth's teeth, apparently been given a vote of confidence. In fact he had caved in; unless he was prepared to let his career end in disgrace, he could not have done anything else. By managing Elizabeth, and with invaluable assistance from Feron, Walsingham had succeeded in hitting exactly the right spot. A reason would shortly be found for abandoning the trip to Scotland;[35] it made little difference. While they were blackmailing him in London, they had managed to persuade Henri III to sabotage him from home. Though he kept up a front to Stafford, the king was extremely nervous about what Castelnau's dealings with and on behalf of Mary had been letting him in for. After Stafford had raised the subject in the middle of March, his letters repeatedly told Castelnau to keep off any dubious connections with Mary as, he said cuttingly, 'I should like to believe (je veulx croire) that you have done in the past'. Even Villeroy, one of his best friends and the most Catholic of Henri III's councillors, joined in.[36] It seems that things went

34 PRO SP 12/171, no. 86. On Englefield, see *DNB*, and Albert J. Loomie, *The Spanish Elizabethans* (London, 1963), pp. 14–51: Loomie indicates (pp. 41–2) that the correspondence with Englefield was a fiction, as indeed it was.

35 *CSP Foreign 1583–84*, p. 541 (Walsingham, 5/15-vi-1584; his notes for it in Diary, f. 76ᵛ); Read, *Walsingham*, ii, 227.

36 *CSP Foreign 1583–84*, p. 413; Henri III to Castelnau, 27-iii/6-iv-1584, also 29-iv/9-v-1584, 25-v/4-vi-1584 (PRO Transcripts 31/3/28, under date; Teulet, *Relations politiques*, iii, 277: BN fr 3305,

a little farther than this. Late in April, just about when Feron's parcel was in transit, Castelnau had written the king a fairly spirited letter obliquely defending his conduct and letting out a little more about his contacts in England than he normally did; or at least, than he had done in the letters home that had gone into the parcel.[37] He was not at all explicit, but by filling some gaps we can conclude that he was not in favour of the sort of Catholic alliance which Mendoza had been angling for, but recommending that the threat of it ought to be kept alive as a means of persuading Elizabeth to accommodate French interests. He claimed that she was still in a panic about it, and that 'they' were convinced that it would come about when Anjou died, as he was now expected to do before long. The king should play upon this fear, and keep secret what he intended to do about the Netherlands; he should also stop his councillors leaking his intentions to Stafford. The implication was that, if they were kept sufficiently nervous, the English would make concessions about a French presence in Scotland, and allow Castelnau to go there; in view of which his connections with Mary and her English supporters would prove valuable. The authorities, he said, were now keeping a very close eye on any notable Englishmen who frequented Salisbury Court; there had been only two of them, 'whom Your Majesty knows to be faithful to him', and these no longer came because one of them had heard that he was about to be arrested. When Castelnau wanted their news he had to send or to go to them by night. Nonetheless he had been able to put the Duke of Joyeuse's secretary, Marion, now on his apparently unpolitical visit to Mary, in touch with her 'friends' around Sheffield.[38]

In short: in spite of the string of arrests before Christmas, he still had some cards up his sleeve, which the king might use advantageously if he wanted to, as Castelnau implied that he ought to do. He did not actually say that he was still in correspondence with Mary, but the king might deduce this. He appeared to be more au fait with Castelnau's clandestine relations than the rest of their extant correspondence has allowed to emerge. I do not know who the two contacts were; the one who was lying low for the time being was possibly Baldwin; but they sound more aristocratic.

Gnomic as it is, this letter looks like a defence by Castelnau of his Catholic and Marian contacts, which might stand out less markedly if more

---

f. 50ᵛ); Villeroy to Castelnau, 29-iii/8-iv-1584 (BN Vᶜ C 472, p. 127): the king's letter 'ne vous doibt metre en peine, mais seullement vous servir d'advis pour vous conformer au bon plaisir de notre Maitre'.

37   No. 37, and note on date.

38   Above, p. 103; he also put him in touch with Douglas, which cannot have done any good.

of his correspondence had survived. If so, it would seem to have been the last. If it had been in Feron's parcel it would have weakened Walsingham's hand in restraining Elizabeth from drastic action against Castelnau. But it was obviously not: the copy is not in Feron's hand, nor in any hand that I can connect with the embassy at this time, and it came to Burghley not to Walsingham. I think we may take up Castelnau's suggestion that things were being leaked from Henri III's council, and conclude that it was leaked in Paris to Stafford, who passed it to Burghley as he would have done. There are two endorsements on it: one of them I cannot read, and the other, by Burghley's clerk, says: 'Letters from France to the Queen' and has been crossed out.[39] The handwriting might possibly be a small version of Jean Arnault's, but I do not think he was in Paris at the time. I guess that the piece was not leaked clandestinely, but on the king's authority, to show that he had nothing to conceal, to support his strong letters to Castelnau, sabotage whatever he might still be up to with Mary, and invite Elizabeth to take such action against him, within reason, as she saw fit. It cannot have arrived in London in time for Walsingham's explanation with Castelnau, and I wonder whether Elizabeth was allowed to see it; it was surely used in some way to hasten Castelnau's downfall. Attacked from his front and his rear, with Feron in his chamber, Fagot at his dinner table and Douglas on his doorstep, Castelnau was henceforth an ambassador in chains. The grip Elizabeth and Walsingham had now got on him would not be shaken during the time he remained in London. I doubt if it is accidental that from exactly this point another two months' worth of his correspondence has disappeared: it was not a period when his doings would look impressive to posterity.

Throckmorton's trial, which was a very grand affair in the London Guildhall, did not go quite according to plan; which is not surprising if the plan had been as hastily contrived as it seems. He was indicted on a charge of high treason for attempting to deprive the queen of her crown by armed rebellion and assassination, and for three particular acts in execution of the attempt: the correspondence with Englefield, the paper of havens, and a treasonable conference with his brother Thomas. The evidence against him was drawn entirely from a set of his confessions which had begun after his second torture on 19 November 1583 with his volunteering to explain everything 'by way of an historical narration' covering six or seven years beginning in the Netherlands in 1576 or 1577. The correspondence with Englefield then begun had continued until about 1582, and it was in the course of it that he had compiled the paper of havens. After a pause of a year he had been brought into the new scheme

39 *HMC Hatfield*, iii, 81; Cecil Papers 149, ff. 117f.

by his brother Thomas, who had come over secretly from France, to tell him of the Duke of Guise's plan and to persuade him to get in touch with Mendoza about it; the rest had followed. He claimed that just before his arrest the scheme had been brought to a stop when they found no answer to the problem, how to get Mary out of captivity before the news of the invasion reached her captors.[40]

Since at some later point he had written to the queen admitting his guilt and throwing himself on her mercy,[41] the Council appears to have assumed that he would plead guilty. But in his solitude and self-contempt he had found strength from somewhere, and in court defended himself briskly. He repudiated his confessions as a cock-and-bull story invented to stop his interrogators torturing him. He then claimed that, even if his confession of the three acts alleged in the indictment were true and good in law, he could not according to the Treason Act of 1571 be convicted on any of them because the statute required him to be brought to trial within six months of the commission of the offence. The judges told him that his offences were not only against this act, which covered rebellion in support of the pope, but against the original Treason Act of 1352, which covered rebellion in general and contained no such limitation. He then said, correctly, that the statute of 1352 required some 'overt act' of rebellion to have been committed, whereas he had committed none. The judges said that setting down the paper of havens was an overt act; he denied having written it. The Attorney-General then adduced independent confirmation of one of the confessions from another confession by William Shelley, to the effect that Charles Paget had come over to Sussex for treasonable purposes; which showed that Throckmorton had not made everything up out of his head.[42] He was found guilty and returned to the Tower, but not executed.

40 A report of the trial, incomplete, in BL Stowe 1083, ff. 17–20; the confessions are expounded in *A Discoverie of the Treasons*, which includes Throckmorton's final confession in a letter to the queen of 4/14-vi-1584; there is an early draft of the first part of the *Discoverie* in PRO SP 12/171, no. 86 (ff. 197ʳ–214ᵛ), from which there are interesting departures in the printed version. Behind this, for the list of the original confessions (*Discoverie*, pp. 192–3), there is Norton's 'The Plott of the Treasons intended' (BL Addnl Mss. 48029 [Yelverton Mss. 33], ff. 64–69); from which, presumably on the advice of Attorney-General Popham (PRO SP 12/171, no. 79), all the confessions involving the Earl of Northumberland were omitted. But Norton was not, as Graves, *Thomas Norton*, p. 269 says, the author of the *Discoverie*; he had died on 10/20 March. The work must have been written between the trial (21/31 May) and 4/14 June, when Throckmorton made his final confession, which was then appended. The author was probably Thomas Wilkes, and the date on the prefatory letter is 15/25 June.

41 BL Stowe 1083, f. 18ʳ: at the trial, the Attorney-General (Popham), after Throckmorton had pleaded not guilty, 'wondereth that he will deny the treasons: mentioneth a submission of Throckmorton's owne hand to the Quene's Majesty' (which does not survive).

42 *Ibid.* f. 19ʳ⁻ᵛ; *Discoverie*, p. 196, which differ.

In fulfilling what I take to have been their bargain with Castelnau, Elizabeth and the Council had been almost excessively scrupulous. Not only was there nothing in the indictment about the supposed confession of 25 March in which Throckmorton was said to have accused Castelnau of actively promoting the invasion; there was actually nothing about the secret correspondence either. It was only mentioned once in the course of the trial, and in such a way as to imply that it was Mendoza who ran it.[43] So half at least of Throckmorton's confessions were not used. None of the other evidence to the correspondence system was used either: nothing from Feron's parcel or his other leakages, which is of course not surprising, but nothing of the evidence about it, like Courcelles' notes, which had been seized at the time of Throckmorton's arrest and would not have exposed Feron; nothing from Parry. Over anything that might indicate that Castelnau had had the least connection with Throckmorton, or had acted as a post-box for Thomas Morgan, there was a complete blackout.[44]

With this the reader may think that our story is over; indeed, so far as it has been a story of intelligence, it now was virtually over, completed by the strategic non-use, or non-use in public, of the knowledge that had been painfully and perhaps expensively acquired. Five days after Throckmorton's trial the memo-book in Walsingham's office resumed service after a gap of six weeks which I have no explanation for. Next day, 27 May 1584, we find, evidently together:

> To dispatche Herle
> The [*sic*] dyspatche Wyllyams.[45]

Walsingham was drawing a line under his year-long enterprise in intelligence. The notes confirm that Herle and Williams, one from north Wales and one from south, had been working in tandem almost from the beginning. We should not have gathered this from the notebook so far; whence I suppose that Herle had been kept from knowing that he was half of a pair, and possibly Williams too, though I think it more likely that he knew. I hope that Walsingham had the civility to celebrate with a drink all round. Herle was off on a thoroughly respectable diplomatic errand in defence

43 Above, p. 100; BL Stowe 1083, f. 18ʳ: under the 'proofs' of the articles of the indictment, his 'mutual intelligence with [Mary] by letters in cipher' is put between two items about Throckmorton's dealings with Mendoza.

44 Above, pp. 115–17. Walsingham's notes for a letter to Stafford, a week or so after the trial (above, n. 35), say: 'The processe delyvered unto the Fr[?a]'; then there is a blot. If this means sent to Castelnau, and I cannot quite think what else it could mean, Walsingham had sent him an account of the trial to show that their agreement had been respected.

45 Diary, f. 76ʳ.

of the Dutch; Williams was off to Wales, with money in his pocket. They
had done a good job.

When they had gone their different ways, it began to emerge that the
heroic effort to keep Castelnau out of Throckmorton's trial had backfired,
since it had left the prosecution with a rather poor case, which did not
prove very convincing to much of the public. There was a feeling, not only
among Catholics but among 'persons not evill affected', that his defence
was good in law, and some sympathy with him over his torture; the reaction was strong enough to persuade the Council that it was no use trying
to bring a prosecution of the Earl of Northumberland, which would
depend on Throckmorton's confessions, before the House of Lords.[46] In
fact the Crown had all the evidence it needed, but it would have to let a
little more of it out of the bag if it were not to suffer a defeat in public
relations. Walsingham, presumably, was told to get something like the real
story into print, and somebody in his office was set to compose what
became the *Discoverie of the Treasons practised and attempted against the
Queene's Majestie and the Realme by Francis Throckmorton*. The need was to
show that his confessions, or enough of them to justify his conviction,
were true, which was awkward for two reasons: first, because the confessions used at the trial, though genuine, were largely untrue; and second,
because it was very tricky to use those that were true without implicat-
ing Castelnau. The apologist began by admitting that Throckmorton's
arrest had been the result of 'secret intelligence' which had been left to
mature for some months. He then had to justify leaving Throckmorton at
large all this time, and did so by revealing, which was perfectly true but
had not emerged at the trial, that he had not been arrested for planning
an invasion but for running the secret correspondence. Something had
now to be revealed about it. Throckmorton was now said, rightly, to have
confessed 'voluntarily' that Morgan had recruited him to correspond with
Mary, and that he had forwarded Morgan's own letters back and forth. He
had declared the 'effect' of his own correspondence with Mary, and sent
the queen a copy of the cipher in which it was conducted. He had said
something about the carriage of the letters in England. He had not, so far
as this version went, said anything about Castelnau or Salisbury Court.
But the reader was going to wonder how the letters had got in and out

---

46   *Discoverie*, p. 191: slanderous rumours given out 'whereby such as are evill affected towards her
     Majestie and the present government' say that his confessions have been exacted by torture, etc.
     The draft had said: 'in so much as some persons *not* [my italics] evill affected, but generallie all
     suche as are Recusants and carrie like mindes towardes her Majestie and their countrey, do not
     only stagger in their conceiptes touching the sufficiencie of the matters prooved against him
     . . .' On the failure to prosecute Northumberland, see Popham's opinion (PRO SP 12/171, no.
     79, and above, n. 40).

of the country, and half a page later he found out: Throckmorton had 'haunted continually *two* ambassadors in London', by whom he sent and received his treasonable letters 'daily'.[47] There had only been two ambassadors in London at the time.

On 1 June the writer's task was complicated by news from the Tower: under pressure from his wife and mother, Throckmorton had decided to make a complete confession. It arrived three days later.[48] When he had explained the story about Englefield, he described his correspondence with Morgan about the real invasion scheme, and quoted, perhaps at length but presumably from memory, letters from Mary to show that she was au fait with it: the published *Discoverie* interrupted his recitation with a couple of prudent 'etceteras', possibly to save Mary's face but certainly to save Castelnau's. He said that he had received some of his letters from Mary via Castelnau, who had received them from a man whose name Throckmorton claimed he did not know: the man must have been More and Throckmorton must have been acting under instruction. He also said that many of the packets he had received from Mary had contained letters to Castelnau as well as to Morgan. In the published version Castelnau was designated by the letters 'F.A.', and lest this disguise should seem too absurdly transparent somebody had the notion of inventing for More the name 'William Ardington', of whom I suppose the less wide-awake members of the public might take F.A. to be a relation.[49]

With this benevolent equivocation the confession was put into print together with a slightly modified version of the *Discoverie*; it was a hasty concoction which made no attempt to solve the contradiction between Throckmorton, who said that his confessions about Englefield were rubbish, and the official statement which still assumed that they were true. When it was published he was still alive, and perhaps it was not a foregone conclusion that he would be executed; but he suffered on 10 July, apparently in retaliation for the assassination of William of Orange, the news of which had just reached London. If that was so, it was a pity to have had him executed (I take it hanged, drawn and quartered) at Tyburn, which must have made him look more like a martyred priest than a political traitor. The only report of his execution says that in his dying speech

---

47   *Discoverie*, pp. 192, 193.
48   *CSP Domestic 1581–90*, p. 179 (Hopton to Walsingham, 1/11 June); Diary, ff. 75^v (26-v/5-vi-1584), 79^v.
49   *Discoverie*, pp. 197–98; the draft does *not* say, to describe someone who is obviously More: 'The man's name is William Ardington.' (*Discoverie*, p. 193) Throckmorton's petition for mercy, preliminary to the confession (*Ibid.*, pp. 196–7), must be the 'supplication' enclosed by Hopton, and hence must have been sent on 1/11 June, not 4/14 as the *Discoverie* says.

he made another turnabout and defended himself briskly;[50] I doubt if it is reliable. Since Castelnau destroyed his letters for this period, we do not know what he had to say, still less what he thought, about the death of someone he had 'loved as himself'.[51] Decent man as he was, I suspect that he may have been rather ashamed.

He was not to get away without some public shame either. A few days before the execution he was visited by an enemy in disguise, Mary's clandestine Jesuit servant Henri de Samerie, alias Monsieur de la Rue, who passed through Salisbury Court on the way from Sheffield to France. He had surely been told to look for treason, and may have talked to hostile members of the household, of whom Courcelles was probably now one; he had read, or got hold of, the *Discoverie*. When he got back to France he spread the word that Castelnau himself had been responsible for the betrayal of Throckmorton; the rumour became current among the Catholic *zelanti* and did Castelnau a great deal of harm when he himself returned home.[52] We cannot be surprised at it: the best-intentioned person who had read the *Discoverie* or knew what had happened at Throckmorton's trial could very naturally have come to this conclusion. Apart from the blatant fact that Castelnau had been protected throughout, there was a sinister passage in the *Discoverie*, immediately following the news about the 'two' ambassadors, where the information about the treasonable contents of the correspondence with France was attributed, not only to Throckmorton, 'but to others of better credite than himselfe'. This could well be taken to mean Castelnau. I think the implication had not been intended, but that wires had got crossed. What the writer had originally put was 'others of better credite and honestie than himselfe'. The 'honesty' was removed before printing, which makes me guess that the person referred to was William Parry, whose honesty it would have been imprudent of Walsingham to vouch for.[53]

---

50 Francis's cousin Arthur (Diary, vol. ii, f. 13ᵛ) says that he was executed at Tyburn. Hicks, *An Elizabethan Problem*, pp. 45f, from a report by Parsons printed in CRS xxxix, p. 266. Hart's 'Tower diary' (above, p. 84) says that the *Discoverie* was published on the day of Throckmorton's execution; but the text seems to presuppose that he was still alive, and the prefatory letter (p. 191) is dated 15/25 June.

51 Above, p. 109.

52 *CSP Foreign 1583–84*, p. 592; *CSP Scotland 1584–85*, pp. 414ff; Martin, *Henry III and the Jesuit Politicians*, pp. 112, 128f; *GB*, p. 131.

53 *Discoverie*, pp. 193–4, compared with draft; above, p. 88, n. 9.

7

OLD FRIENDS

Je vous feray tousiours juge de mes actions et vous y feray veoir comme mon ancien amy aussy cher qu'il vous plera.

(I shall always make you the judge of my actions, and by them shall prove you to be my old friend, as dear as you may wish.)

Castelnau to Walsingham, 16/26 August 1584
(PRO SP 78/12, no. 43)

AFTER THE PASSING of the parcel there was not much mole-work for Feron to do, and perhaps not much work at all. Castelnau, now that he had got rid of the pile of letters for Mary which had been hanging around, kept his word about the secret correspondence; at least, Mary's next two letters arrived in Walsingham's office in what appear to be authorised copies. Mary thought Castelnau might float the idea of exchanging Throckmorton's life for that of the Scottish lords involved in the failed coup; this was a non-starter, since James had already executed one of them.[1] So far as I can see, this was the end of Castelnau's part in the secret correspondence, though not of the correspondence altogether. Baldwin was left at large, no doubt to protect Feron, and not arrested until October; then he was found from the Sheffield end to be communicating secretly with Mary's secretary Gilbert Curle, and sent to the Tower to join the rest of the prisoners. He must have been interrogated, but no evidence of his confessions survives: I should think they were destroyed, as Throckmorton's were, to save Castelnau's blushes.[2]

---

1 Above, p. 104, for the coup. Nos. 39 and 40. I do not recognise the hand, which also seems to appear in No. 47. For the letter previous to these (no. 38), above, p. 105; it is a copy by Feron made on or after 7/17 May and perhaps given to Williams when Williams brought him his money about a week later. Cf. Castelnau to Walsingham, 30-viii/9-ix-1584 (*CSP Foreign 1584–85*, p. 38): 'I send you a copy of the letters that I wrote to the Queen of Scots, and that you may see the originals and all that comes and goes [on] that side.'

2 Clifford, *Sadler Papers*, ii, 402, 409–22, 451; Castelnau to Mary, 17/27-x-1584 (PRO SP 53/14, no. 9, extract); Pollen and MacMahon, *Philip Howard*, p. 132; *CSP Domestic 1581–90*, pp. 272, 450;

His embassy was now virtually over. If the affairs of France had been in better order, he would probably have been recalled in the summer of 1584; as it was, the letter recalling him did not arrive until November, and he did not leave England for almost another year. This was a long time for him to survive as a lame duck or, as he said, a 'voluntary prisoner' at Salisbury Court. His expressions of feeling mingled demonstrative Anglophilia and evocations of his 'old friendship' with Walsingham, which I take to be genuine and not unmerited, with occasional private outbursts of spleen. Elizabeth made sure that he did not get to Scotland, and may have imposed a period of social purdah; in August there was an anti-French riot around Salisbury Court which Castelnau suspected, I think mistakenly, to have been inspired by the English authorities. After this the queen was liberal with invitations to Court, to which he was shepherded by Leicester; at Christmas he responded by presenting her with a fine copy of the works of Bruno, behind which he could shelter as a fan of Elizabeth and a recruit to the anti-papal cause. At his dinner table he cultivated Walter Raleigh and steered clear of Catholics.[3]

There remained some flies in the ointment. One of them was Courcelles, who after Castelnau's withdrawal and by means, I suppose, of Baldwin, had been carrying on Mary's continental correspondence by himself; she was still trying to promote an invasion, though her candidate to launch it was no longer the Duke of Guise, now preoccupied in France, but the victorious Duke of Parma.[4] Another fly was the butler Girault, boss of the downstairs Catholic mafia and of a band of underground book vendors who in the summer and autumn had two best-sellers to distribute: William Allen's *Defence of Catholics* against Burghley's *Execution of Justice*, an unwontedly aggressive manifesto of political papalism; and the sensational polemic *Leicester's Commonwealth*, which threw an amazing amount of mud at the queen's favourite, and drove him to complain bitterly to Castelnau.[5]

CSP Scotland 1585–86, p. 287, 297, 300 (Mary asks Arnault to help him, March 1586). He was arrested on or before 5/15 October; on the 20th/30th Sadler asked Walsingham to tell him what came out when he was examined; on the same day Walsingham made a note (Diary, f. 97ᵛ) 'to take order with Baldwyn', which suggests that he had been examined already.

3 Castelnau to Walsingham, *CSP Foreign 1584–85*, pp. 11, 15, 23, 24, 36, 38, 166; Chéruel, p. 327; No. 44; *Sadler Papers*, ii, 387; Yates, *John Florio*, pp. 69, 73; *GB*, pp. 48–51, 127–9. On the riot, it emerges from Graves, *Thomas Norton*, pp. 369, 382, 386 that William Gryce, who started it, had been a very close friend of Norton; hence I wonder whether he was not au fait with Castelnau's dealings with Throckmorton, and making a point about his getting off scot-free.

4 *CSP Scotland 1584–85*, pp. 488f, 501f.

5 Editions by R. M. Kingdon (above, p. 94, n. 28) and D. C. Peck, *Leicester's Commonwealth* (Athens, Ohio, 1985); Peter Holmes, *Resistance and Compromise: the Political Thought of the Elizabethan Catholics* (Cambridge, 1982), pp. 129–35; *GB*, Texts nos. 4 and 13 and see index, 'La Chassaigne, Girault de'; Castelnau, April–May 1585 (F. H. Egerton, *The Life of Thomas Egerton* [?Paris, ?1828], pp. 43, 48: from BN fr. 4736, ff. 294, 308).

Meanwhile the larger political structure was groaning with readjust-
ments which were a response to Catholic aggressiveness in general and
the murder of William of Orange in particular. Orange was assassinated at
Delft in July 1584 by a loyalist subject of Philip II; the event wrecked the
shaky political leadership of the Dutch United Provinces and threatened
with collapse their revolt against Spanish sovereignty and Catholic intransigence. During the autumn the Council began to usher Elizabeth in the
direction of a decision to send an army to support the Dutch, and so to
promote her cold war with Philip to a hot one. At the same time they
invented, or borrowed from Protestant Scotland or Catholic France, a new
political institution called the Bond of Association, which bound all loyal
subjects to swear upon oath to take revenge on Mary if an attempt should
be made on Elizabeth's life, and excluded her from the succession if she
were found to have had anything to do with it; it was, we may believe, a
portentous constitutional innovation designed to erect the Protestant
commonwealth above the Crown and its inheritance. Elizabeth could just
about cope with that, but there was nothing much she could do about
war with Spain except to put it off for as long as she could. It might be
said that she had spent the first months of the year trying to provoke a
crisis with France: she must have provoked Walsingham hugely by claim-
ing that she could not be expected to fight the Spaniards unless she had
the French at her side.[6]

In July she was persuaded to send Philip Sidney at the head of a distinguished embassy to France, formally to condole with Henri III on the
death of his brother and her ex-fiancé Anjou, actually to propose joint
action in the Netherlands. To smooth his path, Sidney paid perhaps his
only visit to Salisbury Court, and Castelnau duly wrote a letter in his
favour. He must have known that it was a bad idea: the king replied, dev-
astatingly, that he was booked to go on a pilgrimage to Lyon and would
be unable to receive Sidney. Elizabeth scoffed; Castelnau sent Henri III a
rude letter about the English which Feron passed to Walsingham and
Walsingham to Burghley. As Bruno told them, Henri III was no pro-
mising adherent to the Protestant cause: Elizabeth would go into her war
with Spain without any help from the French.[7]

This bad news was compensated by better news from Scotland, whence
King James, having defeated the English coup, came up with a good offer.
He would leave his embarrassing mother to fend for herself, and turn
down any advances he might receive from Spain or France; Elizabeth

6 R. B. Wernham, *Before the Armada: the Growth of English Foreign Policy, 1485–1588* (London, 1966),
    pp. 367ff; Read, *Walsingham*, iii, 71ff; Patrick Collinson, 'The Monarchical Republic of Queen
    Elizabeth I', *Bulletin of the John Rylands Library*, lxix (1987), 394–424.

7 *GB*, pp. 151–3; No. 44; Chéruel, pp. 309, 311–13, 317, 346; *CSP Foreign 1584–85*, p. 23.

would recognise him as her successor and pay him a subsidy meanwhile; her Council would give up fomenting revolts against him and stop interfering with his efforts to control his Presbyterian ministry with a bench of bishops. This, more or less, was the deal eventually struck, though the Council held things up by failing to persuade James that the Bond of Association was not directed at him. Among other things, James's overture finally buried Castelnau's famous trip to Scotland; it also left his mother in a position where she could be sealed off from her allies in the outside world and, if occasion arose, done away with.[8] A new parliament was called for November, to give the nation's assent to as many of these matters as the queen was willing to let it deal with; in an atmosphere of national crisis, it was to enact draconian statutes against Catholic priests and Catholic propaganda.[9]

It was not until Castelnau left England in September 1585 that serious intelligence work needed to be resumed; there was indeed one undercover operation in the meantime, but its substance, so far as one can fathom it, was marginal to our story, though its consequences were germane. Otherwise, I have to record one last piece of Feron's work, which is nicely documented though fairly trivial, and a couple of loose ends.

Walter Williams turns up again in Walsingham's diary around the middle of August 1584: he must have come back from Wales with a tale of woe about how a gentleman in Monmouthshire had refused to sell back to him some land which he had sold when he had been harder up than he was now. Walsingham obliged by getting a number of eminent locals to swear an affidavit that Williams was 'not *compos mentis*', i.e. drunk, when he sold it. In return he was to do a job, or at least to give advice on a matter we should like to know more about. Walsingham made a note that he must 'confer' with him about something to do with Fagot.[10] This is an agreeable surprise, for two reasons: it is the only time that Fagot appears in the diary, or is mentioned from Walsingham's side except in the endorsements to his letters; and it is the only indication that Williams and Fagot had to do with each other, unless they had met at the time of Williams's first interview with Feron more than a year ago. During the major operations about the secret correspondence Herle, I suppose, had dealt with Fagot while Williams dealt with Feron, and it was only now that Herle had gone overseas that Williams and Fagot were to communicate; or so it seems. The note is also the only sign of life from Fagot for a whole year

---

8   Read, *Walsingham*, ii. 235ff; R. S. Rait and A. I. Cameron, *King James's Secret* (London, 1927).

9   Neale, *Elizabeth I and her Parliaments 1584–1601*, pp. 13–57, 94f; Diary, f. 97ʳ: bills to be drawn for queen's safety, harbouring priests, seditious books (mid-October 1584).

10 *Ibid.* ff. 90ʳ, 91ʳ, 91ᵛ (Fagot: see Plate VIII).

from about March 1584 to February 1585; one had supposed that he was too busy writing to take time off for espionage.

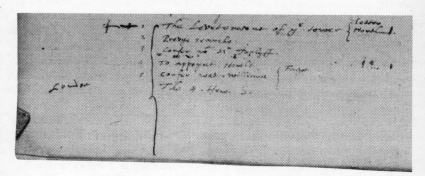

Plate VIII   Extract from Sir Francis Walsingham's office diary. British Library, Harleian Ms. 6035, f. 91v. Perhaps by the same hand as the endorsements in Plates IX and X.

If we take it that Williams was now to talk to Fagot about something, I should guess that the subject was the import of dangerous Catholic books through Salisbury Court. Fagot had complained about it from the beginning, and Walsingham, who had had other things on his mind, had now to do something about the heavyweight items that were coming in. In February 1585, when he was in Paris, Fagot was to repeat to Stafford his denunciation of the butler Girault for bringing in *Leicester's Commonwealth* and other works.[11] But I cannot think of a satisfactory reason for disturbing Fagot about this in the middle of August. Some kind of official complaint had been made to Castelnau on the subject towards the end of June; a large consignment of *Leicester's Commonwealth* was seized in London at the end of September, and set off something of a crisis.[12] But Fagot had nothing to do with this and the dates are remote. Perhaps the likeliest thing is that Fagot was to be asked to produce one or more copies of Allen's *Defence of Catholics*, which he would certainly have been happy to provide; and perhaps the reason for that was that William Parry, who was now, as I suppose, afoot on some undercover venture among Catholics, should have one to pass around.[13] But this is a shot in the dark: we do not know what inspired Fagot's only appearance in the diary, and Williams's last.

Meanwhile Feron was meeting Walsingham on his master's business, and passing him some scraps from the office;[14] but he did not break his silence

11   *GB*, Texts nos. 4, 9, 13, 15, 16.
12   *CSP Foreign 1583–84*, p. 559; Peck, *Leicester's Commonwealth*, pp. 5–7, 279–94.
13   W. Cobbett (ed.), *State Trials* (3 vols, London, 1809), i, coll. 1097, 1103, 1110; and below, p. 154.
14   *CSP Foreign 1584–85*, p. 11 (7/17-viii-1584); Nos. 41–4.

again until November, when he sent a racy account of some mildly comic goings-on in Salisbury Court which shows what we have lost by his taciturnity on other occasions. Patrick, Master of Gray, was by all accounts a pretty young man and one of the earliest of such to catch the eye of King James. In Paris the previous year he had flirted with Mary and her friends, and she had sent him a letter and a cipher in the same packet in which she had sent others to William Cornwallis.[15] Now he had changed tack, and James had sent him to London with instructions to launch his new understanding with Elizabeth. Mary was more or less au fait, but thought he could be made to change back; she sent him, how I do not know, a letter which awaited him at Salisbury Court when he arrived in London at the beginning of November. In it she told him, hopefully, how to conduct himself with people in London: confidentially with Courcelles, cautiously with a person to whom she gave the name 'Negoty' but who was evidently Castelnau, and not at all with Archibald Douglas. He was to insist on coming to see her, and if denied to communicate secretly via Courcelles.[16]

Naturally, the first thing Gray did was to get in touch with Douglas; then he went to see Castelnau, and was given his letter. He could not read it: either he had lost his cipher with Mary, or it was in a different one, or he was unable to decipher a letter even with the key in his hand. He gave it to Douglas, who took it back to Feron, who deciphered it. Before handing the letter to the knavish Douglas, Feron showed it to Castelnau; possibly Castelnau found him doing something that was meant to be kept from him. Castelnau was not pleased by Mary's description of him as a blunderer and a man of uncertain humour to whom Gray should not let on what he was really up to; nor by the instruction to deal with Courcelles, not with himself. He deftly rewrote the passage to say the opposite, and Douglas, smelling a rat, took the doctored letter back to Gray.[17]

15 No. 7 (above, p. ••); *HMC Hatfield*, iii, 12.
16 No. 45; *HMC Hatfield*, xiii, 253–8; Labanoff, vi, 14ff, with Feron's note pp. 26f; also. p. 48. The original of the note, with the 'demi-feuille' in BL Cottonian Nero B vi, no. 186 (f. 371), restores one phrase omitted by Labanoff. The revised version is in the hand of Archibald Douglas. Castelnau to Henri III, 15/25-xi-1584 (Chéruel, pp. 352–4), says that Mary has 'ces jours-icy' sent him 'plusieurs lettres en chiffres pour [the copy has, mistakenly, 'par'] ledit Gray'.
17 The original has: 'Quant au plus important et secret que vous aurez à m'impartir . . . adressez vous a Courselles . . . lequel vous ouvrira la voye pour m'escrire en chiffre. Vous vous pouvez fier audit Courcelles . . .' The rewrite, after 'impartir', goes on (*HMC Hatfield* version): 'Je manderay à l'ambassadeur de France qu'i[l] vous ouvre les voyes pour m'escrire; auquel vous vous pouvez fyer et l'employer en ce que vous avez à negocier par delà.' This replaces Courcelles by Castelnau as the person to be trusted; and consequently turns 'Negoty', the unreliable duffer, into somebody other than Castelnau, probably Courcelles. It was a highly economical, effective and unscrupulous rewriting, and Courcelles will not have forgiven Castelnau for it.

Feron kept in his drawer the uncensored 'half-leaf' of his decipherment. A day or two later, he met somewhere (en quelque lieu) an unnamed person who was surely Walter Williams. Williams, or whoever it was, asked him what was new, and 'considering that it was a long time since [he] had been able to do anything for [Walsingham]', Feron had told him the story. Williams asked him for the original page; Feron said there was no point since Douglas would already have passed his copy on: it is odd that he did not think Walsingham would be interested in the alterations. Williams persisted, and Feron handed the piece over the next day, with a long and chatty note to Walsingham which reveals a secure and contented ex-mole delivered from the panic in which his earlier communications had been made. He knew that Walsingham would look after him, and ended with an *envoi* which would have been perfectly conventional if he had signed it:

Quant a Monsieur l'ambassadeur il n'en a point receu de ce coste-la il y a long temps, et en atendant qu'il vienne quelque chose regardez en quoy je vous pourray servir, vous asseurant que je m'y emploiray d'aussy bon coeur que je prie Dieu, Monsieur, qu'il vous donne en parfaite sante heureuse et longue vye, avec accomplissement de tous voz desirs.

[As for M. the ambassador, he has had no letters from [Mary] for a long time, and while we are waiting for something to turn up see whether there is any way I can serve you. I assure you that I shall devote myself to it as heartily as I pray God, Monsieur, to grant you perfect health, a long and happy life, and the fulfilment of all your desires.]

The letter probably dates from just before 15 November 1584; it may then be that a note in the diary of that date – 'A letter to A. B. from the queene' – records Walsingham asking Elizabeth to write to Feron a note thanking him for his good work.[18] If so, I hope that this time she at least signed it with her own hand, for she owed rather a lot to him. So far as I am aware, no 'quelque chose' turned up during the months he remained at Salisbury Court. His mole-work was done, and his lively messages at an end; it would be nice to have had more of them, but three is quite as many as we have a right to expect.

18 Diary, f. 101ʳ: about the last item in the diary. If this is correct, Feron's note must be dated before this. Gray had not arrived, or not seen Castelnau, by the 4th/14th (Chéruel, p. 349), but he must have picked up his letters shortly after that, since on the 15th/25th Castelnau said he had communicated with him 'souvent' (above, n. 16); by Feron's account there must have been six or seven days between Gray receiving the letter and Feron sending his version. Somewhere between the 12th/22nd and 15th/25th seems right.

The laborious operations of the past eighteen months were now to be made unnecessary by sealing Mary off from the outside world. This entailed moving her from Sheffield to Tutbury in Staffordshire, and from the guardianship of the Earl of Shrewsbury to that of Sir Amyas Paulet, who would not let aristocratic camaraderie or 'foolish pity' interfere with the rigour of his regime.[19] It also entailed the political offensive against Thomas Morgan in Paris, for which Elizabeth had been thirsting for a year. This was actually not much better an idea than the abortive mission of Philip Sidney, and achieved little more: it did not secure the person of Morgan, who was detained comfortably in the Bastille, nor, due to the dexterity of Jean Arnault, his papers.[20] The anticipated arrival on Walsingham's desk of a mega-version of Feron's parcel did not occur, or at least did not occur for another year: I can hardly imagine that Walsingham thought it would. It is a tribute to Courcelles' management of the English end of Morgan's correspondence, and I think a sufficient answer to doubts about his loyalty, that despite the efforts of Feron and the capture of Throckmorton and More not a single item of it had so far fallen into the hands of Elizabeth and her ministers, and that they resorted to this desperate attempt to acquire it.

Hence Courcelles had to be got rid of. The natural conclusion from Feron's last offering was that Castelnau would not risk his skin by defending him, and would probably be relieved to see him go. The problem, as with Throckmorton, was to put up a case against Courcelles which would not incriminate his master; hence, I suppose, the failure to use Baldwin against him in October.[21] A solution emerged in the person of William Parry, whom we have seen hawking inflammatory Catholic books around London and may remember sitting by Castelnau's fireside the winter before helping the ambassador to put a packet of letters into the flames. On 8 February 1585 Parry was arrested on a charge of conspiracy to assassinate the queen a second time, more exactly of seeking to fulfil the vow of pious regicide he had made with Thomas Morgan a year ago, this time in the company of a young Catholic gentleman called Edmund Neville, who now denounced him. He was tried and convicted on 25 February, and executed on 2 March – a notably rapid exit, compared with Throckmorton's.[22] Walsingham's diary ends in December 1584, so we have none

19 Patrick Collinson, *The English Captivity of Mary Queen of Scots* (Sheffield, 1987), p. 4.
20 Above, pp. 23–5.
21 Above, p. 125.
22 Above, pp. 96, 129; to the authorities given there add Neale, *Elizabeth I and her Parliaments, 1584–1601*, pp. 39–41, 48–50.

of the light it gives us on Throckmorton's history to illuminate this extraordinary turnaround in Parry's.[23]

Since his conspiracies, and their connection with them, were the principal grounds for the expulsion of Courcelles and the attempt to get hold of Morgan, we can assume that the need to produce such grounds was one motive behind Parry's summary despatch; which is not necessarily to say that they were a motive for his arrest. To go deeper than this we should have to take a view about whether his dealings with Neville, which mainly occurred in August 1584, were more authentic than I have supposed his vow in Paris and his letters of February to have been. I do not myself believe that they were authentic, but this is not the place to thrash the question out. It seems enough to say here that, in February 1585, there may have been larger political reasons for recycling these five-month-old conversations, more or less independent of whether they had been genuine or not. I mention two of them.

Around Christmas 1584 relations between Elizabeth and her councillors were again in something of a crisis, which had arisen out of the Bond of Association against Mary, a statutory version of which was now going through Parliament, and more particularly out of proposals for a constitutionally radical form of government to be put in place if Elizabeth were to be assassinated. These, in the form of a Bill for the Queen's Safety, were put together by Burghley in January, and it seems clear that a ferocious argument about them came to a climax at the end of the month, after which they were dropped.[24] We may well think that Parry's downfall, which began with a denunciation by Neville on 6 February, had something to do with this. One's first thought would probably be that Parry was brought out of the woodwork to provide *actualité* for the contingency of the queen's murder, and to persuade Elizabeth to go along with the Council's view of what should be done afterwards. My reason for doubting this is that I do not believe that Elizabeth would have been at all impressed by a revelation that for the past five months or longer Parry had been planning to murder her. By now she knew him rather well, and there is good reason to believe that she appreciated his services to her. I have suggested that she had personally employed him in her campaign against Castelnau a year ago; more recently, when Parry as an MP had outraged the Commons by speaking vigorously against a bill imposing new and

---

23 There are two mentions in the Diary from August–September: ff. 89ᵛ ('To wrytte Mr. Parry'), 94ᵛ, apparently to talk to the queen about him; and one of Neville, in May (f. 76ᵛ), The two had been bracketed together as 'spies' by Lady Lee in January (PRO SP 12/167. no. 51).

24 Neale, *Parliaments*, pp. 44–53; Collinson, 'Monarchical Republic' (above, n. 6), p. 420; above, p. 128.

severe penalties upon Catholics, she had made herself very unpopular with
the members by defending him against them.[25] Now, I suspect, she threw
him to the hounds in Council and Parliament so as to get them off her
back and preserve the integrity of her crown. I have little doubt that Parry's
execution was a judicial murder and a grave discredit to whoever was
responsible for it. At his trial, he blamed Elizabeth personally, and perhaps
we ought to believe him.[26]

Parry's downfall must have given Castelnau a fright. True, the year-old
letters to Morgan and Paget, which would have appeared to compromise
him, were not produced in evidence;[27] the letter of indulgence from Cardinal Gallio, which had no doubt come via the embassy, was produced, but
no more was said about it than that Parry had received it at Greewich
on 31 March. All the same, I think Castelnau was terrified that his long
familiarity with Parry would land him in a worse disgrace than he had
escaped in the matter of Throckmorton; when William Waad arrived at
Salisbury Court on 23 February, two days before Parry's trial, with an
account of his treason and a demand for the expulsion of Courcelles, he
caved in once again. To Walsingham he said that Parry was a scoundrel, and
that whatever connection he might have had with Courcelles was nothing
to do with himself; to Elizabeth, if we are to trust what Courcelles said later,
he denounced his secretary as the worst villain in the world.[28]

Courcelles, meanwhile, wrote Walsingham a tough and, from a man who
has not seemed to possess the finesse of Jean Arnault, remarkably subtle
letter. In the guise of a humble secretary who would of course do what
the queen wanted, he managed to make two or three sharp jokes at Walsingham's expense, to send up the case against Parry, and to point out that,
in the matter of Throckmorton which Waad had also raised against him,
the man they really wanted was Castelnau. He gave a jolly account of a
dinner with Parry at which Parry had tried to get him to pass over
seditious books; and admitted that he had come across Throckmorton
once or twice passing through the garden at Salisbury Court: what was
Throckmorton *doing* in the garden but going to see Castelnau, and by
the back door? Perhaps his neatest stroke, which hit both Castelnau
and Walsingham at once, was to appeal to Throckmorton's 'confessions et
interrogatoires' to prove that he himself had had nothing to do with

---

25 Neale, *Parliaments*, p. 41; above, p. ••.

26 *State Trials*, i. coll. 1110, 1112: 'I here summon Queen Elizabeth to answer for my blood before
     God.'

27 As Hicks observed, 'The Strange Case of Dr. Parry', p. 356.

28 *CSP Foreign 1584–85*, p. 301; *CSP Scotland 1585–86*, p. 661; *1586–88*, p. 81. We might connect
     Castelnau's fears with his sending a bottle of white wine to Leicester on 21-ii/3-iii-1585: Adams,
     Household Accounts of . . . Leicester, p. 226.

Throckmorton's treason; he meant, of course, not the real confessions, which had probably by now disappeared, but the doctored version of them published for Castelnau's benefit in the *Discoverie*.[29] This salvo off his chest, he took himself off to Paris, where he could pursue the Catholic cause with fewer hindrances than in London. Should I repeat that he had *not* spent the past two years as Fagot's or Williams's or Walsingham's mole?

When Courcelles got on his boat at Rye or Dover he brought our story virtually to an end. With another six months on his hands in London Castelnau, like many a superannuated ambassador since, was writing his memoirs. Finally he went home with his sick wife at the end of September to attend, as his friend the historian Bernard du Haillan told him, the funeral of France. The Catholic League had launched a general rising in March, which coincided with the attempt to grab Morgan; if he had been handed over, they were ready to rescue him on the way. By July Henri III had had to come to terms with them by redistributing jobs and withdrawing toleration from Protestants.[30] In the new political climate Castelnau's recent performance in London, actual and suspected, did him no good at all; his career collapsed. The personnel of the new regime in Salisbury Court assembled. Arnault followed his sociable letters to Walsingham early in July; then Châteauneuf, the new ambassador, arrived with his wife and a train of Catholic *zelanti*, determined to present an altogether different face from the zany, convivial and leak-ridden ecumenism of Castelnau's establishment.

Bruno and Fagot, like Tweedledum and Tweedledee, remained with him to the end, returning to France with him by the passenger route while Girault took a cargo of household effects and a clutch of English seminary students from Gravesend. Just before leaving, Fagot had been grilled by Châteauneuf about his doings as a priest, about spies in the house, and about Castelnau's dealings with Archibald Douglas (who had now dropped him); as we should expect, he gave nothing away. Passing the news on in the last of his English messages to Walsingham, he offered to go on working for him in France.[31] What he did there and thereafter is none of our business now: it is intriguing, but no more, that Walter Williams turned up twice in Paris in the course of the following year, and may perhaps have

29 PRO SP 78/13, no. 18 (f. 41); *CSP Foreign 1584–85*, p. 261. Courcelles gives the date as 7 February (new style); but this is an obvious mistake for March, and the date is 25-ii/7-iii-1585.

30 BN V^C C 472, pp. 145 (Du Haillan), 189 (Arnault). The English envoy, William Waad, was actually seized by Leaguers on the way home, in case he was taking Morgan with him: *CSP Foreign 1584–85*, pp. 352, 416; BN fr 3181, f. 71; 4736, f. 302.

31 *GB*, pp. 58–61, and Text no. 15; *HMC Hatfield*, iii, 110 (Castelnau and Douglas); BN V^C C 472, p. 159; *CSP Foreign 1585–86*, p. 283.

seen him.[32] Whatever Williams was doing, he was not available to take part in Walsingham's culminating intelligence triumph against Mary in the spring and summer of 1586, during which his place was taken by Thomas Phellippes. Sadly, I can say nothing of Williams's history after this. Nor, just as sadly, can I say anything certain about Feron's. He was mentioned by Châteauneuf, when he interviewed Fagot, as one of the suspects in the house; so he must have been there until Castelnau left.[33] He will not have gone over to France; if he went back to his import-export business I can find no trace of it; he does not appear again in the registers of aliens or in the London tax records. What can have happened to him?

Perhaps we have one pointer; perhaps not. Two days before Castelnau left, on 21 September 1585, Walsingham wrote a note to Leicester from Barn Elms, enclosing a spy's report from Paris passed to him by Pallavicino.[34] The spy said that Madame de Châteauneuf had brought with her a Florentine 'who carrieth the name to be a great practiser'; Walsingham suggested that she should quietly be told to send him back. He added a postscript: 'The party recommended unto your Lordship and unto me gave me warning of this Florentine.'

We can only go so far in deciphering this delphic sentence. The Florentine was probably one Brancaleone, a member of the Franco-Florentine family of Gondi who acted as a contact with English Catholics during Châteauneuf's regime; if Madame de Châteauneuf was asked to send him home she did not oblige.[35] I take the recommendation to have come from Elizabeth, since it sounds rather official, and there would be reason to conceal her name; on both grounds I do not think it can have come from Castelnau, friendly as he was with Leicester at the time.[36] I exclude from figuring as the 'party' anyone who might have given the information but whose identity would not need to be hidden: among them William

---

32 *CSP Foreign 1586–88*, p. 130, 132f; *GB*, pp. 64–9, Texts nos. 16–18 (Fagot in Paris). Williams was also in Dieppe in August 1586 (BL Harleian 1582, ff. 104, 108).

33 *GB*, Text no. 15.

34 Bodleian Library, Tanner Mss. 78, f. 74. I am deeply grateful to Simon Adams for this piece of intelligence.

35 W[illiam] H[erle] to Queen Elizabeth, London, 20/30-xii-1585 (BL Cottonian Galba C viii, f. 203): 'Brancaleone a Florentine and near companion of Parry's, sometimes a follower of Sir E[dward] Hoby's, now governing the French Ambassador peacibly [?], is a person necessary to be noted as a malicious practiser, performer and intelligencer, near of kin to the bishop of Paris [Pierre de Gondi], by whom he is here maintained.'

36 Castelnau took over to France with him a servant of Leicester's called Henry Slyfield who wanted to see the country: Arthur Atye, Leicester's secretary, to Jean Hotman in Paris, 18/28-ix-1585 (Archives du ministère des affaires étrangères [Paris], Correspondance politique, Hollande, ii, f. 12). My thanks again to Simon Adams for passing on to me this letter and the previous one.

Herle, who sent the queen the same warning about Brancaleone three months later.[37]

That leaves us with our two sources of secret intelligence, Feron and Fagot. In favour of Feron is to be said: that he was certainly a 'party', as Williams had described him;[38] that he was staying in London and out of a job, so would be glad of Leicester's and Walsingham's patronage; and that he was entitled to a commendation from Elizabeth, which would have to be anonymous. There are points against him: we do not know that he told tales about what was going on in the house,[39] or that he did anything but pass letters, and it was almost a year since he had passed his last one; I should also be a little surprised if Walsingham had let Leicester into the secret about him. Both points may be wrong, and Feron is certainly a possible 'party'. Yet everything to be said in his favour is speculative, while there is something resembling hard evidence in favour of Fagot. A fortnight before Walsingham wrote to Leicester Fagot, in his letter to Walsingham about his interview with Châteauneuf, had told him about a 'méchant' Italian priest who was to succeed him, and he was to continue sniping at the same priest in a letter from France; he had also mentioned Brancaleone as an active member of Châteauneuf's household, though he had not exactly warned against him.[40] It seems clear that Brancaleone and the priest were two different individuals: nobody said that Brancaleone was a priest, and Fagot did not say that his priest was a Florentine. His report about the two of them brings Fagot very close to being Walsingham's 'party', but not quite there.

Then there is the recourse to the Earl of Leicester. It is in favour of Feron and against Fagot, since Feron would be in England and Fagot in France; but it may not be as strong as it looks. Leicester was off to the Netherlands to fight the Spaniards, and would have had to leave the recommendation in Walsingham's hands; we can believe that Walsingham continued to support Feron in England, but Fagot himself seems to say that Walsingham continued to support him in France.[41] Feron, so far as we

---

37 Above, n. 35; others in the same category would be Sylvanus Scory, recommended by Castelnau to Walsingham and Leicester in June–July (*CSP Foreign, 1584–85*, pp. 547, 584, 587), and John Florio, whom Castelnau left in charge of his affairs, with a testimonial which he sent to Walsingham on 18/28-ix-1585, three days before Walsingham's letter (Frances Yates, *John Florio* [Cambridge, 1934], pp. 65, 68f; *CSP Foreign, 1585–86*, p. 28).

38 Above, p. 45.

39 This assumes that Fagot, not Feron, was the source of *GB*, Text no. 10, and the 'party' there mentioned; but it may now be equally possible that the source was Feron, and the intermediary Williams rather than Herle.

40 *GB*, Texts nos. 15 and 16.

41 *GB*, Text no. 16, Fagot to Walsingham, Paris, about New Year 1586: 'Monseigneur, je vous doibz beaucoup d'obligation pour les benefices et biens que je [= j'ai] receuz journellement de vous . . .'

know, had no claim on Leicester, whereas Fagot had done his best to stop
the diffusion via the embassy of the scandalous *Leicester's Commonwealth*,
for which Leicester, if he knew about it, would certainly have been grateful.[42] That is about all we can say. There would be more to say if Fagot
and Giordano Bruno were the same person, since Bruno had been complimentary to Leicester in print, and by his public devotion to Philip
Sidney had virtually made himself a member of Leicester's clientele.[43] But
this is a consideration we must ignore. Altogether, Fagot seems just about
the more likely 'party'. Our story ends with what, on balance, seems to be
Walsingham's only direct acknowledgement of the person who had
given him the opportunity for his coup; it does not tell us who that person
was.

42   *GB*, Text no. 13; above, p. 129.
43   Bruno, *Dialoghi italiani*, pp. 67–70; he had just published *Degli eroici furori*, dedicated to Sidney.
     Giovanni Aquilecchia, 'Tre schede su Bruno e Oxford', *Giornale critico della filosofia*, lxxii (1993),
     pp. 389–93, argues that relations between Bruno and Leicester were now cool.

Endpiece

ONE OF THE PLEASURES of writing about secret intelligence, in the present state of intellectual haute couture, is that those who are concerned in it are looking for facts. Nobody pays good money for pieces of discourse; and Walsingham agreed with the adage about the *Manchester Guardian* that facts were expensive.[1] I have been telling a story about how he acquired some facts; about the circumstances in which they were acquired, and about what was done with them then. Sir Francis has a high reputation in this field, and the story will not have diminished it: we have something to add to the corpus of knowledge about how he worked, and consequently something to say about how his oeuvre as a 'spymaster' or mole-breeder should be judged.

The sharpest question that arises is whether he, or his queen or his colleagues, was not so much discovering facts as inventing them: promoting and nurturing sham plots, eliciting phoney confessions, tampering with evidence, in order to discredit the Catholic mission, to procure the death of Mary, or to persuade the population to acquiesce in a repressive political and social regime. We have seen this line being taken by Catholic historians like Pollen (prudently) and Hicks (less prudently) against defenders of Walsingham and the regime like Conyers Read; it has been revived by writers under influences ranging from John Le Carré to Michel Foucault, discovering in this region a secret theatre or a culture of surveillance.[2]

Our story has something to say about this: it says, or at least it seems to say, that Walsingham and Williams, via Fagot and Feron, were finding out things about real goings-on, and defending the realm against Catholic aggression. But it would not be fair to present this conclusion without saying something about a more famous case in which invention has been alleged, the events surrounding and including the Babington plot, which

---

1   Charles Nicholl, *The Reckoning: the Murder of Christopher Marlowe* (London, 1992), p. 105; but he seems to be quoting Read, *Walsingham*, i, 24, not Walsingham himself.

2   Nicholl, above, n. 1; John Michael Archer, *Sovereignty and Intelligence* (Stanford, CA, 1993).

began a year or so after Feron had finished his work. Apart from Walsingham, those whose part in them I need to describe are, once again, Mary's activist servant Thomas Morgan, and a seminary drop-out called Gilbert Gifford.

In May and June 1586 the rich young gentleman Anthony Babington, whom we have met selling Catholic books out of Salisbury Court in 1584, conspired in London with a soldier-priest called John Ballard and others to run a *coup d'état* which would comprise a general Catholic rising, an invasion, the assassination of Elizabeth and the liberation and triumph of Mary. The scheme had been set on by Morgan and Bernardino de Mendoza in Paris. It was short-lived, totally theoretical, riddled with holes, and hamstrung by Babington's own political and theological doubts; but it certainly existed.

It was not, therefore, a purely theatrical exercise. The most likely way to get it into the category of sham plots has been to make it subordinate to another plot going on at the same time: a plot by Walsingham to bring about Mary's death. This is not an absurd idea: to do it justice we have to look carefully at the part played by Gilbert Gifford, who before his ordination was a young Catholic gentleman like Babington. Gifford arrived in London from Paris at Christmas 1585, sent by Morgan with a letter of recommendation to Mary, but mainly with the mission of getting from the English authorities some kind of welcome for a movement of dissident seminary priests to be set up in opposition to the missionaries and Jesuits.

On this errand he talked to Walsingham, who was moderately interested in the priestly schism but very interested in the chance that Gifford might make himself *persona grata* at the French embassy, and so take on the position of postman to and from Mary which had been vacant for over a year. His success in checkmating Castelnau's efforts had been all too complete, and a pile of Morgan's packets had accumulated in Châteauneuf's house which, as always, Walsingham was most anxious to inspect. Gifford proved willing to play the part of Throckmorton or Baldwin; the embassy was persuaded; and a complicated but effective system was set up in which the correspondence back and forth could be read by both Mary and Walsingham. So his third attempt to break into the communications between Mary, Morgan and others was a great success, producing a pile of confidential papers much larger and more intimate than what had been passed by Feron.

It does not constitute a 'plot': it was a perfectly proper scheme for achieving what Walsingham had been trying to do for a very long time. Where plot and 'theatre' may come in is in the consequences which followed from Gifford's establishing himself as a valued servant of Mary and the postman for her correspondence. Once Babington and Ballard had floated their enterprise, he was the man to pass their communications to and from Mary. They told her what they intended; she replied that she was delighted; Walsingham, via his decipherer Thomas Phellippes, read everything; Mary had at last, by her own hand, convicted herself of treason. This does not constitute a plot either: it revealed real facts. What may constitute a plot is that Gifford took part in the conspiracy: certainly by encouraging Babington to go on with it after he had got cold feet; and possibly by being, with Ballard and Babington, one of its original authors. Pollen, who examined the question with great exactitude, decided that there were no grounds for the graver insinuation; the less grave, of keeping Babingon at it until written evidence of Mary's consent had been acquired, may certainly be thought to be a dirty trick, but the gambit seems to me in the circumstances not to be really discreditable, and not to turn the plot, feeble as it was, into a piece of puppetry.[3]

The one recourse remaining to anyone who wishes to claim Babington's plot as a piece of theatre is to allege that Thomas Morgan was himself an agent provocateur. But it follows from our story that this can really not be so. By pursuing the identity of our mole, we have been able to scotch the idea that Morgan was a double agent, a creator of sham plots or even an 'exile-adventurer'. While Arnault was thought to be the mole, the case was just about credible; since Feron was the mole, and had nothing to do with Morgan in his life, it collapses. Charges against Morgan arose from a feud among Catholic émigrés and turned up nothing worthwhile except that he had had relations with a number of people who were or turned out to be on the other side, and had commended most of them to Mary at one time or another. He probably, when he was under heavy suspicion in Paris, made an offer to change sides. But he was not a long-term traitor to Mary or a systematic agent provocateur: now that we have straightened out the history of Jean Arnault we can be quite sure of this. From what we know of him, Morgan appears a compulsive conspirator with a knack of finding the wrong man; but most of our knowledge comes from one point in his career, and if we knew more about him we might find him to be a perfectly serious political figure, who did a good deal to maintain the traditionalist forces among the Elizabethan aristocracy, and to keep Mary in contact with them and with her allies abroad. The cause of his difficulties was that he could not cope with the predominance in Catholic activities acquired by the missionary movement and the invasion of his political preserves by Allen and Parsons: fighting on two fronts narrowed

3 I summarise the account in J. H. Pollen, *Mary Queen of Scots and the Babington Plot* (Scottish History Society, 3rd Series, iii, Edinburgh, 1922).

his opportunities and probably affected his judgment, which may well have
been too sanguine anyway.[4]

By identifying our mole we get rid of a creative Thomas Morgan; we
also get rid of what might have seemed an attractive alternative, a creative
Courcelles. If Courcelles had been Castelnau's mole, as there had at one
point been good reason for supposing, there would have been almost no
limit to the dirty tricks he might have performed by way of Throckmorton or Parry or Morgan or Babington or whomever. But he was not: his
Catholic zeal was genuine, and so were his talents, and he devoted both
to the service of Mary and the overthrow of Elizabeth. Do we then fall
back on Fagot (or Bruno), who was certainly working on behalf of
Walsingham and Elizabeth, and was in almost as good a position as
Courcelles for the invention of sham plots? His creativity did indeed
extend to inventing a plot in order to have something to report; but this
is the opposite of acting as an agent provocateur, and Walsingham knew a
fiction when he saw one.[5] Fagot was simply an informant.

If we look down the other side of our cast list, we get two more negative answers and one positive one. William Herle had probably invented
a sham plot in the past, for Burghley, and was evidently willing to do the
same again; he even seems to have had an opportunity.[6] But what he did
was to pass on information. Walter Williams's uncomfortable stay in the
prison at Rye was apparently intended to set him up as a spy in Paris; but
it was a flop, and thereafter he served Walsingham as a competent and confidential servant, dealing with his informants, passing (we suppose) their
packages, looking after their interests and keeping them out of trouble. He
invented nothing. William Parry is another kettle of fish, and he has a place
in our story. I cannot think that any serious person would deny that he
was the author of one sham plot (with Morgan), and it is a good question whether he was not the author of another (with Neville): he is our
one recognisably theatrical character, though we cannot be sure that he
was theatrical all through.

It is risky, and would take us too far out of our way, to say much more
than this. But I may as well state what his interventions in our story have
prompted me to conclude about some of the questions which arise in his
perplexing case. First: In so far as he was an agent provocateur, who set
him on? Not necessarily anyone. Much of what he did (his vow with

4   Above, chap. 1; E. C. Butler and J. H. Pollen, 'Dr William Gifford in 1586', *The Month*, ciii (1904),
    243–58, 348–66; Read, *Walsingham*, ii, 429–33; my 'Character of Elizabethan Catholicism', in T.
    Aston (ed.), *Crisis in Europe, 1560–1660* (London, 1965), pp. 238f, and *GB*, pp. 66ff.
5   *GB*, pp. 34–7, and Texts nos. 11 and 11a.
6   Read, *Lord Burghley and Queen Elizabeth*, pp. 45f; *GB*, Text no. 5: Herle to Burghley, 15/25-xi-1583.

Morgan, perhaps his dealings with Neville) I think he did on his own initiative, as a loyalist Catholic seeking to separate the sheep from the goats,
and of course expecting his reward. What he did not do on his own initiative (say, planting his letters on Castelnau) I think he did on the queen's
suggestion, not on Walsingham's. If we knew what the two of them had
to say about Parry at the interview recorded in Walsingham's diary in September 1584 we should have a better idea; but the diary gives us no clue.
Second: Was Parry's extraordinary pro-Catholic speech in Parliament
another piece of theatre in the present sense? (It was certainly a *coup de
théâtre* in the usual sense.) That is: was it intended to certify his Catholic
bona fides so that he could continue his infiltration of Catholic circles?
No: I think it was genuine. Parry, I take it, thought that most English
Catholics were loyalists like himself, that they should not be persecuted,
and that the queen agreed with him. Third: Assuming that Parry had simply
been playing the part of a conspirator, how did his comedy come to end
as a comi-tragedy? I think we ought to recognise how close Parry had
come to Elizabeth in the year since his return from France: I have guessed
that she had set him on against Castelnau, and she had just shielded him
against the wrath of the House of Commons; I should not be astonished
if she had actually put him up to make his speech. Now, I think, she let
him go, a sacrifice designed to pre-empt the enactment of a statute which,
if she were to be assassinated, would deliver the realm into the hands of a
junta of Protestant magnates. Whether this supposition is correct or not,
Parry's story was a sinister precedent all round, and illustrates a general
decay of decency on both sides.[7]

Parry set apart, we have a plain tale about the acquisition from Feron
of some inside information, first about a danger to the realm, then about
Castelnau's attitude to it. No miracles were achieved: if they had been, it
would not have been necessary to put Throckmorton on the rack. But
things were found out which enabled the queen and her ministers to
respond a good deal more effectively than they might otherwise have
done.

When she was put on trial for treason in October 1586, Mary accused
Walsingham of forgery and conspiracy against her. In his answer, he distinguished between his private and his public person: as a private person,
he said, he had 'done nothing unbeseeming an honest man'; as a public
person, he had done nothing 'unworthy of [his] place'.[8] The problem about
this is not so much to know what he thought it was proper for a secre-

---

7 Above, pp. 96–99 and 133f; Diary, f. 94ᵛ; Collinson, 'The Monarchical Republic of Queen
   Elizabeth I', 420.
8 Read, *Walsingham*, iii, 53, from *State Trials*, i, 1182.

tary of state to do which was not proper in daily life, but to know where
he drew the line between the public and the private. The results of his
'curiosity' in the searching out of practices against the realm seem to transcend the distinction. Was Walter Williams a public person? He had been
in official employment as a messenger, and was to be again, but there is
no sign that he was so employed during the time of our story. He appears
to me to have been running Walsingham's house in Seething Lane and
was being paid by him as a personal servant: that is how he had started,
and that is how everybody describes him. Hence the list of his jobs in
November 1583 which included doing something about some trees and
seeing to the seclusion of the detained messenger George More.[9] William
Herle had started as a client, though not a household servant, of
Burghley, and was very anxious to persuade Burghley that that was still
his status; but he was perhaps deceiving him with Leicester,[10] and was by
now in fairly continuous public employment and soon to be appointed
ambassador. Until then he does not appear to have had a salary. The 'secret
money' which came from official funds, about the amount of which there
has been some dispute, must have gone to people like Fagot and Feron,
and probably to Fowler and Douglas too. But Walsingham is generally
thought to have spent a lot of his own money on his informants, I imagine
to keep them going when big occasions like the Throckmorton investigation or Feron's parcel were not opening the Crown's coffers.[11] This is a
primitive state of affairs. When we are told about the history of the Elizabethan secret service we may think of a headquarters, archives, ranks of
officers, job descriptions, pensions.[12] What we find is Walter Williams. It
is household government, if any; and not, in general, the household of
the queen, but the households of her ministers. Hence the difficulty of

---

9   His job at Seething Lane seems to have been taken over by Walsingham's young cousin Thomas
    Walsingham around autumn 1584 (Nicholl, *The Reckoning*, pp. 116f).

10 *GB*, Texts nos. 5 and 7.

11 Read, *Walsingham*, i, 432, 435f (Beale); Nicholl, *The Reckoning*, pp. 104, 109; above, pp. 87, 106.
    Alan Haines, *Invisible Power: the Elizabethan Secret Services* (Stroud, Glos., 1992), produces some
    huge figures apparently collected by Robert Cecil in 1610, but gives no reference.

12 This seems the danger in the *story* of Marlowe in Nicholls's *The Reckoning*, though the descrip-
    tive chapter 13 is fine, and goes a lot deeper than either Haines (above, n. 11), which is lively but
    overblown, or Alison Plowden, *The Elizabethan Secret Service* (Hemel Hempstead, 1991), a sensi-
    ble and unpretentious narrative. Penry Williams, *The Tudor Regime* (London, 1979), pp. 278f says
    that Elizabethan secret agents were professionals, whereas Thomas Cromwell in Henry VIII's
    reign, as described in G. R. Elton, *Policy and Police* (London, 1972), had only casual and unpaid
    informers. This may confuse the actual spies, some of whom may be thought professionals, with
    agents or 'controls' like Williams and Pallavicino, who were not. Perhaps Thomas Phellippes
    was or became one, but he played a very small part in this story. Nicholas Faunt insisted that
    the Secretary's secret work should be done by his own servants, not by 'inferior officers' of the
    Crown: C. Hughes (ed.), 'Nicholas Faunt's "Discourse touching the Office of Principal
    Secretary of State" (1592)', *English Historical Review*, xx (1905), 500f.

knowing where Walsingham was drawing the line, and some of the difficulty of knowing whether we should go along with his defence, which in general I think we should. If Walsingham had two bodies, so did Castelnau, and one of them was the body of Walsingham's friend.

We can be sure that one of the things which fell into the domain of the public person was the extraction of information by torture. If we have in mind the image of an institutional secret service, we shall expect this to be something it will be doing. If we do, we shall, here again, be getting the wrong end of the stick. I have said that the two methods of acquiring information did not fall into the same category. Unlike espionage, torture was a public matter. Otherwise unprovided for in the law of England, its use in cases of danger to the realm and sometimes in others, which occurred during a period of some eighty years straddling the 1580s, required a public exercise of the royal prerogative, usually by the Council.[13] It was part of the legal process, though it was not clear whether its results could be used as evidence in court; informally, it was subject to the restraints of public criticism and, in Elizabeth's case, of embarrassment in the face of her fellow-princes. The persons to whom authority was given had nothing to do with the business of secret intelligence: to pass from this to torture, as in Throckmorton's case, was to cross an important frontier.

Two Elizabethans are famous for having done it, or supervised it: Thomas Norton, who interrogated Throckmorton and apparently most of those arrested after him, and Richard Topcliffe. Both were men of considerable standing: one did not send warrants for torture to people like Walter Williams. Norton's distinction was intellectual and political: blessed with a sinecure in the city of London, he was 'man of business' to the Council, parliament man, playwright, translator of Calvin's *Institutes* and a great deal else. He did not, as has been supposed, spend a year in Rome spying on the English College. He was not part of any secret service. He was employed in interrogation because he was a determined anti-papist who did many jobs for councillors, and because he had ideas about the most effective way of doing it. He had had some success against Campion and other priests, and had more success against Throckmorton; Elizabeth publicly thanked him for his work. He was under public control: he would obviously have liked to put Henry Howard on the rack, as much to further a vendetta against Howard and his family as to ensure the security of the realm; but he was not allowed to. He died in the middle of our story.[14]

13 J. H. Langbein, *Torture and the Law of Proof* (Chicago/London, 1977), chap. 6, though his list of warrants for torture is dependent on the printed Privy Council registers, and hence has nothing for 1582–6, when they are missing.

14 Graves, *Thomas Norton*, pp. 126, 243–78.

Richard Topcliffe's eminence was social only: his wife was the daughter of a peer, and he had some connection with the queen, possibly from having served in her household when she was young. He was another parliament man, though not of Norton's stature; and he appears to have got into the business of torture by way of a good deal of voluntary work pursuing papists in London. Everybody agrees that the consequences were a grave blot on the reputation of the queen and her councillors, who made inadequate efforts to restrain him: Topcliffe had, in the words of an immortal description of his career, 'an unmistakeable and nauseating relish in the performance of his duties'. At one point he is said to have been permitted to use torture in his own house in Westminster because too much of it in the Tower was going down badly with the public. If this was so, as I think it was, it was a violation of distinctions proper even in this dismal matter. It does not make him part of an Elizabethan secret service. His career as an interrogator was indeed perfectly continuous with his hunting of priests, but that was not at all secret, any more than his supervision of their executions.[15] We can see the difference from an occasion in the spring of 1586, when Topcliffe's colleague and fellow-interrogator, the London Justice of the Peace Richard Young, had to be warned off arresting Walsingham's two most successful workers, the spy Thomas Rogers and the manipulator of Mary's correspondence Gilbert Gifford.[16] We do not in any case have to associate Walsingham with Topcliffe's heyday as a torturer, since it happened after his death. There are indeed two references to him in the memo book of 1583–4. In August 1584 he is to be conferred with at the same time as Williams is to be asked to do something about Fagot: I have supposed that Fagot was to get information about the import of Catholic books, and since the memo about Topcliffe follows one which says 'privy search', we can suppose that Topcliffe was to conduct the search and Williams, via Fagot, to get some inside information from the distribution end. The other mention is in December 1583, when it looks very much as if he was sent for to interrogate William Shelley, the principal witness against the Earl of Northumberland, since Norton and the rest were overworked;[17] if that is so, then Walsingham as a public person did introduce Topcliffe to his nasty career, and we cannot know whether he would have disapproved of it as much as he ought to have done.

15   Everyone should read the classic account (quoted) by S. T. Bindoff, in Hasler, *The House of Commons, 1558–1603*, iii, 513–5 or A. O. Meyer, *England and the Catholic Church under Queen Elizabeth* (London, 1916; repr. 1967), pp. 183f. Also *DNB*; CRS v; Neale, *Elizabeth I and her Parliaments 1584–1601*, index, and a good deal more.
16   Read, *Walsingham*, ii, 333; Pollen, *Queen Mary and the Babington Plot*, pp. lvi, clxxi.
17   Diary, ff. 91ᵛ; 42ᵛ – 'To know who shall examine Shelley'; 43ʳ – Shelley to come to Seething Lane; (next item) 'To send to Topcliff'.

Walsingham's forte, and perhaps his passion, was secret intelligence in the strict sense, and we have now a fairly good idea of how he worked in one case, to add to what is known about others. It is right to remember that his talents were not superhuman, and to consider criticisms which have been made of him, then and since. Conyers Read thought that in making the French embassy the object of his attention rather than the Spanish, he was barking up the wrong tree. The first answer to this is probably that Mendoza's establishment was impregnable: he kept himself to himself, as he was forced to do. Or it might be, if we think that his later establishment in Paris did not prove impregnable to Stafford, that the manoeuvres which would have been required to make an impression on it, like posing as a closet Catholic and letting such as Henry Howard loose as a go-between, were not available to Walsingham.[18] The second answer is that Castelnau's establishment was both very leaky and a good deal closer to treasonable dealings than Read supposed: if it had been completely open to Walsingham, he would have found out all he needed to know. It was not completely open, because Courcelles, who had all the secrets, was not to be won. Feron did not know everything, though he knew just about enough, and it was only by the providential intervention of Fagot that he was persuaded to pass on his knowledge; perhaps, if Fagot had not turned up, he would have found another way of making contact, but on his own he might well have been too frightened to risk it. Anyway, Feron did the trick, and Walsingham's gambit was vindicated.

On his mode of operation we need to take notice of a criticism from very near at hand, made by his secretary Nicholas Faunt.[19] Faunt, citing the Ockhamist principle 'frustra fit per plura quod fieri potest per pauciora' (it is futile to invent more agencies to do what can be done by fewer), said that Walsingham employed too many people, which bred 'much confusion with want of secrecie and dispatch'. Looking at the gang of informants clustered in and around Salisbury Court, we may feel that Faunt was right; but Fowler was got rid of and Douglas, who certainly looks like a spare wheel for the time being, was probably a good investment for the future. The essential arrangements were most economical, and there is no case at all for complaining about secrecy. Feron's identity was kept secret, and so was (possibly is) Fagot's. Walsingham was aghast at having to leave their security in the hands of Elizabeth and Burghley, and with reason: it is only due to their indiscretion in keeping Williams's letter that we know about Feron, and indeed about Williams. I have no doubt that Williams was Walsingham's contact with Fowler before he worked

18   Read, *Walsingham*, ii, 385f, and his 'The Fame of Sir Edward Stafford', 292–313.
19   Hughes, 'Nicholas Faunt's Discourse', pp. 500f; also Beale, in Read, *Walsingham*, i. 427.

with Feron; but in all Fowler's voluminous correspondence we have no confirmation of this; Williams, on principle, put virtually nothing down on paper. If Faunt had been right, it would have been a good deal easier to disentangle this story.

In so far as Faunt was talking about Walsingham's office, which he knew well, what he says seems fair in principle but, in this case at least, untrue in fact. Tomson, the head of it, the filing clerk 'E', whom we shall meet shortly, and probably Faunt himself knew something about Fagot, though possibly not who he was. Faunt was away in the summer of 1583, but it looks as if he compiled the 'book of secret advertisements' and perhaps he was the man who was deputed to compile the evidence against Castelnau. In that case he will have known about Feron, as Tomson did; unless, that is, both of them took him to be Courcelles. The memo book, which everybody read, was perfectly discreet. Few of Feron's papers seem to have come into the office at all, certainly not the parcel; Fagot's drifted around in a loose-looking kind of way, but nothing came of it. A mole among the clerks should have worked out what was going on, but there was no such person: all of them had, what Faunt required, a 'conscience'.[20]

Among more important persons, the queen evidently knew about both Fagot and Feron, though much was kept from her: she was not told about the 'messengers' until very late in the day, or allowed to read Feron's notes. Walsingham will rightly have mistrusted her inclination to put her foot into matters of secret intelligence, and also her way of flaunting before ambassadors what she could tell them if she would. Burghley had had to be let in on the secret when Walsingham was sent to Scotland; Mildmay, and presumably others, was shown the book of secret advertisements; Leicester knew about Fagot, probably from Herle and then from Walsingham himself, but I doubt if he knew about Feron.[21] I doubt if other councillors, like Hatton, were told anything at all. Beale, the secretary of the Council, must have known about the operation in general, but his statement that Walsingham had corrupted 'some of [the ambassador's] secretaries' does not suggest that he knew anything very exact.[22] Faunt was firm about a Secretary's colleagues being kept out of secret intelligence, but not I think any firmer than Walsingham.

I expect there is somewhere a set of further rules which anyone running an enterprise in secret intelligence ought to follow. I can think of three, which Walsingham seems to me to have kept more religiously than others.

---

20 For Tomson, Faunt and Francis Mylles, see Hasler, *The House of Commons, 1558–1603*, ii, 109; iii, 114, 511; and *DNB* for Tomson and Faunt. For 'E', see below, 'A Note on the Date'.

21 Above, pp. 75, 101, 137.

22 Read, *Walsingham*, i, 436; above, p. 13.

One would be, not to let your left hand know what your right hand is doing. Williams, I should think, knew everything that was going on. Fowler knew nothing about Fagot or Feron. Fagot, once he had facilitated the original contact with Feron, appears to have been kept in the dark about what Feron was doing, and they were perhaps told to stay apart. Williams, who kept in touch with Feron, had nothing to do with Fagot from the beginning until the summer of 1584, when the serious business was over; Herle, brought in to keep in touch with Fagot, knew nothing so far as I can see about Feron, and probably nothing about Williams either until they met, or so I imagine, to celebrate the end of the operation. Elizabeth and perhaps Burghley seem to have thought that Walsingham was using two (or four) people where one (or two) would do: hence Williams's protest against putting in someone else, possibly Herle, to do his job; hence also Burghley's breach of the rules in receiving a letter from Feron via Douglas, if that is what he did.[23]

Another rule would be, not to do anything which would reveal that knowledge had been obtained clandestinely, and so endanger its source. Walsingham scores high on this: delaying for 'divers months' the arrest of Throckmorton and More; suppressing much of the evidence assembled against Castelnau; rigidly controlling what was allowed to appear at Throckmorton's trial; leaving Baldwin free. Exposure in this way was a nightmare for Feron, as it must be for anyone in his position; it is clear that Walsingham and Williams did well by him on this score, and fairly clear that Elizabeth, left to herself, would have blown everything up. To those who worked for him Walsingham extended patience, consideration and restraint in the use of knowledge; he also, so far as we can see, extended aftercare. We do not know what Feron got in this respect, unless Walsingham's note to Leicester is about him, which I doubt. But Fagot appears to have been looked after until he went over to Stafford, which was not forgiveable; More was quietly taken care of, no doubt by Williams; and so long as Throckmorton appeared to have changed sides Walsingham put a lot of effort into attending to him in his distracted state.[24] The only person in our story who got a really bad deal was William Parry, and I do not think that was Walsingham's doing.

Our story of secret intelligence is also a story about Elizabethan politics, and in the first place of things that failed to happen. England was preserved from an invasion, and possibly from a civil war. It is perfectly possible that the invasion scheme which Throckmorton was promoting would

23 Above, pp. 77, 121, 128.
24 Fagot: *GB*, Text no. 16. More: above, pp. 80–1. Throckmorton: Diary, ff. 39ᵛ ('To sende a man of myne to attende on Throgmorton'), 49ʳ, 53ʳ, 75ᵛ.

not have got off the ground anyway, but I would not be too sure of that. The forces of political Catholicism in western Europe were extremely strong in 1583 and 1584, and if King Philip was less keen on an English enterprise than the pope and the Duke of Guise it was because he was preoccupied with the recovery of the Netherlands, which was going so well that an intervention in England might begin to seem inevitable. English Catholic loyalism had been eroded by an infusion of zeal, an unmanageable force whose impact transcended the conversion of souls: hence Throckmorton. If there had been an invasion it would have recruited some support and, if it had been preceded by the queen's assassination, as its proponents recommended, would have led to something very nasty indeed.[25]

Throckmorton's exposure also put the lid on an alternative possibility, much canvassed in 1583 and at one point attractive to Walsingham himself, of a deal between Elizabeth and Mary. This looks like a non-starter now, and it was sabotaged from the start by Mary's preference for the scheme of invasion. But it struck a chord with Elizabeth, partly I think because it seemed to open a way to the reconciliation with her Catholic subjects of which Henry Howard spoke in his letter to Mary.[26] Elizabeth's anger about Throckmorton's revelations, and her fury with Castelnau, whom she supposed to have been wheedling her into lowering her defences by a treaty with Mary while secretly conspiring with Mary against her, seems to me a testimony that she had taken the idea seriously.

A settlement with Mary was now out of the question, and her execution, one would suppose, became much more probable. In fact it was nearly a year before anything was done in this direction, while Mary was let off from bearing any of the consequences of her connection with Throckmorton. In the end she was answered, in the autumn of 1584, by the Council's invention of the Bond of Association against her, obliging innumerable subjects to pursue her to the death if there were any attempt to assassinate Elizabeth, whether Mary was privy to it or not.[27] It is generally thought to have been a reaction to the assassination of William of Orange in July, and no doubt was; but it was also a response to Throckmorton and his conspiracy, delayed and given a twist by the problems that had arisen in the meantime. It had been impossible to deal with Throckmorton before dealing with Castelnau, and was impossible to deal with Mary before dealing with Throckmorton; the form that the dealing with Castelnau had taken made it impossible to use Throckmorton as a weapon

25 See my 'The Heart of Robert Persons', in McCoog, *The Reckoned Expense*, pp. 148–50.
26 Above, p. 72.
27 Above, p. 127.

against Mary. I have doubted that William Parry was simply brought in to fill the vacant space; but it does seem perfectly proper to see his execution as some kind of a substitute for Mary's.[28] Mary then locked away, Courcelles dismissed, Castelnau in chains, there was nothing that secret intelligence could do about her for another year.

This seems to be what our story has to say about the most immediate aspect of the security of the realm, its security against Mary. But probably its most interesting contribution to the history of Elizabethan politics is that, in this case, secret intelligence was used by Walsingham, and his colleagues on the Council so far as they were au fait, against the queen, to promote a longer-term view of the security of the realm than she seems to have had herself. Walsingham certainly, and Burghley perhaps, thought at this time that the principal negative object of English policy must be to prevent a Catholic alliance of the Spaniards and the French against the country. So, generally, did Elizabeth: it had been the main political motive behind her prolonged affair with Anjou.[29] By the summer of 1583 this had run on the rocks; a symbol of the wreckage, rather perhaps than a serious proposition in itself, was the continuous murmuring about a deal between Anjou and Spain. It has been said that English policy now marked time for a while;[30] I think we can now see that the hiatus was due to the revelation of the Catholic invasion scheme, and more to the Council's preoccupation with preventing Elizabeth's furious reaction to it from ruining relations with France at the same time as she broke them off with Spain. It was a good six months before the struggle was settled in the Council's favour and they could begin, while taking precautions against Mary, to shepherd Elizabeth towards an active intervention in the collapsing Dutch Republic, while remaining relatively sure that, when Philip retaliated, he would not have a rabidly hostile France on his side.

This was a gamble, the result of which as time went by began to look very uncertain. The idea that relations between states could be conducted without respect to religion, attractive as it was to so many of the politically aware in all countries, had turned out to be, not exactly a mirage, but a great deal easier to proclaim than to practise. It had proved so for Elizabeth in England, and for William of Orange in the Netherlands; it was proving so, despite a heavy investment in it by the Crown and its servants, in France. Castelnau's predecessor as ambassador, La Mothe Fénelon,

---

28   Pollen, 'Dr Parry', 358 is surely right to say that Parry was 'the first victim' of the Bond of Association.

29   Walsingham: above, p. 96. Burghley: Kingdon, introduction to *The Execution of Justice*, p. xxxii, but cf. above, p. 94. MacCaffrey, *Queen Elizabeth and the Making of Policy*, pp. 285–301 (Anjou and the French alliance), 456f (on Burghley's withdrawal from foreign policy).

30   *Ibid.* p. 303.

a man of weighty opinions whose instincts were of this kind, had summed up his experience of seven years in London:

> It is obvious enough that nowadays the whole of Christendom is split in two, and that princes and peoples are divided and in such a state of mistrust and hostility to one another on account of religion that it is impossible to make any serious arrangement [de pouvoir rien establir de bien asseuré] between those whose religion is different.[31]

If Fénelon's view was correct, the outlook for England was not good. It turned out to be just too strong, but it was touch and go, in the small world of Castelnau's embassy and in the larger world of the country he represented. Castelnau, against some advice from his best friend,[32] had spent a great deal of time in London trying to prove that Fénelon was wrong. Now his attempt had collapsed, undermined not only by obdurate external difficulties and schism in his household, but by a nagging counter-persuasion in himself. Hence his shift or drift towards collaborating with the forces of Catholic zeal, which was partly a reinsurance for the future (futile, as it turned out), but partly a matter of simply facing facts of honour, even of conscience. We can agree that he had drawn the line at what, in his view, would have turned him into one of Garrett Mattingly's ambassadors of ill-will.[33] But it had been a close shave, and Elizabeth was perfectly entitled to think otherwise. If she had had her way the least that would have happened would have been Castelnau leaving the country in disgrace, and a trial of Throckmorton which would have exposed his conduct to public ignominy. I wonder how long it would have been before another French ambassador was seen in London. Walsingham's charitable burglary, so to call it, averted this disaster, and enabled the Council to pacify the queen, to blackmail Castelnau into good behaviour, and to gain more than a year of freedom from worry about what was going on in Salisbury Court. In due course Castelnau would be replaced by a zealot, and Walsingham would deal with that in his own way. Meanwhile he had achieved what I am inclined to think of as a back-handed masterstroke of secret intelligence, which bears comparison with his showier performance two years later.

---

31 Fénelon to Catherine de Medici, 8-vii-1575 (Chéruel, p. 224); that this opinion was addressed to Catherine makes it the more incisive.

32 Villeroy to Castelnau, 23-vii-[1579] (BNV^{c}C 472, p. 9): 'Monsieur nous avons ce me semble tous besoin de prier Dieu vouloir conduire ceste entreprise [marriage] à bonne fin. Je n'ose dire ce que j'en pense ... Toutesfois serez vous [Castelnau and Jean Simier] l'un et l'autre subjete de respondre des evenements et les cautionner ...'.

33 *Renaissance Diplomacy*, chap. 21.

If he or Elizabeth supposed that by keeping quiet about Castelnau they could draw King Henri III, at long last, into an active alliance against Spain, they were not dealing with real life. Elizabeth may have done; I cannot imagine that Walsingham did. Philip Sidney would not be given a chance to work his magic on the king; Bruno would lead the chorus of sceptics, and even William Parry would join in.[34] In reality the question ought to have been elsewhere: what, if anything, could they do to prevent a tidal wave of Catholic zealotry from running away with the French crown and launching the country into a Catholic crusade against the priest-murdering, and soon queen-murdering, queen? In the end, and by a whisker, Henri III managed to hold off the Catholic League just long enough to ensure that in July of 1588 the ports of France were not available as staging-posts for the Armada or for a horde of exasperated Frenchmen to pour over the Channel in its wake.[35]

Considering how sensitive Burghley and Walsingham had been of the king in 1584, they do not seem to me to have helped him very much thereafter. It may be that Elizabeth was to blame: she had a habit of writing him, at moments of tension, impossibly offensive letters in which she gave vent to the feelings she had had to bottle up in 1584, and for which her envoys were obliged to apologise. Her Thatcheresque manner of treating him as a bumbling satellite might have driven a touchier king into the arms of Philip II. I think she must have been responsible for the hamfisted demand that he surrender Thomas Morgan for setting William Parry on to assassinate her. It was a poor case, and even if it had been a better one the king could not possibly have complied; it had to be toned down into the demand for Morgan's papers, which inspired, as it was bound to do, the comedy with Arnault and a good deal of malicious pleasure in Paris.[36] It provided a wonderful climate in which the League could launch its manifesto of rebellion. Since she had discovered that Henri III had had no part in any conspiracy against her, she might have been more considerate, as she was in the end after Mary's execution, when her dramatic performance of blaming it all on the Council was put on for his benefit and for that of King James.

For all his prudence, possibly tempered by atavistic feelings about the French, the stresses in the relation were partly Burghley's fault. His book on the *Execution of Justice in England* implied that it was the king's duty,

---

34   Above, p. 127; *GB*, pp. 151–5; Parry to Elizabeth, 14/24-ii-1585 (*State Trials*, i, 1104f): 'The French king is French, you know it well enough, you will find him occupied when he should do you good; he will not lose a pilgrimage to save you a crown.' How had Parry come to know this?

35   Wernham, *Before the Armada*, pp. 398ff.

36   *CSP Foreign 1584–85*, pp. 272ff, 332; 337, *1586–88*, p. 184; for Arnault, above, p. 24.

not simply to expel English lay émigrés who were conspiring against the realm, but to send troops to dissolve the seminary at Reims. What did he think was going to happen then? Elizabeth might well despise a king who bowed to the opinions of the populace, but Burghley ought to have known better. With his customary public politeness, Henri III declined to give the book his royal *imprimatur* in France.[37] As for Walsingham, he looks to me to have kept on his sensible course until the middle of 1585, when he was blown off it by three things: Henri III's agreement with the League at Nemours in July, which included a seeming commitment to suppress Protestantism in France; the arrival of Châteauneuf to replace Castelnau; and his own escalating feud with Stafford in Paris, among whose causes was probably Stafford's belief that the queen should have more faith in Henri III and less in the Huguenots, and perhaps also that Henri of Navarre should convert, as the king desperately wished. After that Walsingham made two contributions to Anglo-French relations, both of them upsetting. When he procured Mary's death by his expert handling of the Babington conspirators he hastened something which was surely inevitable. His other contribution seems quite wilful. Just as a French mission to plead for Mary's life was leaving England, he made public a conspiracy between the ambassador Châteauneuf, Stafford's brother William, and an ex-servant of Stafford's called Michael Moody, to blow up Elizabeth with a sack of gunpowder placed under her bed.[38] This crude invention, soon confessed to be such, succeeded in embarrassing Stafford and convincing all Frenchmen anew of the perfidy of the English. It is said to have persuaded Elizabeth to sign Mary's death warrant, but I doubt if Elizabeth believed a word of it and she did not sign until three weeks later. If it was intended to keep Châteauneuf locked up in his house and so unable to approach the queen until Mary was dead, it showed a neurotic apprehension about the effect this pompous and unaccommodating guest might have on Elizabeth's disposition. It expressed contempt for Henri III at a time when he was struggling to contain an outburst of popular rage. It is the only plot, I think, that Walsingham ever simply created. Perhaps we ought to think of it as a joke; otherwise, it is a reflection on the honour he claimed as a private and public person, and an indication, either that his triumph over Mary had gone to his head, or that his feud with Stafford had unbalanced his judgment.

---

37 Kingdon (ed.), *The Execution of Justice*, pp. 6–9; my Ph.D. thesis, 'Elizabethan Catholicism: the Link with France' (Cambridge University, 1961), pp. 48–50; *CSP Foreign 1583–84*, nos. 491, 536; Henri III to Castelnau, 27-iii/6-iv-1584 (PRO Transcripts 31/3/28, under date).

38 Read, *Walsingham*, iii, 60–3; Rait and Cameron, *King James's Secret*, pp. 130–41; for Moody, see above, p. 100.

One of the few people in France whom this stratagem certainly delighted was Castelnau, whose career at home had been wrecked by scandalous allegations, mainly from Châteauneuf, about his conduct of his embassy. If he had had any sympathy for the League, it evaporated in face of the campaign against him, and during his and Walsingham's last years he wrote to him several times, appealing to their 'inseparable friendship', praising the queen and her Council, and cheering them on against the Armada. When Henri III, as Elizabeth in one of her more sober communications had advised him, had the Duke of Guise and his brother assassinated shortly afterwards, he passed on his delight, at least his secretary did; his last letter shows him in excellent form by the side of the new King Henri IV, as he prepared to do battle with the League in Normandy.[39] One of them begins: 'After so many of my letters which have passed through your hands for the queen our [*sic*] good mistress . . .' Was he, one wonders, being ironic? But no, just blessedly ignorant. I do hope Walsingham laughed, but I hope he laughed kindly, as he should have done.

---

39 *GB*, p. 131. Castelnau to Walsingham, 6/16-x-1587 (BN V^{c}C 472, p. 241); 10/20-x (?xii)-1587 (*HMC Hatfield*, iii, 288); 9/19-vi-1588 (BL Cottonian Nero B vi, ff. 414, 419); François Rybot to Walsingham, 5/15-i-1589 (*CSP Foreign 1589*, p. 17; PRO SP 78/19, f. 5); Castelnau to Walsingham, 3/13-ix-1589 (PRO SP 78/20, f. 7). The quotation below is from the first of these. Elizabeth and the assassination: *HMC Hatfield*, iii, 314; *CSP Foreign 1586–88*, pp. 568, 580.

A Note on the Date of Fagot's Letter

(*GB*, Text no. 4)

Note   The letter is printed in *Bruno* as Text no. 4, and I shall continue so to describe it, and shall refer to other items printed in the same series by the numbers there given. See notes 4 and 7 for other numberings. I here give all dates, in text and footnotes, in old style.

1. *The Endorsement*

The letter, which is Fagot's first surviving letter to Walsingham written in conventional form, has been endorsed: '♃ Aprill 1583/Fagot' (Plate IX). The endorsement has not been written by Walsingham's chief clerk, Laurence Tomson, whose endorsements to Texts nos. 3 and 9 are characteristic, and different. It is a weakish date. It does not record when the piece came into the office, as it would in that case have a day of the month: thus another undated piece of Fagot's, Text no. 13, has been endorsed '8th Marche 1585'. It is a conjecture of the date when the letter was written, and its authority will depend upon who made it, and when and in what circumstances it was made. When I said, in *Bruno*, that I was 'sure' it was wrong, I went too far.[1] I did this for the reasons of content there stated, and under the influence of what appeared to be similar conjectures attached to connected pieces, which were wildly mistaken. Text no. 3 had a conjecture, made after Tomson's undated endorsement, of '1582', which was plainly contradicted by its contents; Text no. 7 was dated '23 November 1584', a year out, and other conjectures of '158[ ]' and '1586' had been offered.[2] Since then I have realised, under the tuition of Simon Adams, that the last two cases were conjectures made by Sir Robert Cotton or his scribe when he assembled or copied this and a large number of related pieces for his own collection in the early seventeenth century: these included the copies of Texts nos. 2 and 4 which I had supposed to have been made in Walsingham's office.[3] The date endorsed on Text no. 4, and

---

1   *GB*, p. 195, cf. pp. 191, 208, 224.
2   *GB*, pp. 191, 204; BL Cottonian Caligula C viii, f. 204.
3   *GB*, pp. 187, 195.

Plate IX   Endorsement on *GB* Text no. 4, with query ('Quere') perhaps by Walsingham. Public Record Office SP 53/12, f. 153v.

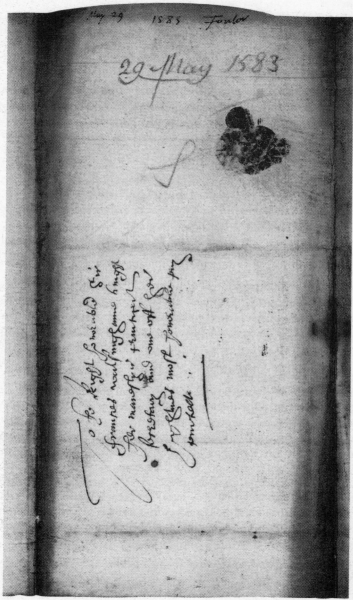

Plate X   Endorsement of Fowler to Walsingham, 29 May 1583 (o.s.). Public Record Office
SP 53/32, no. 51.

followed by Cotton, was not of this kind. It could not therefore be dismissed as having been added thirty years later.

That point taken, it was possible to pursue the identity of the endorser and the circumstances in which the endorsement was made, and in this pursuit Cotton and his scribe became a great help. Among the large quantity of associated material which they had copied into what became the volume Caligula C vii of the Cottonian Mss. was a substantial number of letters from William Fowler; Fowler, as we see from the story, was the precursor and for a time the contemporary of Fagot and Feron in the siege of Salisbury Court. When one looked at the originals of his letters in the Public Record Office[4] one found: (1) that the endorser of Text no. 4 was the endorser of nearly all Fowler's pieces; and (2) that it, and another Fagot piece (Text no. 2), had been copied into his volume by Cotton's scribe along with the Fowler letters and much else. It was therefore clear that Cotton found a collection in which they appeared together. The original of Text no. 4 is not now with Fowler's pieces because, I suppose, it was separated from them by the PRO staff in the nineteenth century, and put into SP 53 (Mary Queen of Scots), volume 12; the original of Text no. 2 is not with them because Cotton, presumably, lost it.

What Cotton had in front of him was a collection or file of Walsingham's papers concerning Scotland, dating from 1583. It could be distinguished into two sections by the character of the pieces and the form of their endorsements. The main section, now forming the bulk of SP 52 (Scotland), volumes 31–3, was the correspondence between Walsingham and the ambassador in Edinburgh, Robert Bowes, which was also copied for Cotton into Caligula C vii: letters from Bowes and drafts of letters from Walsingham to him. All these pieces have an endorsement by Tomson. This always begins with the symbol '♃', which is also on the endorsements of two of Fagot's pieces (Texts nos. 3 and 4), and was probably on the third. As the symbol appears on Fowler's pieces as well, it is obviously nothing to do with Fagot, as I supposed in *Bruno*,[5] but simply means 'endorsed', or possibly 'to go in the Scottish file'. After it, there is a full date and a description of the piece, all in Tomson's long, loopy and legible italic hand. Since Walsingham's drafts of letters to Bowes are not dated, it is clear that the dates on them are the dates on which the drafts were written, entered at the time of writing. Tomson's dates are authoritative.

---

4   I have checked all those in PRO SP 52, vol. 32 (Scotland: May–June 1583), which contains most of them; where simple numbers are given in the text and footnotes here they refer to the document numbers in this volume.

5   *GB*, p. 191.

Along with either one or two of Fagot's pieces (Text no. 4 alone, or no. 4 and no. 2),[6] Fowler's letters formed the other, unofficial part of the collection or file, the product of intelligence. They were not endorsed by Tomson, but by a clerk whom I shall call E; they were not endorsed as they were received; where Fowler had not dated them or not dated them fully, as he usually had not, E was in considerable difficulty. If we take a sequence of eight of Fowler's letters endorsed by E in SP 52/32,[7] three of them are endorsed with day and month, having been so dated by Fowler; three are dated '1583 May'; one '1583'; and one not at all. The natural assumption from this is that E is doing his best to date a pile of letters which he has been given to file some time after they have been received; the assumption can be shown to be correct. On one of the three he has dated to May 1583 (no. 53 in the PRO volume; *Calendar*, no. 493) his endorsement runs: '♃', followed by the symbol used to sign most of Fowler's letters ('M————IS'); in the space above the middle of this symbol he has written '1583/May'. The actual date of this letter is 29 March: it mentions the French diplomat La Mothe-Fénelon, who was in London from mid-February to late March, as having just left.[8]

Why has E endorsed it as of May? He has endorsed six of Fowler's letters as of May 1583, and I take it he had them on the table in front of him at the same time. Two of them (nos. 16 and 19) were both signed and dated by Fowler, and presented no problem: they were of 9 and 11 May. One (no. 51) was dated 29 May (Plate X), but had no signature. Three (nos. 41, 53 and 54) had no date; two of these were signed with Fowler's symbol, one (no. 54) signed 'W. Fouler'. This and no. 53 E endorsed almost identically, with Fowler's symbol and the year and month above or straddling the middle of it. From the signature of no. 54 he might have identified the symbol with Fowler, though he had probably done this already. He wrote 'W. Fouler' under the symbol signature of no. 53; he endorsed no. 41, also signed with the symbol, 'Will. Fouler', then for some reason crossed the name out. He also added 'William Fowler' as a signature to

6 If the title given to the Cottonian copy of Text no. 2 ('Advertisements touching the Scottish affayres') was the endorsement of the original, which it surely was, it will have been written by Tomson (above, p. 160). In that case it will have been in the official file (Bowes), not in the unofficial one (Fowler).

7 Nos. 16, 19, 41, 51, 53, 54, 56 i, 62; *CSP Scotland, 1581–83* [hereafter *Calendar*], nos. 457, 460, 478, 488, 493, 490, 495 enclosure (p. 481), 508. I give the versions of Fowler's letters in the *Calendar* by number, not page, except in the one case where there is no number.

8 *Calendar* no. 493: Sir Thomas Kerr, laird of Fernyhurst, has just arrived in London and is about to leave for France; Fowler thinks he will 'convene' (meet) Fénelon on the way. The piece is of about the same date as *Calendar* no. 724, which also mentions Fernyhurst's arrival and has been misdated by a mile in the *Calendar* to December; by *Calendar* no. 377 this can be dated 29 March or very shortly before. Fowler dates *Calendar* no. 493 'Friday'; so its date is 29 March, Good Friday.

the unsigned no. 51, dated 29 May. So he had three undated letters which
he had identified as Fowler's; they came with three which were dated in
May; he endorsed them as of May. He was right in two cases (nos. 41 and
54; the real dates are probably 14 and 31 May), and wrong in one (no. 53)
by two months. I think he supposed that nos. 53 and 54 were of the same
date because Fowler had dated no. 54 'this Fryday', and no. 53 'this Fryday
at night very lait'.

Three things follow from this account of E's procedure. (1) He was
struggling with both the authorship and the dating of Fowler's pieces, and
where he had no date he was supplying it by conjecture. Sometimes his
guesses were right and sometimes wrong; but they had not been informed
by looking at the contents of the letters or, if they had, by previous knowledge of what Fowler was writing about. (2) He was dealing with a sizeable number of Fowler's pieces at the same time. (3) That time was at or
after the end of May 1583. I think we can be a little more precise than
this. E endorsed four more of Fowler's letters, which date from between
about 5–6 June and 8 July.[9] The last, which Fowler had signed and dated,
is endorsed '♃ ♀ 8 July 1583'. Two are endorsed with Fowler's symbol,
but no date. The endorsement on the fourth, which is the earliest, begins
with Fowler's symbol, under which there is a ♀, and under that '1583
Fowler'.[10] I guess that these represent an early stage in the filing, when E
had used the symbol ♀ for Fowler, an idea he later dropped; he would be
going through the pile backwards, with the latest letters on top. Whether
that is so or not, it must be very likely that E was endorsing the whole
series for filing at the same time. The letter of 8 July was Fowler's last; his
job was finished, and some time after that he went to Scotland. The
obvious time for E to have done his filing is not long after 8 July.

E was, then, what we should now call a filing clerk, and he made something of a mess out of intractable material: in the middle of this mess we
are to place Text no. 4 and its endorsement '♃ Aprill 1583/Fagot'.
Although it is not now in the same series as Fowler's letters, it was certainly with them originally because it was endorsed by E and was copied
by Cotton's scribe into the volume Caligula C vii. I presume this scribe
copied what he found in the order in which he found it, and that this

9   Nos. 56 i, 62, 91, 119; *Calendar* p. 481 (described wrongly as an enclosure in no. 495), nos. 508,
    553, 587. No. 56 i is just after *Calendar* no. 507, which is roughly 5 June; no. 62 is somewhere
    between then and about 22 June, when Robert Beale, whose return from Sheffield it mentioned
    Castelnau as awaiting, arrived back in London (*Calendar* no. 533); no. 119 is earlier than no. 91
    because James's escape to St Andrews, known by at least 3 July (*Calendar* no. 550), was not yet
    known.

10 There are two other letters from this period, Nos. 60 & 61 (*Calendar* nos. 505 & 507), probably
    of 4 & 5 June, which have no endorsement.

order was the result of E's having inserted his additional matter into the existing file of official Scottish correspondence. In that case, the copyist found Text no. 4, which he copied on f. 211 of the Caligula volume and dated according to its endorsement, between two official pieces dated 23 and 25 April 1583.[11] Text no. 2, which he dated 29 April because he or the original endorser had not noticed that it was dated new style, hence actually 19 April, is three folios farther on (f. 214) and was presumably in the same place in the file he was copying; if, as seems to be the case, the endorsement was by Tomson and not by E, E will have found it in the file already when he put Text no. 4 and the Fowler pieces in.[12] On the next folio after that (f. 215) the copyist wrote the heading of one of Fowler's letters which for some reason he did not copy. The heading is: 'From (*M̶̶̶̶̶̶̶̶IS*) to Sir F. Walsingham'; the date is given as '1583 May', and 'May' has been corrected to 'April'. Shortly after that (f. 221) there is the original of a Fowler piece which the copyist has also dated '1583 May', on no grounds that I can see, but perhaps from an endorsement by E which has disappeared; it is probably wrong since the real date seems to be early June.[13] Shortly after that (f. 224 b) there is an extract from the piece (SP 52/32, no. 53) which E had endorsed '1583/May', but where he had been two months out. The letter which the scribe did not copy on f. 215 must be one of the two others which E had endorsed '1583/May' (SP 52/32, nos. 41 and 54); since he copied no. 54 later, at f. 240,[14] it was presumably no. 41, which does not appear in the Caligula volume. If that is so, it is ironic that the only one of these dates which Cotton corrected was the only one that was right. There is something we can be sure of: when E dated Text no. 4 'April 1583', he was in a muddle.

I conclude:

(1)   that Text no. 4 was endorsed and filed with Fowler's letters, by E, certainly after the end of May 1583, and very probably in July or later;

(2)   that it was endorsed and filed at the same time as a group of Fowler's pieces which E dated, conjecturally and sometimes wrongly, to May 1583;

(3)   that it was dated and placed by reference to Text no. 2, which E understood to be of 29 April. This is what he had done with Fowler's undated pieces, where the only dates he had were from May.

---

11   *Calendar*, pp. 405, 418.

12   Above, n. 6.

13   *Calendar* no. 492; which must be shortly before no. 520 (Walsingham to Bowes, 12 June), in which Fowler's information is passed on. Walsingham attributed it to John Smallett (above, p. 58) to keep suspicion away from Fowler, as Fowler had asked.

14   This, and f. 224 b above, from *Calendar*, marginal notes at pp. 477, 479.

In short: the date 'April 1583' is a guess by an ill-informed filing clerk with a headache, who has been instructed, a good deal later and very probably three months later, to place it, along with a pile of other confidential matter recently deposited in Walsingham's office, in the existing file of Scottish material. It has no force. If, as I think, E was working no earlier than July, there is no reason why the real date should not be in June, as the real date of Fowler's no. 53 is in March.

There is one thing to add: E's date appears to have been questioned shortly afterwards. Some way beneath his endorsement, somebody has written 'Quere', meaning 'Query?', in a bold secretary hand (Plate IX). The writer must have been somebody in Walsingham's office, possibly Walsingham himself. Since the query cannot be about the authorship of the piece, it is hard to see what it can be about but the date. I can make a suggestion as to when and why it was made. Text no. 4 was an important piece: it was the trigger of the 'secret intelligence' against Throckmorton provided, as the official account of the case said, 'divers months' before he was arrested.[15] We can assume that it was looked at when Walsingham was assembling the case against Castelnau the following spring; and it, or more probably extracts from it, may have been copied into the 'book of secret advertisements' which he seems to have put together at that time.[16] Wrongly dated, it would create confusion; I take it that the writer, even if not Walsingham, was sufficiently au fait with the story to think that E had made a mistake.

To find a good date for Text no. 4, we must look elsewhere than to E's endorsement. The choice is between dates before or after Texts nos. 2 and 3 (19 and 25 April): somewhere up to and including early April; and somewhere after April. If we choose the latter, we need a date quite some time later, because if Fagot wrote no. 4 after no. 3 he wrote it 'longtemps' after 25 April.[17] In *Bruno* I dated no. 4 to between about 20 and 31 May, which was perhaps cutting it rather fine; since the filing of the letter probably occurred in July, we have June to play with. I think now that the choice is between early April (or before) and June, and propose two reasons against the earlier date and two in favour of the later one.

2. Reasons against an early date

(i)   A very strong reason against a date in April or earlier is that, in that case, Fagot must have written earlier letters to Walsingham, since he says

15   Above, p. 65.
16   Above, p. 101.
17   *GB*, p. 196.

that it is a long time since he wrote. No such letters are to be found. There are numerous pieces from Fowler dating back to November 1582, and Fagot's, if they had existed, would have been kept with them like Texts nos. 2 and 4, or with his Text no. 3 in the French file (SP 78). Walsingham looked after his papers, and Fagot was a more valuable informant than Fowler. If nothing was filed from Fagot before April 1583, we can be virtually certain that Fagot sent nothing before that date.

(ii)   The second reason is the form and some details of the letters. These, in my view, speak strongly for Texts nos. 2 and 3 as earlier than Text no. 4. Nos. 2 and 3 are in diary form, with careful dating and a signature at the end of each item. No. 4 is a conventional letter with one signature. It seems to me natural to suppose that nos. 2 and 3 are the productions of a person new to the job, who is experimenting with ways of doing it; he is also, I take it, experimenting with his signature, which in no. 2 comes in three forms. Then there are the indications that Fagot was not simply new to the job, but new to the house. In no. 2 he does not know the surname of a man called Pierre who brings a letter; in no. 3 he does not know the name of an English lord with whom Castelnau has had a conversation. Most particularly he does not know the surname of Lord Henry Howard. Howard was a frequent visitor to the embassy, and if Fagot had been around for any length of time he would have known both who he was and that it was quite unnecessary to explain to Walsingham that he was a 'Catholique Romain et papiste'.[18]

3. *Reasons in favour of a date in June*

These are: one point of fact in the letter; and the date and contents of Feron's first leakages.

(i)   A theme which runs through Fagot's three communications is the probability of a settlement, perhaps including a marriage, between the Duke of Anjou and the Spaniards. In Text no. 2 this is reported to Castelnau by Jean du Bex, seigneur des Pruneaux, Anjou's envoy in London; in Text no. 3 Mendoza sends a servant to Salisbury Court to pass on the news; in Text no. 4, Mendoza has come to the house to talk about it himself. This is the only datable fact mentioned in the letter.[19]

18   *GB*, pp. 187–94.

19   'L'ambassadeur d'Espaigne a faict son conte en notre maison que Monsieur le Duc s'en va marier l'une des filles du Roy d'Espaigne.' Anjou's dealings with Spain in 1583 are discussed in L. van der Essen, *Alexandre Farnèse* (5 vols, Brussels, 1933–7), iii, 108–18, 151–60, and in Mack P. Holt, *The Duke of Anjou and the Politique Struggle during the Wars of Religion* (Cambridge, 1986), pp. 189, 201f. Van der Essen probably overdoes them; Holt surely plays them down too much. They revived an earlier proposal of 1578–80: Susan Doran, *Monarchy and Matrimony* (London, 1996), pp. 150, 156, 175, 177.

A visit from Mendoza to Castelnau at this time was something to remember. Traditionally they had not been on visiting terms, and during the five years between Mendoza's arrival in England and 1583 I have only found one occasion, in December 1580, when they had a conversation. Some time in 1583 the wind changed. Mendoza seems to have initiated the shift: since both ambassadors were now corresponding secretly with Mary, and had mutual friends in Howard and perhaps in Throckmorton, it must have seemed time for a chat. Perhaps the idea of brokering a deal between Anjou and Spain was, at least on Mendoza's part, an excuse for making contact, though it was not a ridiculous idea in itself, and it made Elizabeth very nervous.[20] Mendoza's despatch of a servant to Salisbury Court, recorded by Fagot on 22 April 1583, looks like an early move in the game, which led before long to a meeting with Castelnau, and to a period when Mendoza was at Salisbury Court quite often, lasting until his expulsion in January. Sylvanus Scory, who proved an active middleman between the two, said that the period began at the time of the return of Mme. de Mauvissière from France, so about the beginning of August.[21] I think that what Fagot recorded in Text no. 4 was either the first of the meetings between Castelnau and Mendoza, or at least an early one, and that it is to be dated early in June 1583.

Why? In a letter to Mary of early July, Castelnau reported a discussion with Mendoza about Anjou, when he had suggested that Mary should help to bring him and the Duke of Parma together. He said he had written about this in his previous letter (say, mid-June), and Mary reported it in a letter to Mendoza of 13 July, when she was replying to letters of Mendoza's of 2 and 12 June, at least one of which must have had something about it.[22] The question, as Castelnau described it, had arisen from a visit to London of a secretary of Anjou called Chartier, which had occurred between about 22 and 27 May 1583. Chartier had come to visit Elizabeth, but their interview did not go well, and Castelnau told Mary that he and Chartier had decided to press on with the Spanish scheme. On his way

---

20 PRO Transcripts 31/3/28 (17-xii-1580); *GB*, p. 107; *CSP Spanish 1580–86*, pp. 438, 454, 465 (probably Howard, possibly Throckmorton as well); Castelnau, 3-vi-1583, 21-vii-1583 (Chéruel, pp. 248–64, 265–68); Henri III, 15-vi-1583 (BN fr 3308, f. 71ᵛ).

21 Mendoza's letters home, in *CSP Spanish* or more fully in [Marqués de la Fuensanta del Valle ed.] *Collección de documentos ineditos para la historia de España*, vol. xcii (Madrid, 1888), do not mention a meeting with Castelnau from January to the end of August 1583, after which they are missing for 2 months. On my account the likeliest to have done so would be those of 10-vi-1583, which were lost (*Collección*, p. 510). PRO SP 12/176, no. 53 (Scory's confession, 14-ii-1585); *CSP Foreign 1583–84*, p. 23 (Mme. de Mauvissière). Also Fowler, 7-v-1583 (*Calendar* no. 452): his only reference to Anjou.

22 BL Harleian 1582, ff. 402–3 (Appendix, no. 1; and below, p. 167); *CSP Spanish 1580–86*, p. 491; *CSP Foreign 1583*, p. 386 (Castelnau-Walsingham, 4-vi-1583). The dates of Chartier's visit are fixed by Chéruel, pp. 258ff, and Diary, f. 13ʳ (Chartier's passport, 27-v-1583).

back Chartier was captured by Parma's troops, and when they met Castelnau suggested to Mendoza that Parma might send him back to Anjou with an offer. This interview must have taken place between 4 and 12 June;[23] hence Fagot's letter, if this is the interview he was describing, will date from something like 5–20 June. We cannot be sure that there was no earlier meeting: neither Mendoza nor Castelnau mentions one, but there is a large gap in Castelnau's letters before the beginning of May. We can say that, on these grounds, a date in June 1583 for Fagot's letter looks good, a date in April or earlier out of place.

(ii)   The reader may have forgotten that the main thing about Text no. 4 was Fagot's news that Feron was willing to betray his master's secret correspondence with Mary. Nobody will believe that Walsingham lost any time in taking advantage of this offer. Hence the date when Feron began to leak the correspondence is a pretty good guide to the date of Fagot's letter. The first item which Feron leaked dates from the beginning of July. It was from Castelnau, and Feron's copy is not dated; but it reports as hot news the escape of King James from Edinburgh to St Andrews, an event of intense interest to Mary which occurred on 27 June and was known in London by 3 July at the latest. So we cannot go far wrong if we date Castelnau's letter to 3 July.[24] This is eminently compatible with a date for Fagot's letter of say 5–20 June. We need time for the letter to get to Walsingham, for Walsingham to raise Williams, for Williams to find out who exactly he was to make contact with (it would have been a disaster if he had contacted Courcelles), and to meet Feron. We also need time for Feron to have a letter from Castelnau to pass over. This fits very snugly. If we date Fagot's letter to early April 1583, we have three months' inactivity or another collection of lost letters to account for, both of which seem to me quite inconceivable.

Finally: Castelnau's letter to Mary of 3 July was the letter in which he told her about Chartier, Anjou and his meeting with Mendoza; the subject also cropped up in Mary's reply, the second letter leaked.[25] This strengthens the case for dating Fagot's letter close to 3 July, and for supposing that it was this meeting with Mendoza that Fagot recorded.

---

23   Dates fixed by Castelnau to Walsingham, 4-vi-1583, mentioning Chartier's capture, and Mendoza's apparently having reported the meeting to Mary on 12 June (both above, n. 22); on the 10th, Walsingham made a note to write to France about 'Chartier's apprehension' (Diary, f. 15ᵛ). Also van der Essen, *Alexandre Farnèse*, iii, 132. Fowler was hanging around Salisbury Court a lot on 5 and 6 June (above, pp. 60, 162), and does not mention a visit from Mendoza; he would surely have been got out of the way for it, but this may suggest that the meeting occurred after the 6th.

24   Above, n. 22, and p. 67.

25   Appendix, nos. 1 and 2, and above, pp. 67f.

There is one, and I think only one, point to be made in favour of an early date: the earliest of Castelnau's letters which survives in Walsingham's papers in a copy by Feron dates from April 1583. It was not part of the secret correspondence; it was perfectly harmless; and we know exactly how and when it got to Walsingham. Castelnau wrote the letter to the French agent in Scotland, François de Maineville, on 16 April; he gave it to an Italian fencing-master called Rocco Bonetti, who was working for the English and gave it to Walsingham on the same day. Walsingham sent it off and kept the copy. The only problem is about the copy, which was made by Feron, not in Walsingham's office. Feron must have made it for Bonetti. Since Castelnau knew, and Walsingham knew he knew, what Bonetti was up to, it is plain that Castelnau wrote the letter knowing that it would be intercepted; and indeed the letter reads just like it.[26] If Feron turned an honest penny by making a copy of it for Bonetti to give to Walsingham (it is very long), it does him no discredit; and I should think he had cleared it with Castelnau. The piece is no evidence that Feron was betraying his master in April, and hence no evidence for an early date for Fagot's letter. At the most, we may think of it as some kind of trial balloon floated in Walsingham's direction, but I doubt if it was even that. Otherwise something would have happened in the next two months.

3. *Two other points*

(i)   A date in June 1583 is in keeping with the other piece of information, or quasi-information, that we have about Fagot's communications: William Herle's statement in November that he had reported information about Throckmorton, presumably from Fagot, to Walsingham 'this last summer'.[27] Herle had met Fagot on 22 April, and had possibly had a confidential talk with him on 20 May or just before. I doubt if he meant to say that he had been the carrier of Fagot's letter in June. My inclination is to think that Herle was deputed to keep in touch with Fagot after the receipt of the letter and the consequent arrangement between Feron and Williams; he implies that he reported to Walsingham conversations with Fagot, not that he carried him a letter; he also told Walsingham something that was not in the letter, that Throckmorton had been to mass at

---

26 PRO SP 53/12, no. 50 (ff. 117–22); *Calendar*, pp. 380–3. Its history is explained *Ibid.* pp. 345, 377f, 380f. Endorsed by (I think) Tomson: '26 Aprill' 83. A letter of Mauvissière's intercepted written to Maineville in Scotland.' Compare the (probable) endorsement by Tomson of Text no. 2 (above, n. 6), which also repeats the new style date, '29 April 1583'. Hence this letter just preceded Text no. 2 into the archives; but it was not kept with this, or Cotton's scribe would surely have copied it into Caligula C vii.

27 *GB*, Text no. 5, p. 201; cf. pp. 25–7, 28–31.

Salisbury Court 'at several times'.[28] But he strongly supports a June date for Fagot's letter, whether he carried it or not.

(ii) One effect of a June date for the letter is to remove an obstacle to identifying Fagot as Giordano Bruno, who arrived at Salisbury Court in April. But it raises another problem here. If we think that Fagot and Bruno were the same man, we must observe that Bruno was away from London, on his trip to Oxford with Philip Sidney and the Palatine Laski, for some ten days between about 6 and 15 June 1583.[29] In that case the possible dates for Fagot's letter are rather tight: 5 June is possible, but looks too early; otherwise we must date it between the 16th and the 20th, or whenever we think will leave enough time for Williams to make his arrangements with Feron before 3 July or so. If we choose the first, we may like to imagine Bruno handing his letter to Sidney as he stepped on to the Queen's Barge which was to take the party festively towards Oxford, for Sidney to pass to Walsingham on their return: what could be safer? But the later date, and a less distinguished postman, seem much more likely.

---

28 Cf. Fagot, in *GB*, pp. 188, 198: Throckmorton comes either at night, or to dinner – which admittedly is probably mid-day, and hence perhaps after mass.
29 *GB*, pp. 22–4, 195; Yates, *Giordano Bruno and the Hermetic Tradition*, pp. 206–11. The party must have left on 6 June or so, because they arrived at Rycote near Thame on the 8th: Diary of Arthur Throckmorton, under date (Canterbury Cathedral Archives, Ms. U.85, f. 93ʳ); they visited John Dee at Mortlake on the way back, 15 June: J. O. Halliwell (ed.), *The Private Diary of John Dee* (Camden Society, xix, 1842), p. 20.

Documents

(a)
Williams Writes to the Queen

31 August/10 September 1583: Walter Williams to Queen Elizabeth, London

Hatfield House, Cecil Papers 162, no. 114 (from BL Microfilm M 485/43)

Holograph No address; top of endorsement cut off but seems to end 'Williams'/'31 Aug 1583'.

Soverigne lady,

yt may please your heighnes that the letter which your Majestie sent, the partie standeth in dowbt whether it be your heighnes hande writing or not for he saieth he hath seene of the same sundrie tymes, but this resembleth not, and [is] in great feare, as a thing wheron his life dependeth. he sayth thre may kepe counsell if ther be too awaye, meaninge therby if any more be made accquaynted, not to proceed any farther in his course begonne, he marvayleth why your Majestie should desire to knowe the messengers who are allready knowen to be but too, assuring himself that if they should be apprehended, then were ther but one waye with him, for he onely hath ben employed for this six yeares in writing all matters of importaunce, and now specially in the absence of Corsselles, who was accquaynted with the delivering of theym from tyme to time, yt can not be but he only must be suspected to be the revealer of secretts, what reward he maye attend, I leave to your heighnes wisdome, In most humble wise I therfore beseche your Majestie that it maye please you to have a care of sooch which desire to do you faythfull service, and to burne all his writinges which shall come unto your highnes, for he feareth greatly to be bewrayed, so fitt an Instrument is not to be loste, and I hope he will do your Majestie very great service, and therfore I thinck that as tyme breadeth daylie newe matters and ripeing of the oulde, so a fitter tyme maye serve to take the practisers and dealers agaynst your highnes state and quiet with lesse suspition for your servantes discoverye, and greater confusion and shame to the trecherous and evell mynded agaynst your Majestie.

Thus most humbely craving pardon for my over much boldnes In all humilitie I pray the kynge of all kinges to grawnte your Majestie a peaceable and quiet kyngdome in this world and after the same everlastinge joye in the heavenly kingdome which never shall have ende. At London the last of August 1583

I most humbly crave of your Majestie to burne this letter

Your Majesties most bownden in this life
Walter Williams

(b)
Castelnau and the Messengers

[About 14/24 December 1583]: Castelnau and Courcelles to Mary, Salisbury Court

BL Harleian 1582, ff. 385, 386, 382 (Appendix, no. 15)

Draft in Hand II

Madame, J'ay escript dernierement a *Votre Majesté* par Baudouin[1] et luy ay envoyé tous les pacquetz que vous pensoit envoyer le S*ieur* de la Tour[2] lors quil fut prins prisonnier mais je suis adverty quil y a commission de prendre le*dit* Bodouin de par le chemin dont je suis en grand peine et quil fust trouvé avec tant de lettres Le pauvre homme a bien [*something missing* = 'been told'] de ce donner de garde et nier fort et ferme et constamment tout ce quon luy pourroit demander sinon que par le commandement expres de Walsingham il auroit prins quelque argent de moy pour vous porter. quant au*dit* S*ieur* de la Tour il avoit monstré quelque constance au commancement et respondu en homme desperit mais depuis le torment de la torture ou il a este remis quatre fois depuis luy a faict dire ce quil scavoit et ce quil ne scavoit pas, de sorte que par lun des moindre pointz de sa confession il ne peult rechapper aussi suis je adverty que la sepmaine prochaine il sera condamne et faict mourir. Il a confesse avoir intelligence avec V*otre Majesté* mais que cela estoit venu par mon moyen et ma mande quil a este contrainct de le confesser ainsi par ce que Je ne puis porter de peine me priant de nier tout et dire que laspreté du torment luy a faict dire tout ce qu'on a voulu son frere[3] est aussi prisonnier en denger sil na pis de nen sortir de longtemps Ilz ont este trouvez plaines de lettres chiffres et autre choses escriptes de leurs mains qui monstre bien leur imprudance et malheur de quoy je les avoys advertyz souvent et de tout ce quil leur est advenu . . .

[P.S. to Claude Nau, Mary's secretary]

. . . et [? plainderay] de tous ces accidans avenus a tous les bons serviteurs de sa M*ajesté* dont jen ay tant de regret que jen meurt [*sic*] sous le pied Il semble que le Si*er* de la Tour ayt voulu cherché son malheur en toutes

---

1 Thomas Baldwin: see above, 92f, 109, 125.
2 Francis Throckmorton.
3 George Throckmorton: see above, p. 83, 87f; just possibly the description is a code, and means George More: see above, p. 66, 79–81.

choses pour avoir gardé plusieurs lettres et papiers dont il a esté trouvé saisy entre autres dun plant de sa main de tous les ports et havres de ce royaume et des lieux plus commodes pour faire decente aux estrangiers et quil a gardé des petits morceaux de pappier ou Courcelles luy mandoit quil luy envoyoit des pacquetz . . .

Madame, I wrote just now to Your Majesty by Baldwin,[1] and sent him all the packets which the Sieur de la Tour[2] was going to send when he was arrested; but I am told that there is a warrant out to seize Baldwin on the way. I am extremely worried about this, and about all those letters being found on him. We have told the poor man to look out for himself, and to deny absolutely everything he may be interrogated about, except to say that by the express order of Walsingham he had taken some money from me to carry your letters. As for the Sieur de la Tour, he showed some resolution at the beginning and replied as a man of spirit, but since then the agony of the torture, to which he has been subjected four times, has made him tell them what he knew and also what he did not know, so that a single one of the least important offences he has confessed to will be enough to hang him. I am told that he will be condemned and executed next week. He has confessed that he has been in confidential contact with Your Majesty, and that it was I who had put him in touch with you. He has sent to tell me that he was forced to confess this because, he says, 'I cannot bear the pain'; and he has begged me to deny everything and to say that the severity of the torture made him say whatever his examiners wanted. His brother[3] is also a prisoner, and in danger of not getting out for a long time, perhaps of something worse. They were found loaded with letters, ciphers and other things written in their hands, which shows how very rashly and misguidedly they have behaved. I have frequently warned them about this, and about everything that has happened to them . . .

[I am sorry] for all these misfortunes which have happened to all Her Majesty's good servants, about which I feel such misery as crushes me underfoot. It seems that the Sieur de la Tour has brought disaster upon himself all round by keeping numerous letters and papers which have been found in his possession: among other things, a plan in his hand of all the ports and havens in this kingdom and of the places most convenient for a foreign invasion, and also some little pieces of paper on which Courcelles had written to him that he was sending him packets of letters . . .

(c)
Mary Smells a Mole

25 February/6 March 1584, Mary to Castelnau, Sheffield

BL Harleian 1582, ff. 311–13; Labanoff, v, pp. 424–5 (Appendix, no. 31)

Copy in Hand II

Monsieur de Mauvissiere, vous verez par les lettres cy encloses comme des la dacte dicelles je mestois mis en devboir de faire responce a vos dernieres, par la voye desquelles il ne m'a este possible denvoyer ma*dicte* responce, dautant que le gentilhomme[1] a esté adverty y avoir jour et nuict des espions a lentour de vo*tre* maison pour observer tous ceux qui y vont et en viennent et oultre par la descouverte de toutes mes intelligences qui ont hante chez vous plusieurs subsonnent grandement que quelque ung de vos serviteurs naye esté corompu comme a la verité je nen suis pas moymesme hors de doute partant, je vous prie tresinstamment que dicy en avant vous faciez traiter avec ceux que je vous adresseray par tel de vos serviteurs que vous connoissez fidelles non en vo*tre* maison, mais dedans ou dehors la ville par forme de rencontre que aysement vous pourrez appointer en certains lieux et temps sans que autres que ceux que vous emploirez en ayent connoissance autrement je ne trouve homme qui se veulle davantage hazarder en no*tre* intelligence . . .

Monsieur de Mauvissière, You will see by my letters here enclosed that since the date when they were written I have done my part in replying to your last; but it has not been possible for me to send my reply by the way by which yours came, since the gentleman[1] has been informed that spies have been set day and night around your house to watch who comes in and goes out of it. Furthermore, owing to the discovery of all my contacts who have frequented your house, many people have a grave suspicion that one of your servants has been corrupted; which, to tell the truth, I rather think myself. Hence I beg you with extreme urgency from now on to see to it that any dealings with those persons I send to you are conducted (1) by such of your servants as you know to be loyal, and (2) not in your house but in or outside the town, at a rendezvous whose place and time you may easily determine; without letting anyone else than the servant in question know anything about it. Otherwise I shall never find anyone willing to risk his life again in carrying our correspondence . . .

1 Thomas Baldwin: see previous letter.

(d)

Castelnau on his Secretaries
(Plate VI)

[21 March/1 April 1584]: Castelnau to Mary, [Salisbury Court]

BL Harleian 1582, ff. 370–3, at ff. 371ᵛ–2ʳ (Appendix, no. 34)

Draft or Copy in Hand II

... en vous suppliant treshumblement de croire quil ny a un seul homme en mon logis qui ayt eu connoissance de ce que je traicte avec V*otre* Majesté ny de ceste escriture que arnault quant il estoit icy et laurent[1] qui ne bouge de ma chambre qui escript tout devant moy et en ma presence et courcelles qui porte les pacquets aux uns et aux au*t*res et parle a ceux qui sont de v*otre* p*ar*t de sorte que la R*eine* d*Angleterre* ni son conseil nont jamais eu connoissance de chose veritable si eselle [*sic*: = icelle] nest imaginee par quelques espions qui vont et viennent et ne faudray de prendre telle ordre que voudront ceux qui viendront de v*otre* p*ar*t lesquels lordonneront eux mesmes ...

I beg you very humbly to believe that there is not a single man in my house who has been informed of my dealings with Your Majesty, or understood this cipher, except Arnault when he was here, Laurent,[1] who never leaves my chamber and writes everything in front of me and in my presence, and Courcelles, who takes the packets [of letters] to their addressees and talks to those who are of your party; so that neither the Queen of England nor her Council have ever known anything genuine [about our communications], but only what has been imagined by various spies who come and go. I shall not fail to make such arrangements [about secrecy] as those who come from you will require; they may specify these themselves.

1 For this transcription, see above, p. 46, n. 4; the reader may check it on Plate VI.

(e)
Castelnau Responds to the Council's Directions
(Plate III)

5/15 May 1584, Castelnau to Walsingham, Salisbury Court

PRO SP 78/11, f. 205 (no. 91)

Holograph

Monsieur, sur lasseurance que jay tousiours eue que le S*ieu*r Archibal du Glas estoit gentilhomme veritable Je lay bien voullu croyre de tout ce quil ma dit de v*ot*re part comme de chose resollue au Conseil de la Royne v*ot*re bonne mestresse et sur cella Jay ecrit plusieurs letres fidellement sur le memoyre quil men a baille Toutefoys peu de temps apres il mest veneu dire le contraire de quoy Je me suys emerveille Neantmoins Je luy ay respondu acez amplement et prie de vous retourner trouver de ma part Je vous pry Monsieur de le croyre comme vous feriez moymesme et Je pry dieu quil vous donne [*sic*]

> Monsieur en sa saincte et digne garde
> de Londres ce xv^e May 1584
> V*ot*re bien hu*m*ble et affectionne a vous obeir et fere service
> M. de Castelnau

Monsieur, Assured as I have always been that M. Archibald Douglas was a true gentleman, I have been willing to believe everything he has said to me on your behalf as something resolved in the Council of the Queen your good mistress. Thereupon I wrote several letters in accordance with the *mémoire* which he handed me [containing the resolution]. However, shortly afterwards he turned up again and told me the opposite; which astonished me. Nonetheless I gave him a pretty full reply and asked him to return and speak to you on my part. I beg you, Monsieur, to give him credit as you would to myself . . .

Appendix

Letters Passed from Salisbury Court, July 1583 to November 1584

The numbers at the top of the columns mean: (1) number of letter; (2) date; (3) from/to; (4) nature of document (draft, copy, etc.); (5) hand(s) in which written; (6) location of document, and of printed version if any.

I include two letters (Nos. 8 and 37) not passed by Feron, and three (Nos. 39, 40 and 47) probably passed on Castelnau's instructions, according to his agreement with Walsingham (above, p. 113f). I give dates in both styles. Dates without brackets are from the document; dates in square brackets are conjectural: I discuss them in the notes to the letters, at the end of the list. 'C.' is Castelnau. Hand I is Castelnau's; Hand II is Feron's working hand, and the hand of his copies for and notes to Walsingham; Hand III is Feron's official hand for fair copies of Castelnau's letters. Where I say that a letter is a fair copy, I mean that it is an attempt at a fair copy, later scrapped. Hand IV is the (italic) hand of the copyist of No. 37, probably a secretary in Paris, possibly Jean Arnault (above, p. 119). Hand V is a fair-copy hand different from Hand III: it seems to be that of the authorised copies and, if not Feron's, to belong to another secretary or clerk, possibly one Pasquier.

I have used the following super-abbreviations here, in both list and notes: Cal 83 – *CSP Scotland 1581–83*; Cal 84 – *CSP Scotland 1584–85*; E – D'Esneval Ms. (folios); H – BL Harleian 1582 (folios); Hat – Hatfield House, Cecil Papers (vol. no. and folios or number); HCal – *HMC Hatfield*, Calendar; Kér – Kéralio; Lab – Labanoff. Other abbreviations are as used elsewhere.

(i)
Letters passed between July and November 1583

(1)	(2)	(3)	(4)	(5)	(6)
1.	[c. 3/13-vii-1583]	C. – Mary	Copy	II	H 402–3
2.	14/24-vii-1583	Mary – C.	(a) Copy (b) Copy	II –	H 320–1 E 190^r–192^r Lab v, 349–52
3.	22 & 25-vii/1 & 4-viii-1583	Mary – C.	Copy	II	H 306–7 Lab v, 357–60
4.	[c. 20/30-vii-1583]	C. – Mary	Copy	II	Hat 162, 21–2 HCal iii, 9
5.	[probably 12/22- viii-1583]	C. – Mary	Copy	II	Hat 13, 74–7 HCal iii, 123–8
6.	3/13-ix-1583	Mary – C.	Copy	II	Hat 133, no.31 HCal xiii, 234–5 Lab v, 361–9
7.	[c. 10/20-ix-1583]	Mary – C.	Copy	II	Hat 162, 23–4 HCal iii, 12
8.	5/15-xi-1583	C. – Mary	Decipher	Phelippes	PRO SP 53/12, no. 62 Cal 83, 654–6

(ii)
The Contents of Feron's Parcel, April 1584

(1)	(2)	(3)	(4)	(5)	(6)
9.	[c. 12/22-xi-1583]	C. – Henri III	Fair Copy	I–II–III	H 361–3
10.	17/27-xi-1583	C. – Anjou	Draft	I	H 327–8
11.	9/19-xii-1583	C. – Henri III	Fair Copy	I–II–III	H 329–31
12.	10/20-xii-1583	Henri III – Mary	Copy	–	H 332
13.	[c. 10/20-xii-1583]	C. – Mary	Draft	I–II	H 377–81
14.	[c. 12/22-xii-1583]	C. – Mary	Draft	II	H 383–4
15.	[c. 14/24-xii-1583]	C. – Mary	Draft	II	H 385–6, 382
16.	[16/26-xii-1583]	C. – Mary	Draft	II	H 398–401
17.	[c. 21/31-xii-1583]	C. – Anjou	Draft	I	H 392–3
18.	22-xii-1583/1-i-1584	C. – Henri III	Draft	I–II	H 334–7
19.	22-xii-1583/1-i-1584	C. – Catherine	Fair Copy	I–III	H 338
20.	[before 5/15-i-1584]	C. – Henri III	Fair Copy	I–III	H 324–6 Kér v, 345
21.	[before 5/15-i-1584]	C. – Catherine	Draft	I	H 369
22.	5/15-i-1584	Mary – C.	Copy	II	PRO SP 53/13, no. 1 Cal 84, 5 Lab v, 399
23.	5/15-i-1584	C. – Henri III	Draft	I	H 341
24.	[between about 1/11 & 9/19-i-1584]	C. – Mary	Draft	I	H 389

25.	[14/24-i-1584]	C. – Henri III	Draft Copy	I–II II	H 342–5 H 339–40, 348 Kér v, 384
26.	14/24-i-1584	C. – Catherine	Fair Copy	I–III	H 346
27.	[January 1584, n.s.]	C. – Mary	Draft	I	H 387
28.	4/14-ii-1584	C. – Henri III	Fair Copy	I–III	H 349–50 Kér v, 365
29.	11/21-ii-1584	C. – Henri III	Draft	I–II	H 351–52 Kér v, 370
30.	[? 11/21-ii-1584]	C. – Catherine	Draft	I	H 388
31.	25-ii/6-iii-1584	Mary – C.	Copy, with postscript by Feron	II	H 311–13 Lab v, 423
32.	21/31-iii-1584	Mary – C.	Copy ? Decipher	II ?	H 313bis–14 PRO, location now unknown Lab v, 433
33.	[c. 21/31-iii-1584]	Mary – Courcelles	? Decipher	?	PRO, as no. 32 Lab v, 479–80
34.	[22-iii/1-iv-1584]	C. – Mary	Draft	II	H 370–3
35.	[probably 7/17-iv-1584]	C. – Mary	Draft	II	H 374–6
36.	24-iv/4-v-1584	C. – Guise	Draft	I	H 355–8

(iii)
Letters passed between April and November 1584

(1)	(2)	(3)	(4)	(5)	(6)
37.	[c. 25–iv/5–v–1584]	C – Henri III	Copy	IV	Hat 149, 117–18 HCal iii, 81
38.	30–iv/10–v–1584	Mary – C.	Copy	II	H 321bis–323 Lab v, 457
39.	23–v/2–vi–1584	Mary – C.	Copy	V	H 315–17 Lab v, 468
40.	31–v/10–vi–1584	Mary – C.	Copy	V	H 404 Lab v, 474
41.	7/17–vii–1584	C. – a Scottish lord	Fair Copy	III	H 365
42.	[12/22–vii–1584]	C. – Henri III	Draft	I	H 359–60
43.	[c. July 1584]	C. – Adamson	Draft	I	H 366
44.	[mid –viii–1584]	C. – Henri III	Draft	I	Hat 149, 115–16 HCal iii, 41
45.	1/11–x–1584	Mary – Gray	Revised copy Part-copy of original, with postscript by Feron	A. Douglas II	Hat 133, no. 50 BL Cotton Nero B vi, f. 371 Lab vi, 14–27 HCal xiii, 253–8
46.	16/26–x–1584	C. – Henri III	Copy Copy	II	H 353–4 E 260 Chéruel, 342
47.	18/28–x–1584	Mary – C.	Copy	V	PRO SP 53/14, no. 11 Cal 84, 510 Lab vi, 35

Notes on Dating

1   Dated by C.'s just having had news of James's escape to St Andrews, which
    occurred on 27-vi/7-vii-1583 and was known in London by 3/13-vii (Cal
    83, pp. 519, 524); cf. p. 526, where Fowler reports, on the 8th/18th, that C.
    has written about it to Henri III. There is a gap in C.'s letters home at this
    point.

2   Dated by Labanoff from D'Esneval copy, since H has no date; cf. Mary to
    Mendoza, presumably 13/23-vii-1583 (*CSP Spanish 1580–86*, p. 491); received
    by C. before 21/31-vii (Chéruel, p. 267). We must suppose that Mary used
    old style in the letters both to C. and to Mendoza, since so far as I can see
    that is what she always did; but this makes some difficulties with the next
    item, and in that case C. would have received his letter rather quickly.

3   Labanoff's date, assuming old style. But Feron's copy is dated 12th and 15th.
    Labanoff, p. 357 n. 1, records this but says that he has found another copy
    with the dates given, and regards these as correct (1) because this letter was
    evidently written after the previous one; and (2) because in the p.s. dated
    25th Mary says that since writing the main letter she has received one from
    C. of the 13th/23rd (which does not survive, and is not No. 1). These points
    seem conclusive. There remain the problems: (1) Where on earth did Labanoff
    find his other copy? It is not in D'Esneval. (2) Why on earth should Feron
    misdate his own?

4   The date is roughly settled by C. to Catherine de Medici, 31-vii/10-viii-
    1583 (Chéruel, pp. 276–7), since both report Walsingham as still being in
    favour of the treaty with Mary, and this one seems to describe an earlier
    stage in the dealings. It *may* be a reply to No. 2, which C. had received by
    the 21st/31st (above), in which case the date may be a little after the one
    suggested. The date I gave in *GB*, p. 24, n. 17, 'c. 6/16-viii-1583', now seems
    too late; what is in its favour is that the piece is at Hatfield, which means
    that it was either received by Walsingham shortly before he left for Scotland
    on 17/27-viii and passed by him to Burghley, or received by Burghley after
    that date.

5   Between 8/18-viii-1583 (since C. refers to his letter to Walsingham of that
    date: Cal 83, p. 579) and Walsingham's departure for Scotland on the
    17th/27th; hence probably the letter of 12/22-viii whose receipt is acknowl-
    edged by Mary in the next item (Lab v, 362). Misdated in HCal to 1585.

6   Dated from Labanoff, assuming old style.

7   After No. 6; replies to Nos. 4 and 5. Must have been received before about
    10/20-x, or it would have gone to Walsingham. Endorsed in Burghley's
    office: 'L[ord] Archibald Douglas concerning the Q[ueen] of Scottes'. Does
    this mean that Douglas brought the letter?

8   The occasion of Throckmorton's arrest. Dated by Phelippes's endorsement,
    which records C's new-style date and is not, as I supposed in *GB*, pp. 102f,
    28 an old-style date of Phelippes's own. It is a little surprising that there is
    no sign of the original.

9   Date more or less fixed by Feron's marginal note: 'Fault faire un certifficat pour E. du R. du xxii novembre' (H 362ʳ). Answers letters brought by Courcelles, who arrived back just before 3/13 November.

11   So dated, I think rightly; but says that Lord Paget and Charles Arundell had left the country 'depuis quatre ou cinq jours', whereas Paget was in Paris by 2/12 December (PRO SP 12/164, no. 6). Perhaps an example of Castelnau's looseness with this kind of date; cf. No. 13.

13   About the day after No. 11 because the departure of Lord Paget and Arundell is given as 'six' days ago, and one page of it is written on the rest of a page on which No. 11 has been started. A number '24', possibly to do with filing, has been written at the end of it; cf. No. 30.

14   Shortly after No. 13.

15   Between Nos. 14 and 16; mentions No. 14 as written 'dernierement'.

16   E. of Northumberland put under arrest 'yesterday', i.e. 15/25 December (*CSP Foreign 1583–84*, no. 313). Mentions two recent letters and another from Courcelles, which seems to be No. 15.

17   Probably after death of John Somerville, 19/29-xii-1583 (CRS xxi, p. 41); some time before 9/19-i-1584 (order for Mendoza's expulsion); and before No. 24.

20   Dated 7/17 January; but before No. 23, since in that C. reports Elizabeth apologising for a quarrel described in this.

21   Same day as, or day after, No. 20.

23   So dated; but if the date on No. 20 is right, must be after the 7/17th.

24   Some while after No. 17, and before order for Mendoza's expulsion: Mendoza has had a letter from Philip II turning down peace feelers discussed in No. 17.

25   Dated by No. 26.

27   After No. 18, because C. has had dinner with Leicester, the invitation to which he had reported then.

30   Seems to be same date as No. 29. A number '20' has been added, which may not be a date: cf. No. 13.

31   Labanoff dates 26th, but the reading is certainly '25th'.

33   The reference to Edward More in both, and the place where Labanoff found them (State Paper Office), indicate that this is of the same date as No. 32. It seems that the PRO copies of both of these have been lost or stolen.

34   C. says he received Nos. 22 and 31 on 18/28 March and is being pressed (by Baldwin) for a reply though he wrote two days ago. On 30 April/10 May (Lab v, 457; No. 38) Mary reported receipt of four letters, of which the first two were of 29 March and 1 April. This is therefore the second of these; the first does not seem to survive.

35   In the letter mentioned above, under No. 34, Mary reports the receipt of letters of 6 and 17 April; here C. says that Baldwin says he is leaving for Sheffield in two hours, so this is perhaps the second of them; mentions an interview with Elizabeth which he also mentions in a letter home of 13/23

April (Chéruel, p. 292). Reports the liberation of the Earl of Arundel, which is dated by Pollen (CRS xxi, p. 56), very roughly, to 8/18 April.

37   Between the departure of Marion for Sheffield on 20/30-iv-1584 (*HMC Bath* v, 49) and his return, about 29-iv/9-v-1584 (Lab v, 454f).

38   Received by Castelnau on 7/17-v-1584 (C. to Mary, 10/20-v-1584: Le Laboureur, *Mémoires*, I, 594) 'par ceste voye', which probably means Baldwin. Feron did not pass Castelnau's reply of the 10th/20th, which accompanied a set of packets from Morgan and others.

42   So dated in Ms.; but looks as if it might be a draft for the letter of 6/16-vii-1584 (Chéruel, pp. 304–11).

43   Seems to be about the same time as No. 41.

44   Between 18/28-vii-1584 and 18/28-viii-1584 (Chéruel, pp. 313ff, 318ff); *Ibid.* p. 323, of 24-viii/3-ix-1584, reports the same conversation with Elizabeth about the triviality of Scotland, which suggests quite a recent date for this letter.

Index

Persons asterisked are described in the *Characters* (above, pp. xii–xiii).
Names in italics are those of historians.